Arti Boss

Anthony Caro's studio assistants and issues of legacy in British sculpture.

First published in 2016 by Wunderkammer Press

Wunderkammer Press
Bath School of Art and Design
Bath Spa University
Sion Hill
Bath BA1 5SF

Printed in the United Kingdom

ISBN: 978-0-9935511-0-9 [paperback]
Artist Boss: Anthony Caro's studio assistants
and issues of legacy in British sculpture.
Jenny Dunseath and Mark Wilsher (eds)
91 Illustrations

Design: Extra Strong
Type: AauxPro

www.artistboss.org.uk

WUNDERKAMMER

BATH SPA UNIVERSITY
Annely Juda FINE ART
BARFORD SCULPTURES LIMITED
BENNINGTON COLLEGE
NewArtCentre.
NORWICH UNIVERSITY OF THE ARTS
WINCHESTER SCHOOL OF ART
Mtec

Contents

Foreword: Karen Wilkin

Excerpted from 'The state of sculpture', which originally appeared in the May 2014 issue of *The New Criterion*, Volume 32 (2014), p. 40.

Anthony Caro's sudden death in October 2013, at the age of eighty-nine, ended the unbroken lineage of the 'new tradition' of radically modern abstract sculpture constructed in metal that began with Pablo Picasso and Julí González in the late 1920s, and continued through David Smith to Caro himself. Yet there are several generations of sculptors from all over the world who studied with or were mentored by Caro, or worked as his assistants. Judging by the number of them who attended his memorials at Tate Britain, London, and the Metropolitan Museum of Art, New York, some coming long distances, they continue to admire and respect both the man and his work. It's an extraordinarily diverse list that includes, among British artists alone, such well-known figures as Phillip King, William Tucker and Tim Scott, at one end of the aesthetic spectrum, and at the other, Gilbert and George, and Richard Long, along with some very young practitioners, such as Caro's recent studio assistants, Neil Ayling and John Wallbank, who are just beginning to attract attention. Many others from elsewhere in Europe, the United States, Canada, Latin America, Africa, Asia, and Australia could be added, yet few of these artists make work that could be described as 'abstract sculpture constructed in metal'. Whatever they absorbed from Caro, whatever they found stimulating and compelling in his example, was something far larger than a particular approach, material, or way of working.

Foreword: Tim Marlow, 2015

Artistic Director
Royal Academy of Arts

Georgiana Street was the first major artist's studio I ever visited. It felt both serious and playful; functional and creative; private and generous. It never lost that aura for me – a place of material transformation utterly without glamour but full of magic.

It was an old piano factory, and the musical analogy with Caro's sculpture played out easily enough, but the sounds were jarring: the crackle of an oxyacetylene torch, the shriek of a metal grinder. It was Tony's voice that resonated the most though. 'What do you think?' he would ask, not seeking approval but rather continuing the self-questioning that never seemed to stop in his mind. And so it was with his assistants – artists in their own right whose opinions he sought and respected; whose careers he valued and helped to nurture.

As an assistant himself, Caro had learned from Henry Moore. The lessons were not so much about process or form but rather what it took to become an artist on one's own terms. This, I think, was the presiding ethos of Georgiana Street. It was a place where hard and serious work was done, but ultimately a critical space where people were encouraged to think for themselves, speak their minds, understand what they wanted to do and learn what they didn't want to do. Nearly thirty years after my first visit, I've never encountered anywhere remotely like the Caro studio.

Interview:

ANTHONY CARO & PATRICK CUNNINGHAM – PART ONE

Studio assistant 1968 to present day

Camden studio, London, UK

Group interview (November 2010)

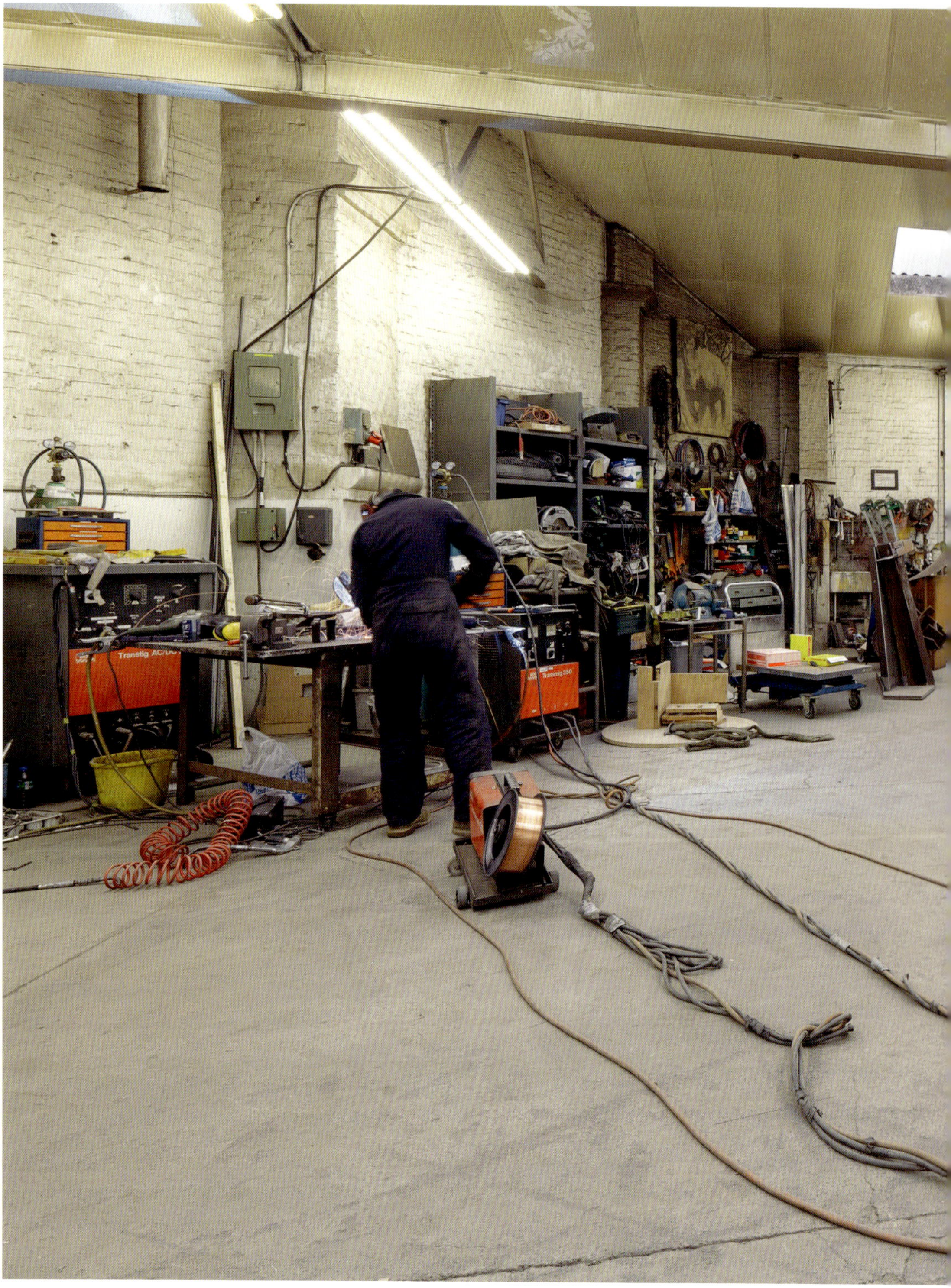

fig. 1

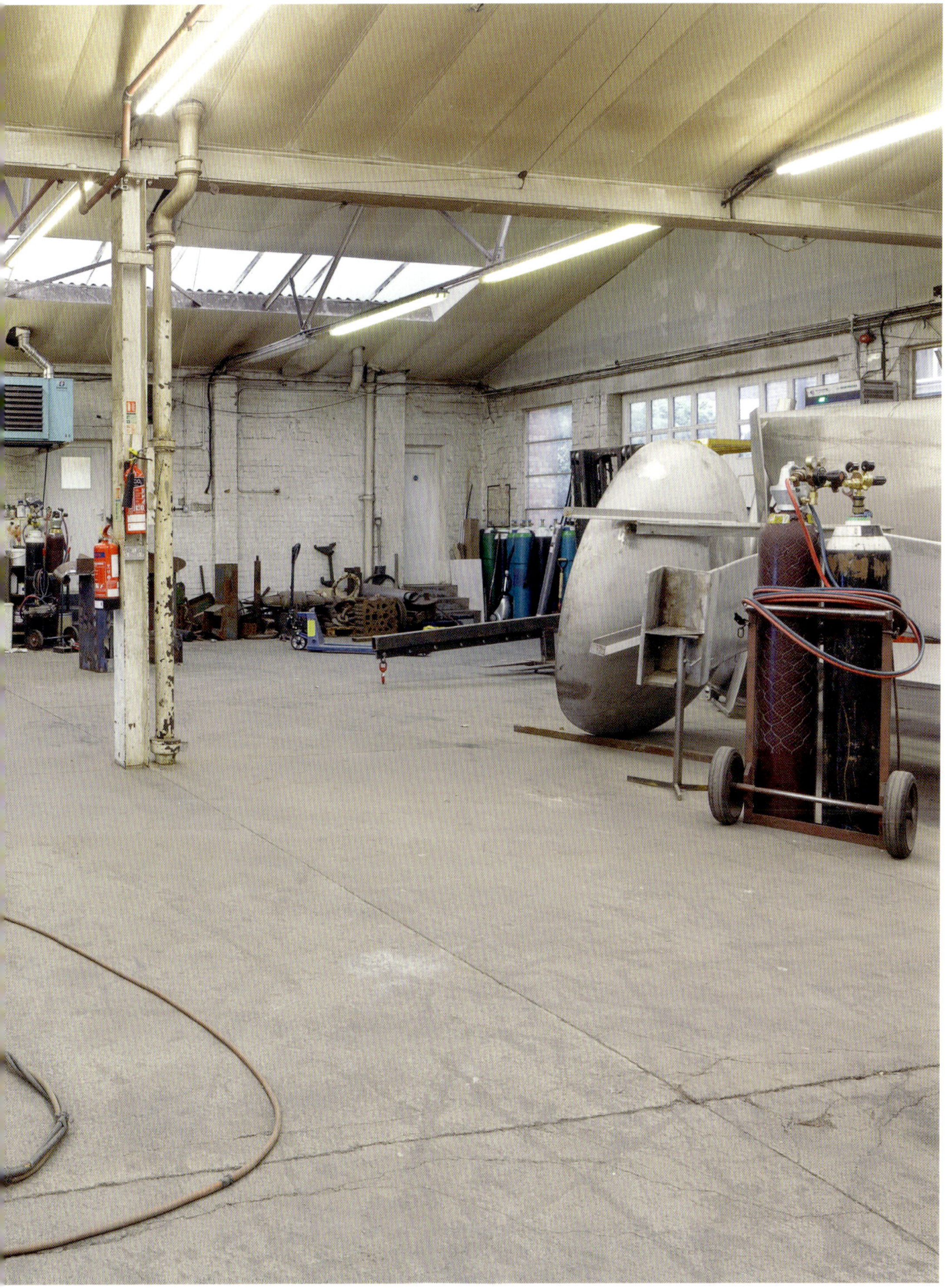

Camden studio, London, UK (2013)

JENNY DUNSEATH *I am interested in your experience of employing studio assistants and what impact, if any, it had on the production of your work. To begin: when did you start employing assistants?*

ANTHONY CARO There were people around to help move and lift things. Maybe 1966–68. No, go back further to when I made things like *Early One Morning* and *Hopscotch*, and those things up in the garage at home. People would come and I'd say to Mike [Bolus], 'Would you come and give me a hand?' Mike helped with *Early One Morning* and we did it together. David Annesley helped me with *Hopscotch*. They'd come for a few days and we'd knock the thing out.

JD *How did you know Mike and David?*

AC I had taught them at Saint Martin's [School of Art] and they were on the staff there. Tim Scott and Isaac Witkin, they all helped in those very early days. They were all from Saint Martin's.

JD *While you were teaching at Saint Martin's, did the environment encourage practical teaching?*

AC I wasn't teaching them in my studio; they were drilling holes and doing all that stuff. In the studio I could only do one thing at a time, so I'd only make four or five sculptures in a year, or even less. Then I went to America to teach at Bennington [College]. I needed help there and I got hold of this man who was the worst technician I've ever known!

JD *Why was that?*

AC Just mad! He had an aeroplane, which he made himself. I thought, 'This one's going to fall out of the sky!' That was so nice having somebody help me like that. No... I've got my dates a bit wrong. I had gone to Aeromet before that because I didn't know how to weld. I didn't know how to join two bits of steel together. I knew nothing!

In the end I did learn how to weld. In those days we had a welding torch. You took the whole end of it off and you put on a different thing for cutting. You didn't have a little buzz box; you didn't have anything like that.

PATRICK CUNNINGHAM No electric welder.

AC No. The first person to have a buzz box in those days was Reg Butler; we thought he was terribly advanced! I said to the rep who came round with the bottles and things, 'Do you know a firm that knows anything that could help me?' And they said, 'Yes, there's a good one called Aeromet.' I went down to this little firm and they made our sculptures, and this chap Charlie Hendy was working there and he was the sort of number one.

JD *It was a welding firm?*

AC Yes, you see Pat was there.

PC We did exhibition work. All the shows... We did Earl's Court and Olympia, the Boat Show. We put up all the stands. Aeromet went bust, then he went on and started another one.

AC When I came back from America, Charlie worked on sculptures like *Wide*, but he was still working for Aeromet. He was so good because he would just invent. *Wide* had a flat piece with three prongs coming out and it was not going to be able to be moved. I remember Charlie invented three prongs that were like sleeves, which fitted over the spigots, which was amazing. I'd never seen anything done like that before. It was beautifully done and, of course, it came to pieces. Charlie was the person who made it possible to make *Prairie*, which was really hard.

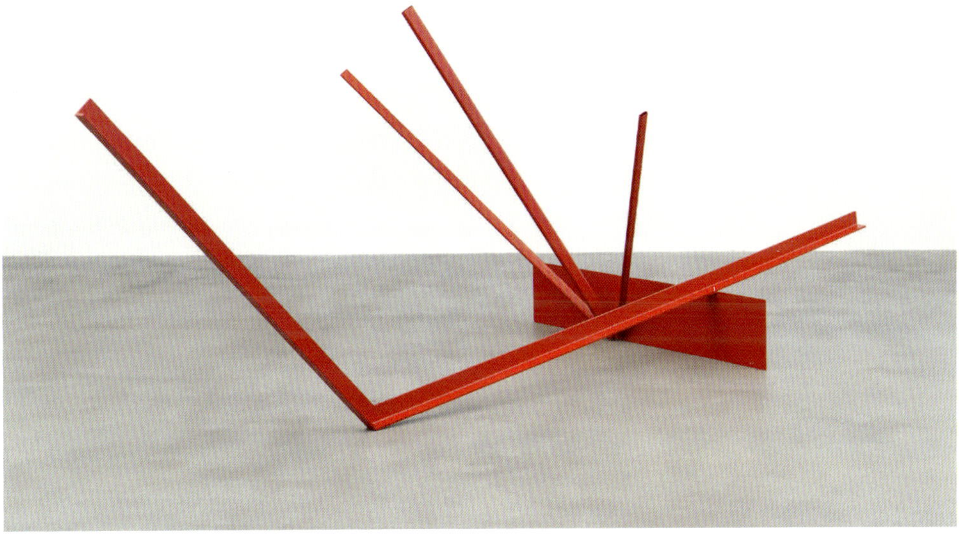

fig. 2

Anthony Caro
Wide (1964)
Steel and aluminium, painted burgundy
149.5 x 152.5 x 406.5 cm

PC That was really hard. You had bolts right up inside the pipes and you had to sit there and tighten them and the air moves and it takes hours to set the sculpture up. There were three or four extension bars inside. It was so advanced – you couldn't do these things today.

AC Nobody could do any of these things at all, except either Pat or Charlie. There was a time when Pat was away and I had to get other help and they didn't have the first clue. Even people who had worked in places like Aeromet couldn't do it.

JD *Would this have been in the 1960s?*

AC The late 1960s, I would say. Mike had that same sort of ability and also an inclination in that direction. So Mike would come and help us. Pat, what year did you start with me?

PC 1968. You had Guy Martin with you then and Charlie was here, then he left.

AC Charlie had a sort of change of life thing. He decided he would be a young man on the run. He was going to work on an oilrig and all sorts of things!

PC Guy Martin was with you when I started in 1968.

AC Guy Martin was the son of Frank Martin and he was very good at making things. He made *Child's Tower Room*, and I thought Mike made that...

PC He did and Mike did too and John Gibbons. A lot of people worked on that sculpture.

AC Was John Gibbons working with us then?

PC Yes. He came back and helped us with *Child's Tower Room*. We used to have people come in and work on the timber at night, prepare the rough planks so that Guy and the carpenters could work on it.

AC So we didn't have any young people working with us then?

PC Yes, Jon Isherwood was working with us at that time. The *Child's Tower Room* was at one end of the studio and at the other end were sculptures like *Ocean*.

AC So that was quite late, the 1980s. So I think the only young person we had working with us at that time was Jon Isherwood.

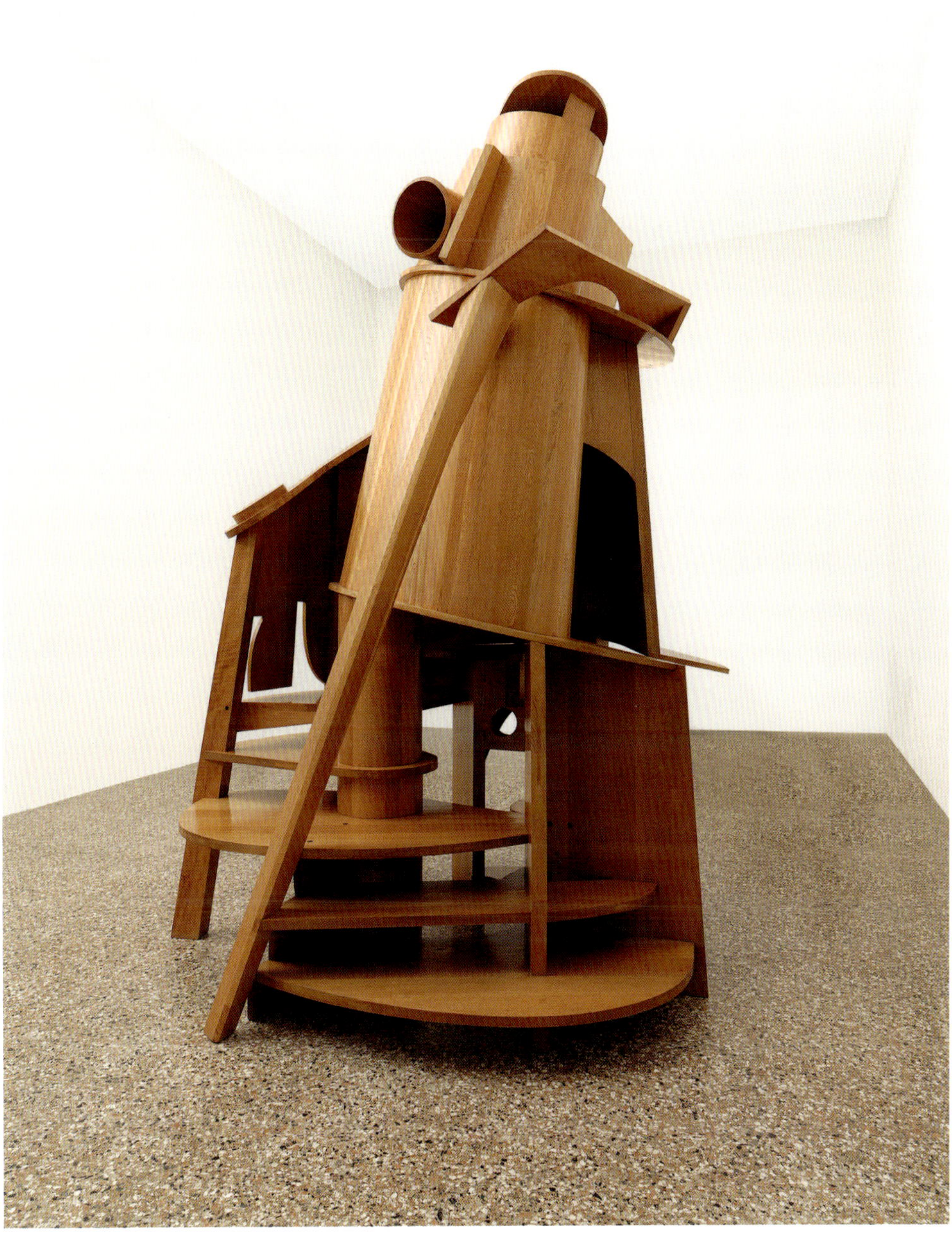

fig. 3

Anthony Caro
Child's Tower Room (1983/84)
Japanese oak, varnished
381 x 274.5 x 274.5 cm
Museo Correr, Venice (2013)

JD *How did you find people like Jon Isherwood?*

AC John Gibbons put us onto Jon. They came to us from Saint Martin's and they came to us in the summer holidays... By that time Pat had left Aeromet, or it had gone bust, and had come to work here permanently. Charlie Hendy was here. Did you overlap with Charlie Hendy?

PC Yes, I did, and then Guy Martin left and we brought Lofty back in.

AC Lofty and those people from Aeromet would come in and do a few days welding or grinding or something. At that time we had nothing but the donkey saw; we didn't have an upright drill!

JD *How was the work done? Was it taken over to Aeromet?*

AC No, we just did it. When did we start having younger people?

PC It was shortly after I came. We would take people from Saint Martin's. The first time I met John Gibbons (Tony knew him from Saint Martin's when he was a student), you asked me to come with you to meet this young Irish fellow, and he asked if we had any work. You asked me what I thought and I said I thought we could try him out for a few days. He did that whole gallery and did all the plumbing, before he was teaching.

AC He painted the cottage for me. Then he went into teaching and he's been the source, in all his years of teaching, of almost everybody I've had working here. I was ringing John and saying, 'Have you got anybody you can recommend who is at a loose end or you think would be good?' Some people like Gavin [Morris] and Beth [Cullen-Kerridge] had been there and gone on to the Royal College [of Art] and occasionally they had said, 'I know somebody else who is good'.

JD *So people work on a range of things while they work for you... Do you employ people for their specific skills?*

AC Well, Beth had done a casting course of some sort at the College. She knew about bronze and she was good at it. I think that's pretty well the history. You find out what people are good at and what they like doing, and if you can get them to go in that direction, then it goes well. If it's something that's horrible, they don't enjoy it and then it's not good to anybody.

JD *How has using assistants affected or influenced your work?*

AC It makes it a hundred times easier. You know I am absolutely useless at making things. I'm very bad at it! Phillip King is very good at it. Quite a lot of sculptors are very good at it. Pat naturally knows how things work and I don't.

I'm very lucky to have Pat. Pat left for a while to go to America, I think. In that time I had some chap who was absolutely no good at it. I was working with him when Willard [Boepple] came in, watched him and said, 'You've got to get rid of this chap; he's not really paying any attention. He's getting it all so wrong.' I mean, you've got to get it right. You've not only got to get it right, but you've got to understand my language and the subtlety.

Somebody had the idea of making a pop-up model of *Early One Morning* for sale at the Royal Academy [of Arts]; they made one that was quite sturdy, and yet it was so mechanical it had no feeling at all of the work. It's perfectly made but it's just horrid! I said, 'You can't do it', and the man said, 'Why, what's wrong with it?' And I said, 'It just hasn't got the feel of the thing. It hasn't got the feel of it at all.' I don't think he knew what I was talking about, but the fact is, if you've got people like that working for you, it doesn't work. You've got to get people on your wavelength.

JD *Is it dependent upon the relationship, the understanding and the communication?*

AC Somehow yes; learning to get a feel for each other.

PC The way it's meant to be and the way Tony wanted it to be.

AC When you ask how has it influenced me, I think in a sense I pick up on the people and realise what they are good at. But if you get somebody who is solid and won't change, it's no good having them there at all.

JD *Is it similar to how you talk about your relationship with Henry Moore when you refer to it being a very close relationship? About understanding the way they work, being visually aware, and listening to instinct?*

AC Well, it was a bit different. My relationship with Henry was not like the relationship I've had with people here. I suppose the one who's had the nearest relationship to my relationship with Henry was Jon Isherwood, because we talked a lot about sculpture and the possibilities of sculpture and things like that. And, of course, Pat. I talk about it all with Pat.

There were three people working at different times with Henry who were students. There was Alan Ingham; he was very, very good at casting. He could do all sorts. We did things like piece moulds; he could piece mould anything. You know, you could give him an ear and he could piece mould it. He was wonderful. So that was his sort of expertise.

Then there was Peter Atkin and also Peter King, who said very interesting things about sculpture and knew a lot about Surrealism. Somehow I wasn't much good at doing the sculpture work.

It's a bit close to the way I work with Neil [Ayling] and John [Wallbank] now. Giving only a very, very open possibility of something and saying, 'Make that'... I explain what I'm doing but don't say what it's meant to be.

So you see, they'll give me something and I'll say, 'Let's adjust that', or, 'That bit's good and that bit's not so good'. This happens with very few people.

John [Wallbank] and I did some work together on the heads just after the church [Eglise de Saint-Jean-Baptiste], because we got this new machine and we sort of worked together. By that time, I knew John well enough to say, 'What do you think?' That's good.

So I was having that relationship with Henry and actually doing waxes with him, which was very good. But people can't get that at the beginning; it has to take time before they can grasp what you are wanting. You were getting to do the same thing. I think really what I am saying is that it could be an alternative to art school, but I don't think there's too much teaching that goes on.

I sometimes say, 'Shall we get so-and-so?' But Pat says, 'We'll have to teach him everything', and it will take too much of me, and in the end I'm not gaining anything. You may get somebody who is very fast or, again, somebody who is very slow, and it doesn't mesh.

PC Now in the old days, when we had time, you could show and teach people, but it depended on how many people were there and what you were working on.

AC I like a small group – three or so. I think our team is very important because in a way we get to know each other as people. I think we begin to speak each other's language and it's a shared thing. I am very much for grouping, particularly in sculpture (more so than in painting). I like people helping each other, because I think that some painters are lone wolves and I suppose some sculptors are – who would you say was a lone sculptor Pat?

PC John Gibbons.

AC Yes. And David Smith, but he did have an assistant, a sort of Pat. Leon Pratt was very, very good. He lived a very lonely life, out in the wilds. Henry, as I say, had two or three of us. Henry saw people more than David Smith.

During the conversation the discussion moves between the 1960s and the 1980s. To clarify the chronology, the dates referred to are: *Early One Morning* (1962), *Hopscotch* (1962), teaching at Saint Martin's School of Art (1953–81), teaching at Bennington College (1963–65), *Wide* (1964), *Prairie* (1967), *Child's Tower Room* (1983–84).

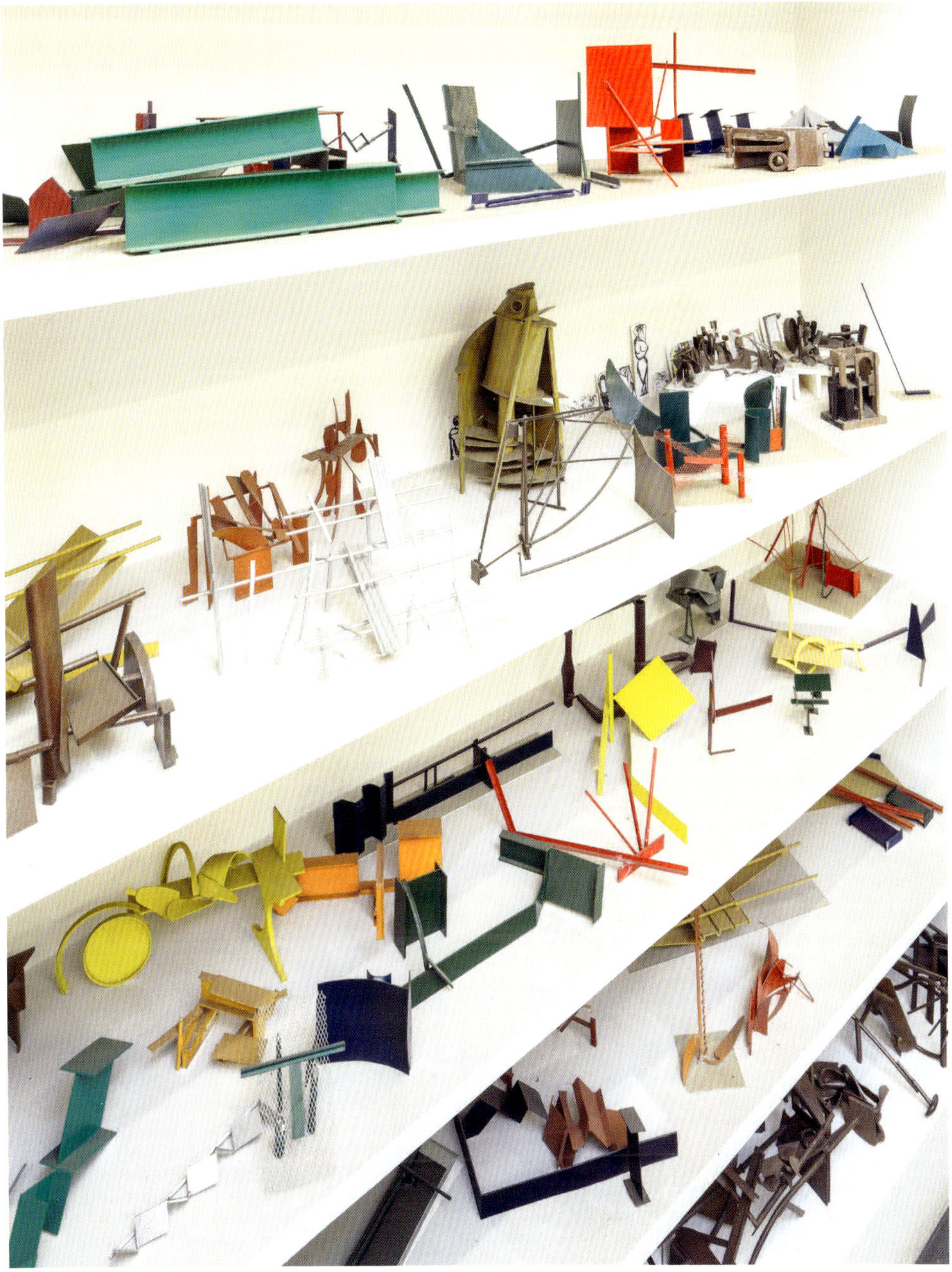

fig. 4

1/20th scale models by Jaana Fowler
in the tearoom at Camden studio (2013)

Essay: Artist Boss

ANTHONY CARO'S STUDIO ASSISTANTS AND ISSUES OF LEGACY IN BRITISH SCULPTURE

Jenny Dunseath
Mark Wilsher

"Generosity and sharing provide an alternative to contemporary individualism and the traditional role of the romantic artist as a solitary genius"[1]

(Lind 2005, p. 66)

Making art is a form of collaboration: between artists and curators, critics, buyers, audiences, those who commission and those who judge. As cultural theorist Brian Holmes reiterates, 'even the lone artist in their studio is dependent upon contributions from others'.[2] Successful artists have always used assistants to enable a greater volume of production or to deal with the more mundane parts of the process. Sculpture, with its greater physical demands and complicated, messy processes, has often demanded the most help. In the nineteenth century the establishing of a working studio was a key point in a commemorative or monumental sculptor's working life, and there are numerous accounts of the studios of artists such as Thornycroft and, of course, Rodin.

This study looks at the studio of Anthony Caro, perhaps the greatest sculptor of late twentieth century Britain. We are publishing for the first time a series of original interviews and responses from Caro and his assistants that focus specifically on the role of the studio assistant in the making of sculpture. How did this affect the production of signature works? What new kinds of production are enabled? Does the role of a studio assistant sometimes grow to become collaboration? But also, and just as interesting, what is the impact on the artistic lives of the assistants and how do we perceive its legacy for sculpture today?

Based on many hours of taped conversations and responses with several generations of studio assistants, *Artist Boss* allows more intimate access to the work of Anthony Caro. It provides insight into his thought processes, and opens up a range of complex perspectives on the sometimes-contentious role of the artist's assistant and the collaborative mode of sculptural production. Across five decades of production, those closest to Caro in the studio speak frankly about what life was like working for this internationally renowned artist. The study describes the context that brought forth many acknowledged art historical masterpieces, and the impact working together had on the careers and lives of the artists he worked closely with. With original material and unseen images of the studio, this first full-length study sheds light on the working relationships of Caro (1924–2013) and provides first-hand insight into the studio methodologies of mid-career and emerging artists in his orbit. New perspectives are given on the working practices of three more British sculptors; Oscar Nemon, Sir Charles Wheeler and Henry Moore.[3]

The historic use of studio assistants is well documented, but recent shifts in modes of production and the kind of sculptural training available through an art school education invite us to look again today at this traditional role and its impact on making. The interviews and responses take place with artists at different stages in their careers, from around the UK and across the Atlantic. They reveal as much about human endeavour as they do about creative careers, education and art.

The varied responses illustrate the different ways in which the evolution of sculptural language has been negotiated. Some artists become guardians of tradition, some fight against it, while others find themselves caught in a struggle to break free.

Working as an assistant to a more established figure is a rite of passage for many artists. It offers a window into the creative process, a glimpse of a professional career in the art world, and a modest income. For over fifty years, Caro worked with numerous people in many different capacities: his longstanding role as tutor at Saint Martin's School of Art perhaps the most well known.

This publication necessarily represents an incomplete selection of studio assistants, defined as those employed to work directly toward the production of Caro's work. It is by no means a definitive or exclusive selection and does not represent all who worked for and with him.

We do not include, for example, the close relationships he had with architects such as Frank Gehry, Tadeo Ando and Norman Foster; artists such as skilled sculptor Hamish Black, or specialist ceramicist Hans Spinner.[4] It does not reflect the well-documented lineage of his students: William Tucker, Phillip King, Tim Scott, Richard Deacon; or those who would later react against his legacy: Bruce Mclean, Barry Flanagan, Gilbert and George, to name a few.

Here we focus on the intimate relationship between a studio assistant and the Artist Boss.[5] In this relationship, the assistant is typically employed at the outset of his/her career, paid to produce work for and with the artist, to learn and respond to the artist's instructions. This is a snapshot reflecting studio assistants across generations who were willing to respond and contactable at the time of writing.

The interviews and responses all reflect individuals talking about their own experience, work and values. After much consideration, it became apparent that a conversational approach would be more akin to the experience of daily studio conversations described by many. They are presented in the format in which they were originally given to provide a documentary insight into this unique experience. When the voice of your employer resounds loudly in art history, it becomes essential to be able to maintain the honest and distinct voice of each participant.

The written responses capture the thoughts and internal monologues of the artists. The transcribed interviews capture the meandering tangents and the unguarded inflection of how the artist responded at that moment in time. Some were shared posthumously, some were written decades after employment. The fallibility of memory and overarching concern of what will be held in print was palpable. Often what is inferred, implied or omitted was just as important as what was said. The uninterrupted transcripts and responses all give form to a larger developing and reflective conversation.

Caro started employing studio assistants in 1966, claiming he was 'absolutely useless at making things', and with the employment of assistants, the process of making was made 'a hundred times easier'. He would often hire recent graduates or artists in the early stages of their careers, and here similarities can be drawn to an apprenticeship, where skills are learned from the experienced master while the pupil earns a wage.

As Tim Marlow and Karen Wilkin identify in their forewords, Caro's studio nurtured people and challenged work. Caro and Patrick Cunningham discuss how imperative it was to employ people 'on your wavelength'. For Caro, decisions were tested on other people, as Willard Boepple's response explores: 'He thought outside his head'.[6]

The community produced by the studio was an important feature of Caro's working methodology. The testing of work on assistants, critics, writers and guests is perhaps suggestive of the studio as a directed community, affirming his role as the Artist Boss.[7]

The interviews reveal a high turnover of assistants. Working relationships in the studio were paramount. Caro wanted to maintain a 'freshness' and interest in the working environment. The majority of assistants were employed during or after studying for a bachelor's degree or master's. A large number worked for approximately three years, with many returning to work part-time while sustaining their own practice. Others would work for a short duration to complete a body of work or finalise projects, and a few stayed for decades.

Travelling between the UK and US, Caro employed assistants in both countries as required. Some would travel in order to work and would eventually settle, helping to affirm bilateral transatlantic relationships.

Many assistants continue to maintain their own practice. A few provide insight into working exclusively on Caro's practice and subsequent changes in careers. Interviewees discuss how experiences in the studio would feed into their practices and roles as heads of department (Winchester School of Art, Bennington College and Winthrop University), teachers, technicians and tutors in establishments across the UK and US, often becoming unofficial recruitment agents for the next generation.

The interviews present a celebratory but sometimes complex account of the master/assistant dynamic. Regardless of Caro's persistent, inquisitive nature, there is no doubt about who was ultimately in charge.

Guy Martin notes that 'friendly exchanges of ideas can occur, but only at the master's pleasure', while André Fauteux remembers that 'Caro's self-centredness was exceeded only by his generosity'. Patrick Cunningham clearly understood his role and how he 'may have participated and helped, but he [Caro] said when it's finished'. In the end, individual tastes are not quite absorbed within the overarching goal. As John Gibbons describes, 'He likes Mozart and I like Bach'.

With a group of young artists working together under the eye of a benevolent master, the comparison to apprenticeships and art school education is inevitable. In their interview, Neil Ayling and Olivia Bax discuss the transition from art school to the working studio, reflecting on the different opportunities that each provide.

The shifting role from student to employee for an established practitioner is an exciting domain, and is particularly interesting when assistants begin to articulate their own practice ideals in comparison to Caro's work. Beth Cullen-Kerridge describes how she could only make 'Caro-esque sculptures for years after', and the 'borrowing' of ideas is touched upon by Willard Boepple, Ian Dawson, John Wallbank and John Gibbons.

One of the initial motivations for this research was to trace the complex paths of influence that run in both directions between master and assistant, and how they might become legible in the artworks themselves. The work and responses produced by assistants reveal a huge amount of information about a process of thinking through making, materials and the shifting notion of sculpture itself across generations.

Recurrent questions Caro would ask were 'Is it sculpture?' and 'What is sculpture?' There was a strong impetus to produce work that purposefully pushed the boundaries of the definition of sculpture. But definitions have since blurred, and practices shifted. In a 2012 study of the discipline of art, Van Winkle recognised that 'there are no longer any criteria to determine what it means to be a visual artist'.[8] The definition is no longer exclusively based in the idea of material, process or technique.[9]

The questioning and re-evaluation of sculptural terms by the assistants reveal an important shift in sculpture legacy. To question and re-evaluate the sculpture Caro embodied was paramount to many of the assistants. The interviews reveal an awareness of the shifting dynamic around the idea of a specifically material practice. Many expose their internal struggle with the agenda of then and now; relationships between theory and practice and polemic definitions of sculpture.

By taking Caro and his impact on art education in the 1960s as a pivotal moment in British sculpture, the responses reflect on a fundamental shift from hands-on, process-based studio sculpture towards the expanded field and a post-medium condition. The works and responses produced by his assistants explore a kind of learning that is rooted deeply in the processes of the studio, and in spending time with someone committed to medium specificity.

An art school education today is very different to that of forty years ago. Current orthodoxy in British art education is that students are taught holistically and are not limited to media-based pathways. In his provocatively titled book *Why Art Cannot Be Taught*, James Elkins recognises that there is no longer 'a hierarchy of genres, a sequence of courses, a coherent body of knowledge, or a unified theory or practice'.[10] Today, professional career skills are taught alongside studio practice, and with student debts hanging in the background there is an acute awareness of possible career paths and ways of making a living.[11] In his interview, Jon Isherwood offers discussion about the impact of professionalisation on US art education, identifying an important juncture in higher education provision today.

The interviewees speak candidly about wanting a career in the art world; some commented that employment in the studio validated their career choices, but that the experience provided them with 'business balls' not otherwise obtained in art school learning. Alongside honing their technical skills and gleaning something of art-world etiquette, the role model of Caro coming to work each day gave a unique insight into what it takes to sustain a high-level international reputation. As Gavin Morris discusses in his interview, Caro had a 'hard line and relentless work ethic'. The studio environment provided the assistants with a working model, a direct example of learning by doing, daily studio activity with making and remaking, and a hard-working ethos.[12]

The micro-economy of the studio, with teamwork at its core, emphasised a division of labour that maximised exploration and productivity. Assistants speak of the unique work environment and the perception of the role by their peers. Discussions reveal the shifting economic pressures impacting on individual career paths and trends in employment.

The socioeconomic impact of the job went far beyond monetary gains to affect confidence and dedication, and provided vital support networks for the artists. Perhaps, as Lind suggests, legacy is the notion that coordinated effort and collaboration is the intrinsic critique of individualism and profit-seeking.[13]

In his interview, Ian Dawson discusses a shift in employment for young artists in the 1990s. As art production by specialist large-scale fabricators increased, the traditional assistant's role declined both in esteem and availability. Although this might have meant more day-to-day technical work in fabrication to order, the special quality of contact with the artist was perhaps lost.

The concept of a learning community, where personal relationships and face-to-face transactions facilitate the most effective learning, is echoed throughout all the interviews. This isn't a model whereby the master imparts knowledge to the student, but one in which everyone continues to learn through ongoing discussion and debate. In their seminal book *Situated Learning* from 1991, Lave and Wenger identify a 'community of practice that promotes learning'.[14] Attention is diverted from the solitary experience that draws from the personal and inward to what psychologist Donald Winnicott describes as a cultural experience or 'shared reality'.[15]

Young assistants brought new knowledge, opinion and energy into the studio, ensuring that art making never settled into the known and comfortable. It was, perhaps, a unique space of freedom in British art history, thanks to the resources that Caro was able to draw upon.

Caro had several studios during the course of his career, including a garage in Hampstead and a converted piano factory in Camden. He would work in the studio every day right up until his death in 2013, directing assistants to assemble new compositions, solving problems and experimenting with new materials. There are many interesting details and stories about particular pieces contained in these interviews that shed light on their production.

All the assistants stress the value of making and the importance of a well-established working process, which provided the free space in which the work could progress. Patrick Cunningham and Tim Peacock speak of their dedication to and enthusiasm for making work entirely for someone else without the pressure or distraction of their own work.

For others the influence of the experience on their practice is rich. Guy Martin 'learnt to nourish my own work', André Fauteux 'learnt to extend myself in all respects... and not accept the comfortable, to push further' and Shaun Cassidy identifies 'an interest in discovery as opposed to sustaining an ideal vision'. William Fausset cites how 'important discussing the work is with people'.

For some, the enduring impact of Caro's work is something to be more directly negotiated. James Wolfe, André Fauteux, Hywel Livingstone, Jonathan Gildersleeves and Shaun Cassidy's responses return us to questions of the modernist ideals of rationality, geometry and abstraction that have evidently been given new urgency by their experience. All of the artists have sympathies with the work of their employer, but how do you find your own individual voice under the weight of that monumental influence?

Caro's own assistantship to Sir Charles Wheeler (1942–44)[16] and his well-documented role as assistant to Henry Moore (1951–53) is reflected in discussions about his employment of assistants.

As many of the interviewees discuss, the role gave them far more than just a wage. It provided a shared experience, an insight into a studio methodology and an example of how to operate as a sculptor. All the experiences speak of the kind of learning that cannot be replicated exclusively in the studio or through an art school education.

The interviews and responses raise awareness about artists' ambitions for their work and their careers, and what they had hoped to gain from the assistant role. There are many tensions and dilemmas, especially after spending several years in the sculpture studio. Can one assist and be fully focused on one's own practice? Or can it rather be a source of engagement with art and the art world? Is an assistant meant to be nothing but a skilled pair of hands, or is it important that there is an individual artistic practice to inform the decisions that are made?

The title of our project reflects issues of authorship that cut across almost all of the interviews. One effect of this publication is to problematise the current reading of sculptural production, which still tends to foreground authorship and the self-expression of the individual artist's hand. While it is clear that processes and decisions are evident in all stages of the creative process, it is especially relevant when artists are held up as emblematic of anthropomorphic self-expression prior to the challenges of postmodernism. Art writing around Anthony Caro's work has tended, from the beginning, to focus on the idea of the artist's unique sensibility – his way of arranging forms, his touch. We would like to unpick this idealised notion a little, not to undermine his achievements but to explore his actual working methods in greater detail and with more recognition of his directing and orchestrating skills.

With the long-term use of assistants, studio experiences and actions are reordered, reshaped and experienced differently by those involved. The potential to change the nature of the activity itself through 'shared experience and interactive negotiation' introduces a new dynamic.[17] Collaborative practices between artists, or between artist and audience, are increasingly paradigmatic within contemporary production, and this project locates the roots of such relationships within the traditional artist's studio system.

With issues of ownership and authorship already jumping between discussions throughout this book, to edit and standardise the original interviews seemed one step too far. We have kept various irregularities because it is important to give an honest representation of the complex and multifaceted insights that individuals provide.

The use of oral histories and responses within this context allows us to reinsert narratives of production, pedagogy and economics into our understanding of British sculpture and, in doing so, expand the convenient but reductive shorthand of art history. These voices reveal shared experiences that resonate around thoughts of lineage, sculptural connections, and approaches to production and understanding in the studio, with an emphasis on 'thinking through making'[18] at the core. The conversations, interviews, responses and essays place individuals within a wider context, and simultaneously remind us that the larger narratives of art history were built from the work of many individuals.

The interviews are arranged broadly chronologically based on the period the assistants were employed in the studio. They are all held within a two-part conversation between Caro and his assistants, and finish with the voice of the longest-serving assistant. We intersperse the interviews with critical essays that subdivide the decades and elaborate upon themes raised. The external voices of the essays extend conversations to help trace the changing definitions of the themes of legacy, production, authorship and pedagogy.

In his essay 'Making a show of yourself', the sculptor, author and curator Dr Michael Petry offers insight into the global shifts of current sculpture production. With reference to other artists' studios (Bernini, Rembrandt, Damien Hirst, Jeff Koons, Joana Vasconcelos and Angela de la Cruz to name a few), he draws attention to historical modes of making alongside contemporary examples to show the context of sculpture production today, discussing issues of authorship, brand and style.

One of the overarching themes of this whole project has been that art making is a collaborative process, and in his short essay 'Omnivorous, restless, decisive: Caro in context', Sam Cornish compares works produced between 1962 and 1977, and argues against the interpretation of Caro as 'an isolated generator of sculptural ideas'. Art history tends to focus on individuals rather than communities; the cliché of the inspired expressive genius rather than the realism of day-to-day experimentation and productivity in the studio. In this essay, Caro is seen as an artist constantly alive and responding to the work of others in his milieu.

Expanding upon the notion of communities, Professor K. Patricia Cross of the University of California, Berkeley, illuminates a pedagogic approach. Here we reprint her 1998 essay 'Why learning communities? Why now?', which explains a model of people learning together through situation, action and discussion that we believe so important in the current context. A scholar of educational research, Cross's essay is used to extend the recurrent discussions around apprenticeships, studio communities and the roles of teachers and tutors beyond an art discourse. This study seeks to revise our interpretation of British sculpture.

By documenting and studying the experiences of those who helped to make it, we aim to insert new narratives into art history. By engaging scholars with the need to enquire into these methodologies, this study aims to set the foundations for fresh analyses of creative identity, artistic practices and the economics of art in the modernist period and beyond.

1 Maria Lind, 'Complications: on collaboration, agency and contemporary art', in *Public: New Communities*, 39 (2009), p. 66. <public.journals.yorku.ca/index.php/public/article/viewFile/30385/27912>. This text expands on the author's 'The collaborative turn', *Taking the Matter into Common Hands: Contemporary Art and Collaborative Practices* (London: Black Dog Publishing, 2005), p. 15-31; and 'The future is here', *Framework: The Finnish Art Review*, 6 (January 2007), p. 56–9.

2 Brian Holmes, 'Artistic autonomy and the conUTlunication society', in *Third Text*, 18:6 (2005), p. 53; cited in Lind, 'Complications'. This quote is followed with 'this is especially true for many male artists who have been able to rely on more or less invisible support from surrounding women' (p. 53).

3 Mapping the Practice and Profession of Sculpture in Britain and Ireland 1851–1951, <sculpture.gla.ac.uk/about/index.php>

4 Similarly we do not include – but want to acknowledge – specialists who worked for Caro: artist Garry Doherty, who worked on surfaces and colours; internationally acclaimed British photographer John Riddy, who photographed much of Caro's work; artist Jaana Fowler, who made thousands of 1/20th scale models of Caro's sculptures; and the dedicated PAs who work tirelessly to maintain the day-to-day running of the office.

5 The term Artist Boss is used in response to Dean Kenning's discussion of Miwon Kwon's text 'One place after another: notes on site specificity', *October*, 80 (Spring 1997), p. 85–110; about current interpretations of authorial presence in his article 'The artist as artist', *Art Monthly*, 337 (June 2010).

6 Willard Boepple 'Anthony Caro: 1924–2013', *Abstract Critical*, (published online 19 November 2013). <abstractcritical.com/note/anthony-caro-1924-2013>

7 Lane Relyea and Barry Schwabsky discuss ideas of the studio as a space of sociability, bricolage, and ideological resistance to acknowledge them as networks and social spaces. Lane Relyea, 'Studio unbound' in Mary Jane Jacob and Michelle Grabner (eds), *The Studio Reader: On the Space of Artists* (Chicago: University of Chicago Press, 2010), p. 341–355. Barry Schwabsky, 'The symbolic studio', ibid. p. 88–99.

8 Camiel van Winkel 'Chapter 4: artists and critics in the culture of design', *During the Exhibition the Gallery will be Closed: Contemporary Art and the Paradoxes of Conceptualism*, PhD Thesis (Amsterdam: Valiz uitgeverij, Faculty of Humanities, Amsterdam School for Cultural Analysis (ASCA), 2012), p. 165. <hdl.handle.net/11245/1.366403>

9 Key books that encapsulate much of the rethinking on aesthetics of modern sculpture include Rosalind Krauss, *Passages in Modern Sculpture* (New York: The Viking Press, 1977), William Tucker's *The Language of Sculpture* (London: Thames & Hudson, 1974) and Thomas McEvilley's *Sculpture in the Age of Doubt* (New York: Allworth Press, 1999).

10 James Elkins, *Why Art Cannot Be Taught: A Handbook for Art Students* (Champaign, IL: University of Illinois Press, 2001).

11 Reference to Howard Singerman, *Art Subjects: Making Artists in the American University* (Oakland: University of California Press, 1999.) Singerman places an art degree in a historical framework and ideological context, arguing that where artists trained made a difference in the forms and meanings produced. He demonstrates how the university structure performed a critical role in the production of modernism in visual arts.

12 As Heider (1958) and Wiener's (1974) attribution theory suggests, here the assistant or learner develops a self-attribution explanation of effort direct from experience. Fritz Heider, *The Psychology of Interpersonal Relations* (New York: Wiley, 1958). Bernard Weiner, *Achievement Motivation and Attribution Theory* (Morristown, NJ: General Learning Press, 1974).

13 Lind, 'Complications' (2009), p. 66.

14 Jean Lave and Etienne Wenger, *Situated Learning: Legitimate Peripheral Participation* (Cambridge: University of Cambridge Press, 1991). This book developed the idea that learning 'is a process of participation in communities of practice, participation that is at first legitimately peripheral but that increases gradually in engagement and complexity', p. 138.

15 Donald Winnicott, 'Chapter 1: transitional objects and transitional phenomena', in *Playing and Reality* (London: Tavistock Publications, 1971).

16 Sir Charles Wheeler was one of only two sculptor presidents of the Royal Academy of Arts (1956–66). The other was Caro's student Phillip King (1999–2004). Discussed by Penelope Curtis, *Modern British Sculpture*, exhibition catalogue (London: Thames & Hudson, 2011), p. 14.

17 Excerpt from Chris Follows's discussion on LPP, 'How can tacit and explicit knowledge be communicated and experienced online?', *Process.Arts* (published online 8 June 2011) <process.arts.ac.uk/content/how-can-tacit-and-explicit-knowledge-be-communicated-and-experience-online> in response to Lave and Wenger, *Situated Learning* (1991).

18 A term applied by Professor Tim Ingold in his lecture of the same name (Scotland: University of Aberdeen, 2012) and later in *Making: Anthropology, Archaeology, Art and Architecture* (Oxford: Routledge Press, 2013).

Interview:

GUY MARTIN

Studio assistant 1966–87

Somerset, UK

Email correspondence (January 2011 to December 2015)

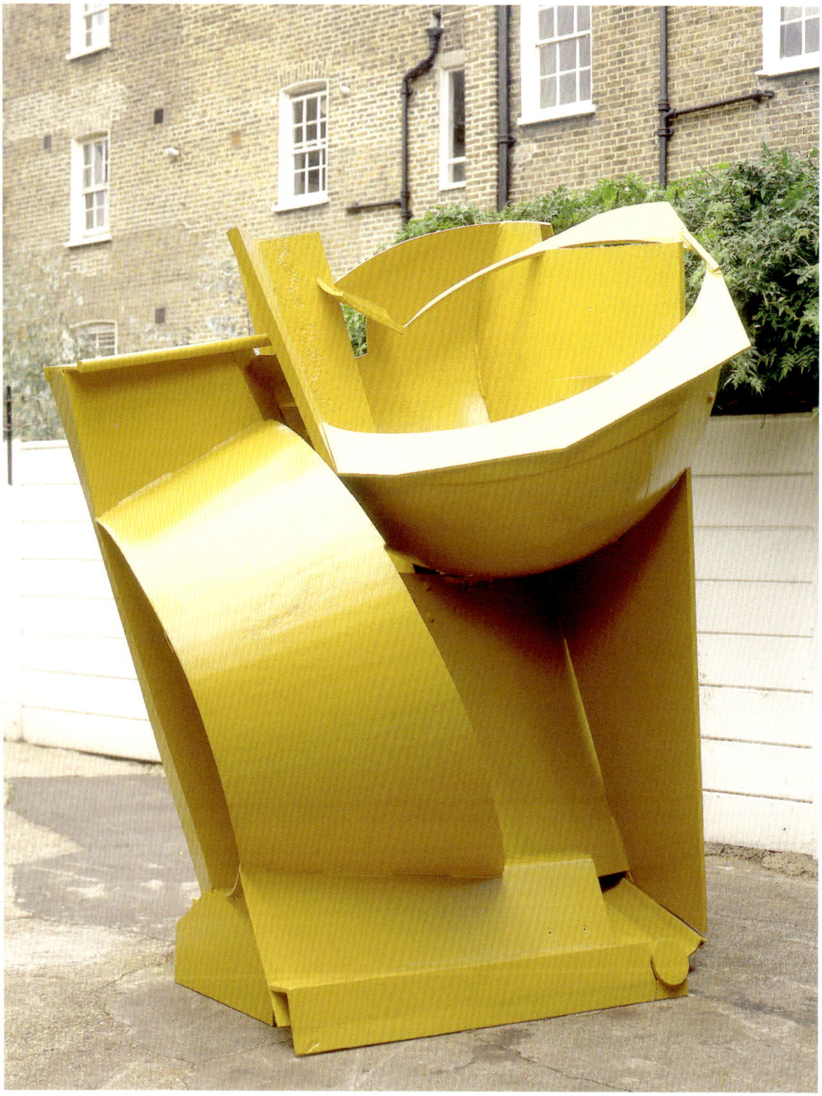

fig. 5

Anthony Caro
Eastern (1983–85)
Steel, painted grey, cream and yellow
Recoloured 1991
244 x 213.5 x 175.5 cm

I attended Saint Martin's from 1966 to 1969, graduating with second-class honours. I first worked for Tony in 1966, his first full-time assistant. He had just acquired the Loudoun Road studio, so I helped him set up the practical side. He gave me a pretty free hand and limited budget to buy equipment and tools. I was there about eight months.

In September I started at Saint Martin's, but kept in touch with Tony, working some holidays and weekends. During that first year (to Bill Tucker's disapproval) I took a few weeks out and travelled to the States for Tony, to help with a show at the Emmerich Gallery in New York. While there, I went to stay with clients in Seattle to repair a sculpture, also to Boston and stayed with the Cabots – other friends and patrons of Tony's. All this was a terrific adventure, I thought; a great beginning to my career and worth the time out from the course.

Some of my fellow students cold-shouldered me. Maybe they were jealous, or felt that I hadn't earned my place there. Social outcasting is something to think about. Carrying a psychological stigma can be damaging if not dealt with in some way. Bill Tucker, who was in charge of my year group, also expressed a prejudice – it was subtle, but it emerged from time to time.

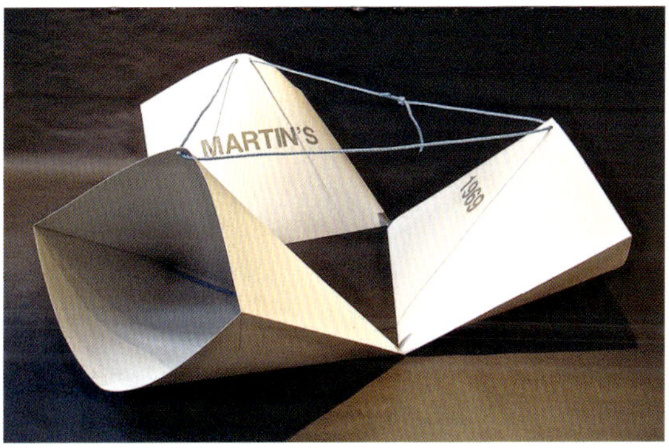

fig. 6

Guy Martin
Saint Martin's 1969 (1969)
Heavyweight paper and rope
46 x 166 x 190 cm

How did I come to be with Tony? You could say through a nepotistic nudge (hence Tucker's reaction). My father and Tony were friends and fellow students at the Royal Academy. Tony happened to be looking for an assistant to fit in with his move away from his garage at Frognal.

I had started a course at Portsmouth School of Art, which was a disaster. I only completed four terms, so I was thinking about an alternative. The timing was right.

Tony had known me as a child. He and Sheila spent holidays at my parents' home on Hayling Island. He knew that I possessed an aptitude for making.

I could try to list some of the sculptures I made, but my memory isn't so good these days. *Cleeve*, *Drop* and *Stream* were among the first. Then

Trefoil, Argentine, Sun Feast, Orangerie, Georgiana, Canal, Serenade, Side Step and others, plus many table pieces, including *LXXXVIII (The Deluge)*. Later on, in the mid 1980s, *Black Russian, Eastern... Egyptian Table* was about the last. I'll mention one other further on.

In the beginning, I had to learn a bit more about fabricating steel, welding, cutting... I developed many new skills, and I am indebted to Tony for allowing me the time and freedom to learn. He paid me £15 a week at first, full-time.

Before the larger studios, Tony was having pieces made by a steel fabricator, Aeromet, and a brilliant technician called Charlie Hendy, whom Tony subsequently employed full-time. I seem to remember that Pat Cunningham also worked for Aeromet initially. As you know, he's still there. Tony outgrew Loudoun Road and [John] Kasmin found him the Georgiana Street premises. I rejoined him there after Saint Martin's, but for personal reasons I decided to move on after a couple of years.

I was unable to stay away, however, when Tony invited me to work on some new pieces in a casual way, finding innovative solutions to working with new materials. I worked on most of the lead and wood pieces, and the first pieces in silver, beginning with *Jubilee* (a gift for Sheila on their 25th wedding anniversary). I would often spend a week working in the studio and sometimes take pieces back to Devon (where I was living) and get them to a stage where Tony could develop them further.

An important year or so was 1983/4, when the Arts Council invited Tony to participate in the 'Four Rooms' touring exhibition. He wanted to make his contribution in wood. He knew that I possessed wood-working skills, so I began the most complicated piece of wood engineering I had ever embarked upon: *Child's Tower Room*. He wanted to treat it like steel and, of course, it's not the same. It was finally finished after nearly a year, with help from invited wood-working friends, to meet the opening in Liberty's top floor exhibition space. As is Tony's nature and uncontrollable desire to get things 'right', he had me cutting a piece off the top five minutes before the doors were opened.

There were other assistants; people came and went. I forget their names. Although Tony could be extremely demanding, he helped a great many people; or they wanted to help him to realise his uncompromising, ambitious nature. It's those characteristics that make him unique, and such an international force.

John Gibbons and Mike Bolus helped with *Child's Tower Room*. I was fortunate enough to travel to every venue and, later in 1987, to Australia, because the secret of its assembly was locked in my memory (or so I liked to believe).

I don't think a true pedagogic relationship can ever exist in that sort of professional environment. Inspiration and influence undoubtedly, but maybe with a price. When I joined Parnham College to run the design element of the course, I began to reflect on my experiences with Tony. My relationship with him probably extended beyond that of most assistants. There is much

I haven't mentioned. Asking for his reference certainly secured me the post.

On reflection, I consider the roles of master/assistant to be very different to that of teacher/student (I hesitate to use the word teacher). The assistant serves the master. The teacher serves the student; however, they agree (sometimes openly, sometimes tacitly) through the structure of institution, to embark on a collaborative journey. The teacher creates the conditions for life to flourish, hopefully.

In the master's studio and business environment, one can learn many things, but largely about professional practice. One learns through listening (with all the senses) and by providing a good service. If the service fails the master, he (or she) may think twice. At times, within the practice of an artist where assistants are employed, friendly exchanges and valuable dialogue and exchanges of ideas can occur, but only at the master's pleasure.

A master's studio possesses limitations, and certain boundaries cannot be crossed. The art student/teacher relationship is the opposite. It should encourage exploration, present different and diverse areas of stimulation and inspiration and almost demand that boundaries are crossed.

A clear pedagogic relationship exists within a structured teaching/learning environment, but between master and assistant it is vague or pretends to be operating.

Tony, in one sense, is larger than life – he makes things happen; he was, and is, a great inspiration. I worked for him, intensely and casually, for over twenty years, and I have learned to take only what I need from that experience to nourish my own work.

It is only recently that I have found the courage to return to making sculpture. I also understand the design process to be very different to that of finding ways to make sculpture. There are overlaps: both seem to be about developing the whole person and involve professional practice, the nuts and bolts of making it work to make a living. It is only my opinion.

Postscript by Guy Martin, July 2015

On reflection, I should add that both Tony and Sheila possessed a generosity of spirit that extended beyond the professional studio environment, and I am thankful to have been touched by their love and creative energy; it will always remain with me.

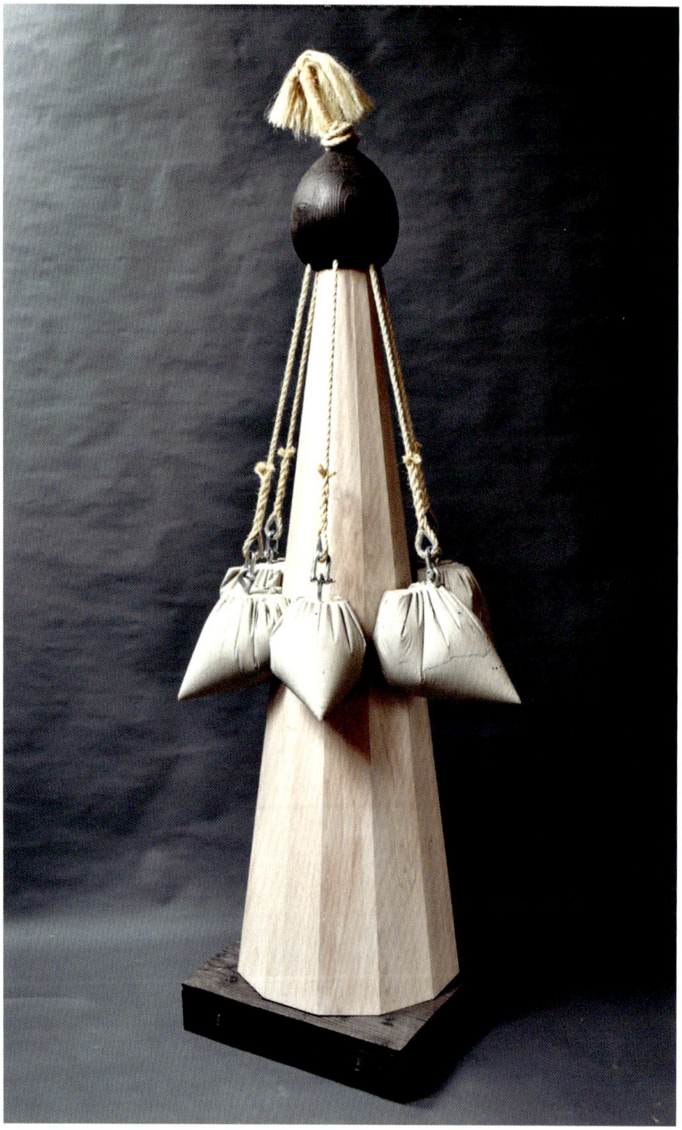

fig. 7

Guy Martin
Standing in Silence (2012)
Macrocarpa and larch woods,
concrete, steel, rope and raffia
2120 x 80 x 80 cm

Interview:

JAMES WOLFE
Studio assistant 1970–78
Maine, USA
Email correspondence (March 2011 to March 2015)

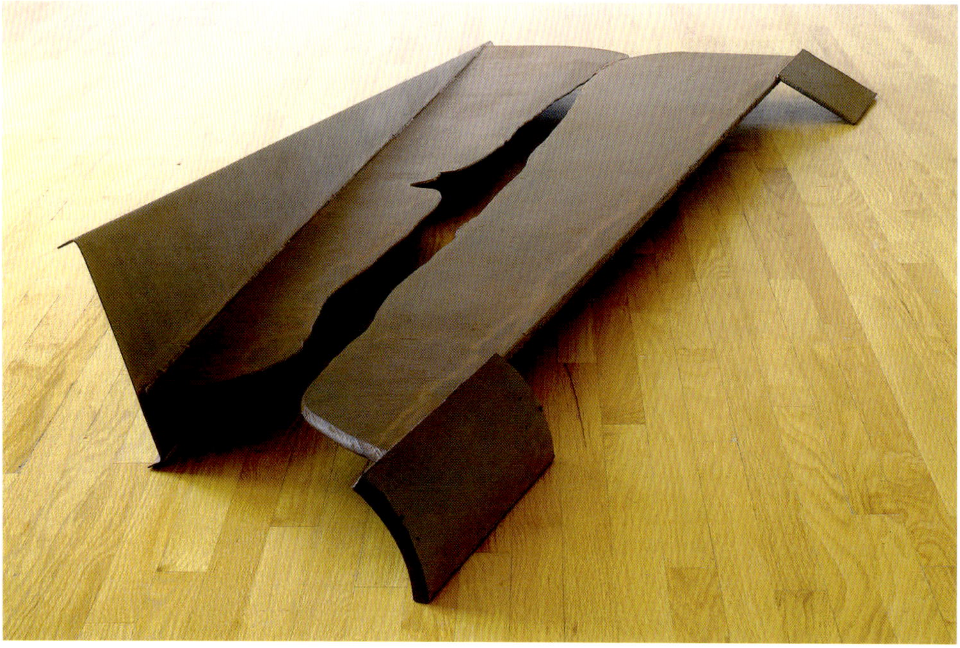

fig. 8

Anthony Caro
Veduggio Fan (1972–73)
Steel, rusted and varnished
28 x 287 x 99 cm

Did you have an art school education?
No.

When did you work for Anthony Caro?
1970–78

How did the job come about?
I was a sculpture assistant at Bennington College and studio assistant to Isaac Witkin, who had studied with Anthony Caro in England. Kenneth Noland needed someone to take care of his animals and house while he lived in New York City during the winter. While I was there, he brought the steel and equipment from the David Smith estate so he could make sculpture, and he asked me to assist him. Caro came to visit and wanted to come back for a few weeks and make sculpture when Ken was in New York. Over several years he came and worked at Noland's.

Why did you want to work for him?
Caro was charming, and I thought working for him would be fun. Curiosity and money also counted.

Which sculptures did you work on?
We made over thirty in Shaftsbury, thirty in Veduggio, thirty in Toronto at York Steel. I worked on his commissioned sculpture for the East Wing of the National Gallery. While working there he also made four small sculptures.

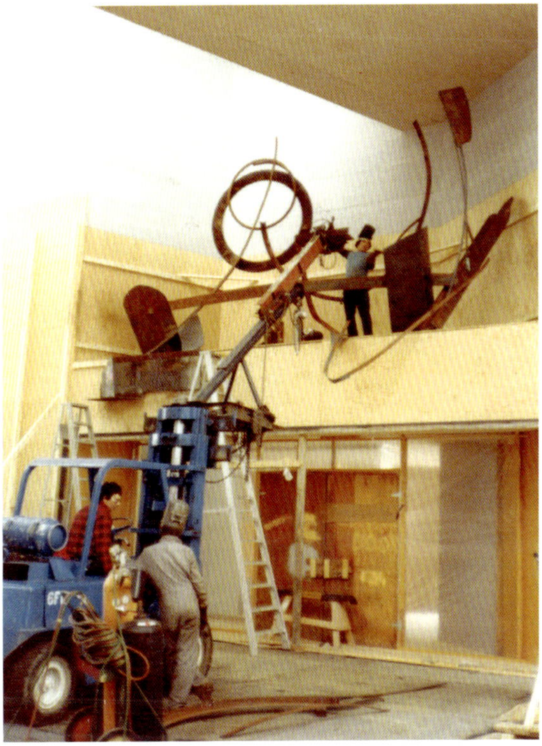

fig. 9

Caro working on *National Gallery Ledge Piece* (1978)

How has – or has – working for Caro influenced you?
I learnt how he went about creating his sculpture; talked with him about the sculptures he was working on and listened to him talk about the direction sculptures might take in the future.

How was your role of assistant received by your contemporaries?
Some positive, some negative. The negative was the belief that he would be an overwhelming influence.

Do you still make work?
Yes.

Has being an assistant informed your teaching methods in any way?
Yes. Creating is more important than theory.

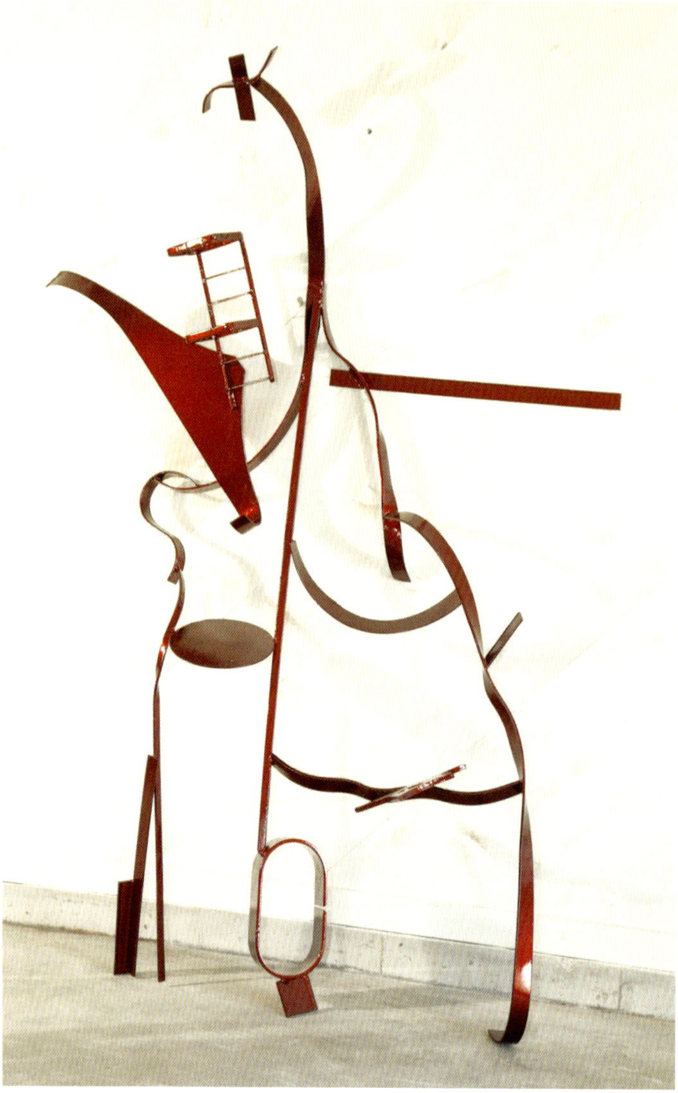

fig. 10

James Wolfe
Changing Scales (2012)
Powder coated steel
228.6 x 140 x 61 cm

Interview:

WILLARD BOEPPLE

Studio assistant 1971–78

New York, USA

Email correspondence (October 2015)

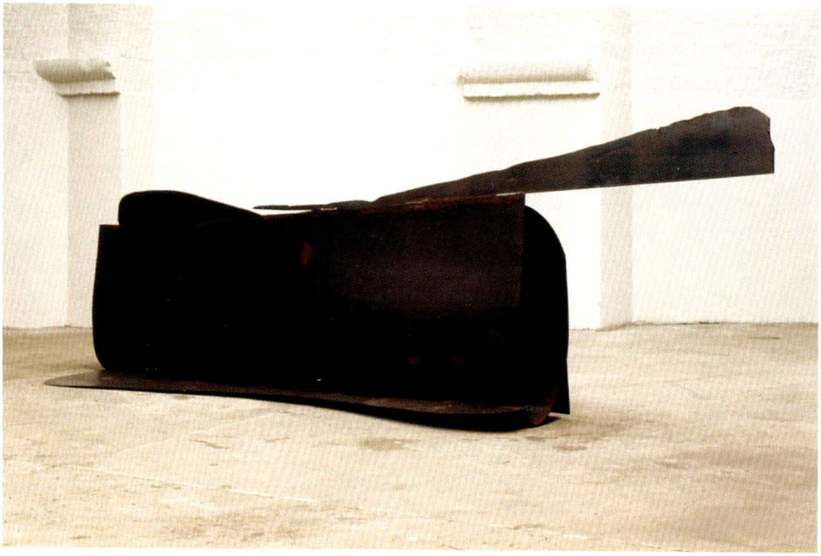

fig. 11

Anthony Caro
Durham Purse (1973–74)
Steel, rusted and varnished
122 x 373.5 x 76 cm

It was in the early 1970s at Ken Noland's place on Buck Hill Road in Shaftsbury, Vermont, that I first went to work for Tony Caro. He was hard at it with Jim Wolfe, making a steel sculpture in the hot sun, and needed a welder. It was good work and the beginning of a long friendship like no other in my life.

When I think back about what it was like to work for Caro, one thing stands out sharp as a fact: Caro thought outside his head. Let me see if I can make sense of this...

In the studio, as has often been noted, Caro frequently made decisions after reacting to the responses of others. He would ask, 'Is this sculpture better with this bit here or over there?' Or, 'Is this sculpture better standing this way up or on its side?' He would ask any and everybody at hand: assistants, friends, visitors, startled passers-by... Anyone. It wasn't simply that he valued your opinion (because often as not he would reject it) but it was as though a decision would become clear in his mind only when he tested it out on others, when he could react to another person's reaction to it. It is said that in quantum physics there are nanoparticles that don't exist until they are measured. Measurement itself becomes a physical act with a reaction. It's as if some version of this was at work for Caro: another viewer's reaction gave him the measure of a thought, made it real. He thought outside his head.

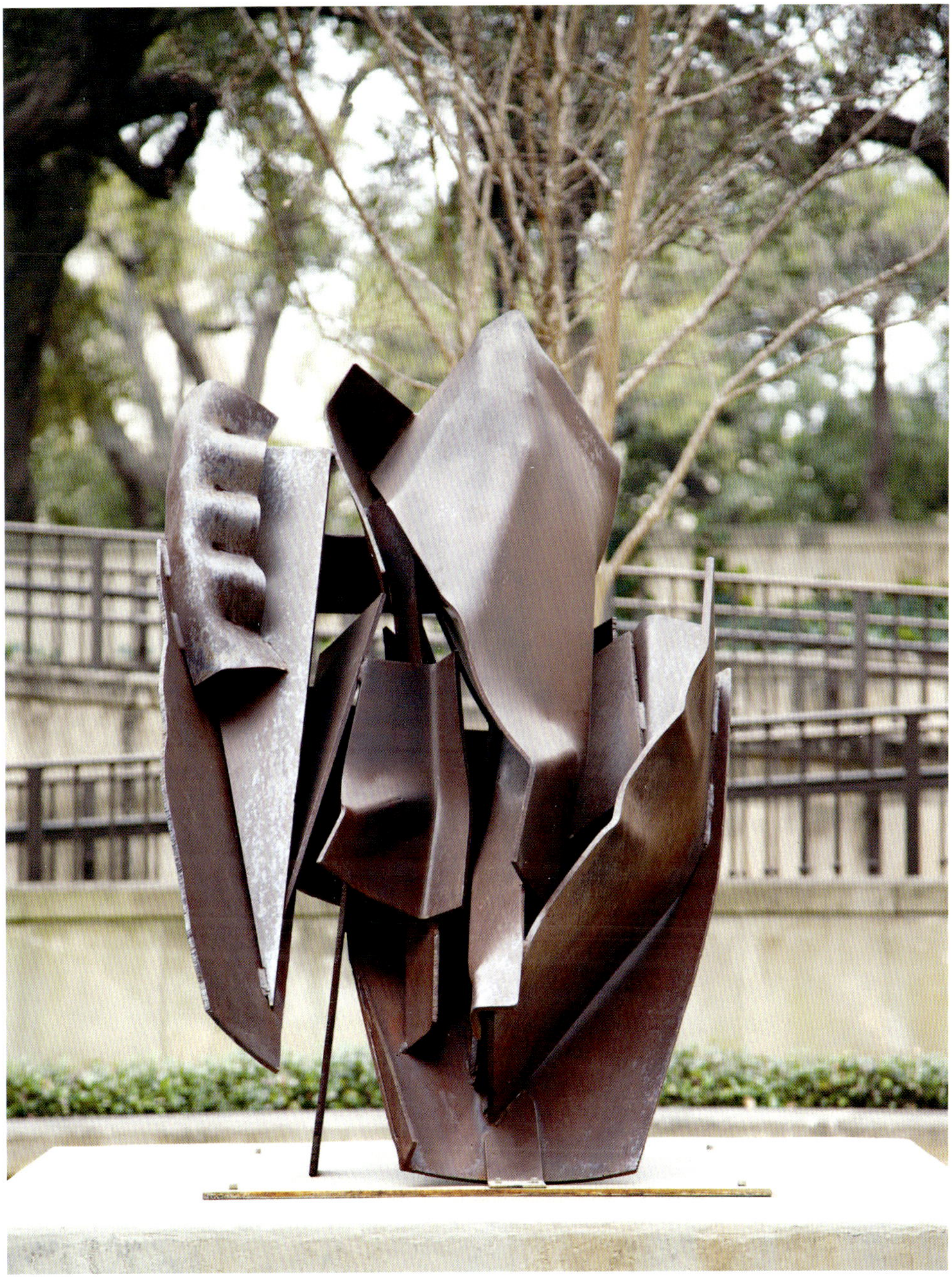

fig. 12

Willard Boepple
Eleanor at 7:15 (1977)
Steel
124.5 x 89 x 114 cm

This working method was at the same time incredibly generous and voracious. It was generous in the way his shared 'public' thinking seemed to open his mind for all to see; open to see how he was going about making a sculpture. And he was voracious in his aggressive, relentless hunt anywhere and from anyone for solutions to the puzzle of a sculpture. 'Where's my crib?', he would ask, and look for inspiration to Rubens, Duccio, Picasso, Matisse, contemporaries. Art books, snapshots and magazines lay open around the studio. And he didn't just borrow. Caro took sculpture-making off the pedestal of traditional art-making and into the realm of a hunt, a game, a great adventure for all in the room. It was an adventure propelled by what Clement Greenberg used to call 'the Caro vortex'; an irresistible enthusiasm that sucked in all bystanders. His was not the way of the private, angst-filled artist struggling alone in his studio; his angst was broadcast, was public, ricocheted around the studio for all to see and share and feel. Working for Caro on his sculpture was a thrilling process that did nothing less than send me rushing back into my own studio, which for my money is the highest compliment one artist can pay another.

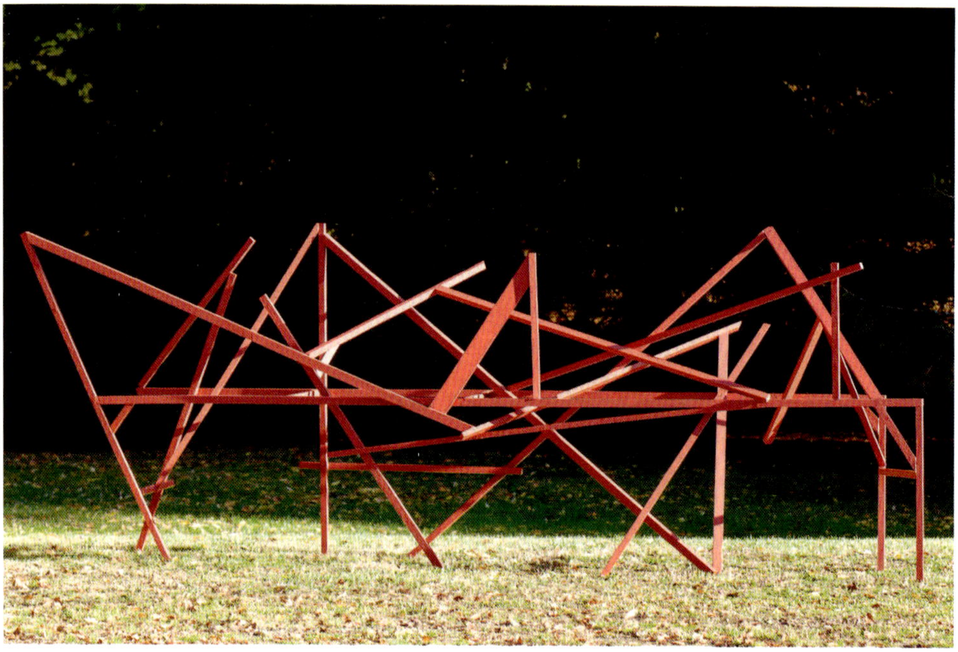

fig. 13

Willard Boepple
Bison (2013)
Aluminium
175 x 467 x 96 cm

Interview:

ANDRÉ FAUTEUX

Studio assistant 1974–75

Ontario, Canada

Email correspondence (February 2011 to August 2015)

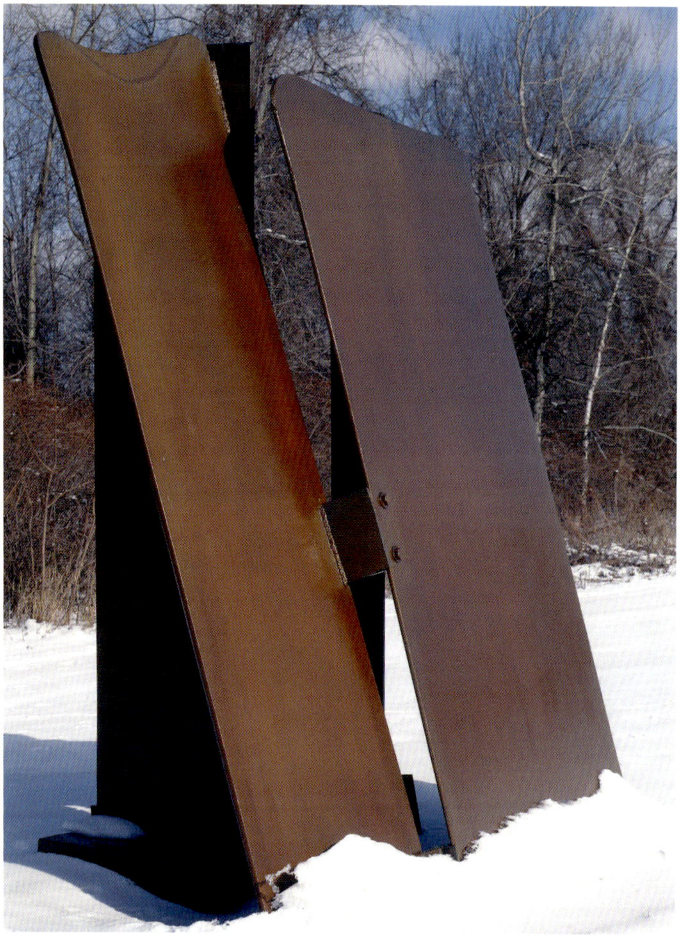

fig. 14

Anthony Caro
Toronto Flats (1974)
Steel, rusted and varnished
330 x 190.5 x 302 cm

Did you have an art school education?
I attended Central Technical School in Toronto, but left halfway through the course because my work in my own studio was much more engaging than the work I was doing in class (with the exception of life drawing).

When did you work for Caro?
In the summer of 1974 I went with Toronto critic Ken Carpenter to see Tony Caro's work in progress (the York sculptures) in a field at York University in suburban Toronto. There I met Jim Wolfe and Willard Boepple, both sculptors from Bennington, Vermont, who had been working for Tony from the beginning of the project. I was an experienced metal fabricator and had just been laid off work a week earlier. Jim and Willard were overwhelmed with the project, whose scope turned out to be much larger than they imagined. They promptly offered me a job and I enthusiastically accepted. I worked with them for about a month;

when they went back to Vermont I continued work for three more months with some assistants that I had hired, until the snow arrived. I didn't meet Caro until two months after I started, when he came back to review the work with Clement Greenberg, Ken Moffett, Ken Noland and Friedel Dzubas. The job started up again in the spring for about three months and then for another two months in the summer. I am still in touch with and interested in the work of Jim and Willard.

Do you believe that a pedagogic relationship existed?
Not in the traditional sense, in which the master verbally imparts his wisdom to his student or apprentice. The word 'mentoring' appeals to me more than 'pedagogic'. Tony Caro's sculptures, not his words, are what have influenced me the most. After seeing Tony's 1970 show (which included *Orangerie, Sun Feast* and *Cadence*) at the Emmerich Gallery, New York, I was blown away and stopped painting and turned to sculpture. To this day, the York sculptures that I worked on seem a step back from this 1969 show.

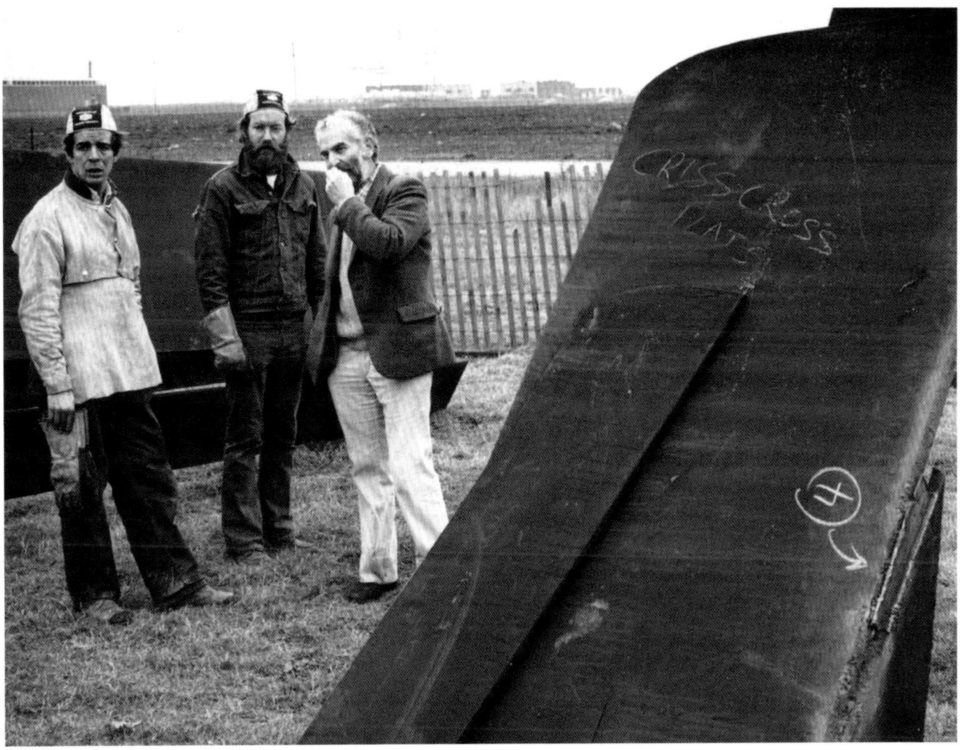

fig. 15

Fauteux, Wolfe & Caro (1974)

The role of the artist and artist-assistant is complex. The artist must get more than he gives or his work would not move forward. The artist-assistant needs nurture both financial and physiological. My experience working for Caro, and the experience of people I know, was that this relationship was always a productive balance. I would jokingly say to friends, 'Tony Caro's self-centeredness was exceeded only by his generosity.'

There is an interesting difference between the artist-mentor and critic-mentor. The artist's experience of your work has to do with what they are concerned with in their own art (object) or what change you can bring to their art (object). The critic-mentor's experience of your work has to do with what they are concerned with in their own art (philosophy) or what change you can bring to their art (philosophy). For me the second has been more fruitful, because it allows for my originality.

How has – or has – working for Caro influenced you?
The most important thing I learnt from Caro was to extend myself in all respects – money, scope, taste – and not accept the comfortable, to push further.

How was your role of assistant received by your contemporaries?
I never thought about this.

Do you still make work?
Yes, I am still working and I rarely employ assistants.

Have you taught in art schools?
Only as a guest lecturer. In North America I was a tradesman, a welder. It made more money than being a professor, and there's no politics.

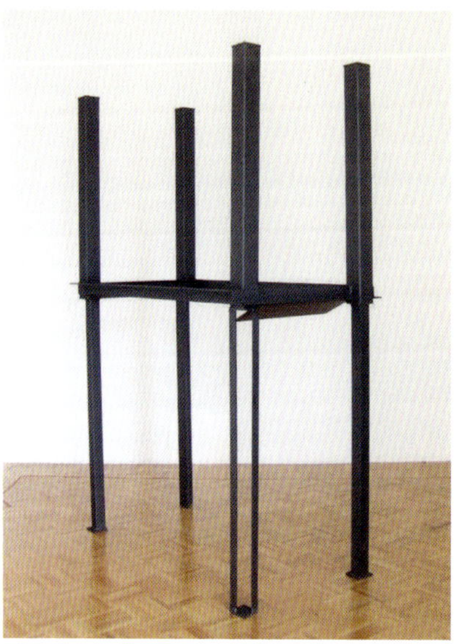

fig. 16

André Fauteux
Nite Watch (1974)
Steel
200 x 73 x 127 cm

Interview:

JOHN GIBBONS

Studio assistant 1976–78

South London, UK

Interview (August 2013)

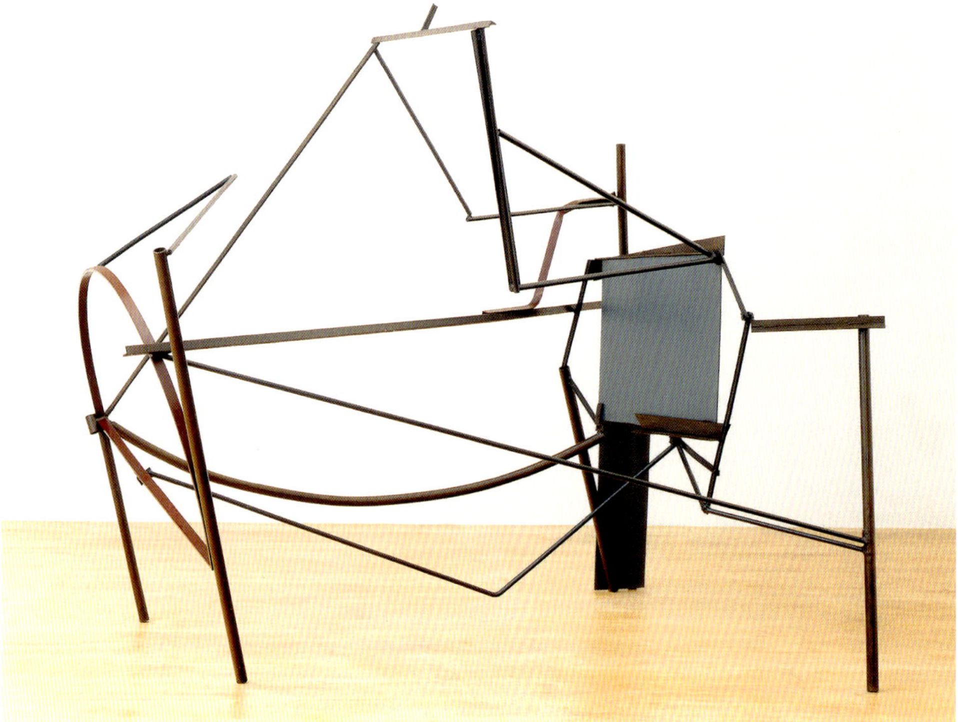

fig. 17

Anthony Caro
After Emma (1977/1982)
Steel, rusted, blackened and painted
244 x 274.5 x 188 cm

JENNY DUNSEATH *I am interested in your experience as a studio assistant and what impact, if any, it had on your practice, career and teaching. To begin: when did you start working for Caro?*

JOHN GIBBONS It was either 1976 or 1977, but before that I worked for Oscar Nemon. He was the Queen's sculptor and his studio was in Clarence House, St James's Palace. I started working for Nemon in 1971 and that's where I really started to learn stuff – how to look, cast, mould, carve and model.

JD *Is that while you were a student?*

JG I was studying in Ireland and getting very frustrated, so in the summers I would come back to London to work. I was working as a gardener in the Houses of Parliament, attached to St James's Park, where I met the Queen Mother's gardener. She told me about this sculptor she knew, Oscar Nemon. One day she asked if I could cast; I said, 'Of course I can',

(I'd only made one waste mould in my whole life!) so she brought me over to meet Nemon.

He brought out this head and asked how I would cast it. I started telling him but quickly realised the logic behind the smaller divides was beyond me, until I noticed that the head – which was made of plaster – had the cast lines still evident, and so I followed those. Of course, he cottoned on straight away that I didn't know what I was talking about, but said to come the next day. I turned up the next day and he said, 'I'll show you how to do things once and once only.'

We got on very well and after working for him for a few months I decided not to go back to art school in Ireland because I was learning so much.

JD *What did you learn from your time with Nemon?*

JG Looking was the first order of the day, and then discussing various ideas about what to do; this was exciting and opened my mind. He showed me how to make moulds, how to enlarge, and all those studio demands. He told me how to make string moulds – a very quick method to make a clay cast of a work in progress. I would take three clay casts, and he would work on each one with different expressions. One would then be chosen as the final work.

We had lunch in the studio and always talked about all kinds of things. One day he said I should go to the Tate; I thought he was being amusing because I related Tate with sugar. I didn't know anything about galleries or museums so I went and the McAlpine Collection show was on – I'd never seen anything like it before and was totally amazed. I bought the catalogue and checked out where all the artists went to school and decided to apply to Saint Martin's.

I worked with Nemon until that Christmas, then I went back to Ireland and made a portfolio of work inspired by the sculptures I'd seen and applied to Saint Martin's. It was an exhilarating and demanding period, working on my own work at Saint Martin's and in the evenings and weekends with Nemon.

JD *How did working for Nemon differ to working for Caro?*

JG When I started working for Tony, I was surprised to see that there was no essential difference to working with Nemon. The studio language was the same: 'Up a bit, down a bit, cut that, try that there...' Nemon would work on a variety of poses and whittle it down to one figure, which would then be cast into an edition, whereas Tony would work on a series and finish each one with its own particular character – essentially the same process.

JD *Were you working at Caro's while studying at Saint Martin's?*

JG No, at the end of my third year I went up to Tony's studio at weekends to help out, move steel, and I got to know Pat and began to do more there. I wasn't terribly good at welding so I did lots of grinding and finishing.

JD *What sculptures did you work on?*

JG There's only one sculpture I worked on with Tony, in the real sense of that word, and that was because Pat was away. You go into the zone and you are working together; it's very fast moving, there are no boundaries. It's not like you're ticking boxes – you're in the zone and you're both on this sculpture. He is leading and, in the end, they are his decisions and that's it.

Tony said, 'Well, what do we call this?' It was part of the *Emma* series he made in Canada so I said, 'After *Emma*'.

All the other work I did in the studio was either working with Tony, Pat and other studio assistants or under Pat, finishing work. Pat actually showed me how to weld properly.

JD *What was it like being an assistant to Caro?*

JG It was a very different creative place from working with Nemon: open and fluid. With Nemon it was more formal, you had very different agendas to work to. It was amazing seeing Tony and Pat working, it was pure chemistry.

After Emma was the only time I've worked with Tony where I have actually been assisting him in the real sense of that word. With Nemon, I was doing it all the time. When I was at Saint Martin's I would go over in the evening and we'd chat about what he was working on during the day, then decide what I would do and make ready for him the next morning. I'd have to have my eye in all the time. I remember one day I wasn't looking and he just screamed at me.

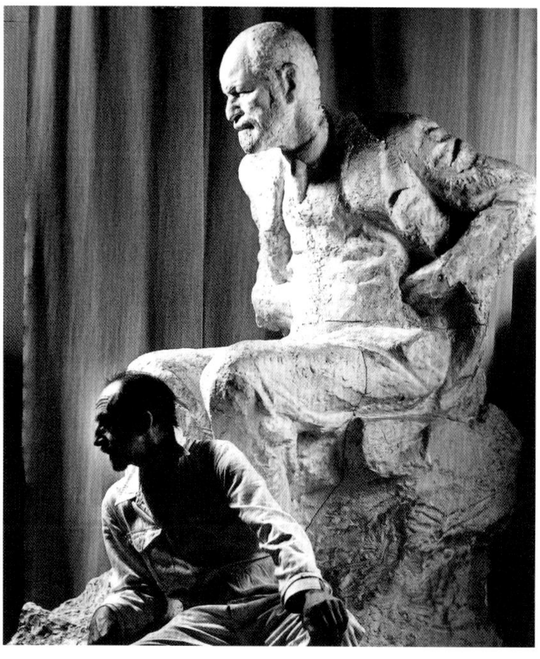

fig. 18

Oscar Nemon with his statue of Sigmund Freud (1971)
Vintage print

JD *Were there similarities between being an assistant to Caro and Nemon?*

JG Actually it was the same language, and I thought, 'Well, that's logical', because Tony worked for Wheeler. Our language is still the same. You know when you listen to how musicians talk: 'That needs to be softer, it's bit sharp, a bit quick'?

When you work with an artist, you get an insight into their creative thinking and what happens to the end product. When you work on a commission or a gallery show, you're working towards that objective all the time. As a student I didn't work with those objectives – you're feeling your way into something and it's important that you are given space to find your voice within the subject.

When you're assisting in the studio you're serving somebody else, you're serving their voice. You have to be receptive to their way and have to be fully in their service, and that forces you to learn different things. It also makes you think much more carefully about how you think and how you work. It's very important not to lose your own identity, because that happens quite a lot. People get very seduced in studios, for all kinds of reasons.

Nemon was good at making you do things you'd never done before. We were working on a large Churchill commission and had to make the hands – I had to enlarge the hands from a cast I made of Nemon's and was really pushed. I learnt a lot about scale and lateral thinking from doing that. On the *Lord Portal* sculpture I'd get to the studio in the evening and he would say, 'It's all wrong'. That commission was a nightmare, and I swore then I'd never do commissions.

JD *What was the commissioning process like in Caro's practice?*

JG Tony talked about the Bourbourg church project [Eglise de Saint-Jean-Baptiste], and it all sounded so familiar. He told me that he had three different parties involved: the bishop, heritage and someone else. He worked on other projects but that was the one that cooked it for him.

JD *Taking* After Emma *as your example of assisting, did you influence the outcome or were you just facilitating the process?*

JG Oh, I couldn't be objective about that, and it's not something I think about. I saw the piece in the Hepworth and knew from a distance what it was, and had a strange recognition. Suffice to say that if you're playing around with ideas and notions of stuff you pick something up from those around you, you need that. You need people with a good eye, because they open things up. Tony feeds off people, that's what artists do. Things move very fast; it's not about ownership, you're on a journey with someone and they're driving. I guess that's why I say that the only time I was truly his assistant was with that sculpture. With Nemon it was different, because I was assisting him all the time and was the only one working there.

When you work with someone you have to enter into their zone and some people are more aligned than others. I can't say that I was really fully aligned with Tony in that sense.

JD *You've maintained contact with Caro?*
JG Yes, we have visited galleries and museums, and we discuss work.

JD *Do you class it as friendship?*
JG It's fun going around galleries and museums with someone, especially Tony, and seeing their reactions to things in contrast to yours. For example, we went to the Paul McCarthy show. I loved taking him to shows like that, shows that are challenging and are rich with a lot of references. I've never seen his jaw drop so quickly! We went to Copperfield Street first and then to the Whitechapel; he was getting off on the set pieces – they were very sculptural. I really liked the drawings and he said, 'What! You like those?' But he went on to say, 'Well, they are a bit French… well, sweet'. It was really very funny! It was the same looking at ancient work. I remember going to see the Henry Moore show at the RA and Tony pointing out the Moores he worked on.

JD *What else did you learn from being an assistant to Caro and Nemon?*
JG Working as an assistant you get a sense of the business, and I think that's very important. Nemon's business was commissions; Tony's was galleries and museums. I saw two pathways that I could follow and got a sense of our profession; that's very important.

JD *The McAlpine Collection influenced your decision to study sculpture at Saint Martin's. Could you tell me about your time there between 1972 and 1976?*
JG Saint Martin's at that time was an extraordinarily open place. In the second year, sculpture divided into the A and B courses. The course had become very conceptual and, in the year before I came, some students rebelled because they wanted to make objects. So Frank [Martin], who was head of sculpture, said, 'Well, we will divide into object makers and conceptual people.'

In the second year, Peter Kardia fronted the A course, and Bill Tucker the B course. We were split into two groups and had to go into the 'white room' as an experience of the A course. The fascinating thing was that we ignored the split into conceptual and object makers because the place was so anarchistic, so it was mixed anyway, and because of that it was truly amazing. You had makers on the A course, and filmmakers and performance artists on the B course.

I describe it as being feral – no-one could control us because there was such a diverse range of opinions. I remember my first crit: I came away in a spin after experiencing tutors talking the heads off each other. I had to go to the library and figure out who all these people were and where they were coming from. Only then did I begin to figure stuff out. Because it was like that, we felt we could do the same, so we did!

I had two very good tutors in David Annesley and Bill Tucker, who had very different mindsets, and it was extraordinary – an amazing and very privileged place to go. I remember David coming in and saying, 'This is a bit boring', so we went off and did a sound thing in the main hall.

Thirty or forty people joined in, bashing bits of steel, pots and pans. It wasn't recorded or documented, we just did it.

Some days we would all work on one drawing or sculpture and David would be orchestrating it; it was something to amuse ourselves with, using different materials and ideas. There was no, 'You're a sculptor, you shouldn't be doing that.' It wasn't like that. It all had value to us as individuals and if it didn't, it wouldn't have worked.

JD *Were you aware of Caro at this point?*

JG I didn't know who Tony was; it was Bill who said I should go and see his show 'Straight Through'. I wasn't impressed; I thought it was very formulaic and not really interesting, but interesting enough for me to check him out in the library. I was left in no doubt as to Tony's significance.

JD *What else did you learn at Saint Martin's?*

JG Bill was writing his book, *The Language of Sculpture*, and we were his research students. He picked out certain students to present a seminar on each artist, then he would ask questions and bring it into a contemporary context. He recorded everything. It was like a brainstorming session. There was no-one else like Bill in the place. What was interesting about him was that he never gave us his opinion; he would probe everything we said. There were huge arguments among the students – it was really stimulating. You had to be articulate to have that kind of input.

Bill curated 'The Condition of Sculpture' show at the Hayward during my time there. So you had this kind of austere, intellectual man in Bill, and David, who was this very open and generous, gregarious, fun guy and equally very intelligent. There were other people there as well, but those two guys really did it for me and were great fun to work with. It was very challenging.

It was anarchistic; we didn't think, 'Could we get away with this?' rather, 'This is how we think about this and this is how we are going to do it.' Some of the students would go on walkabout and we might not see them for three weeks. But we knew our responsibilities: to work hard, to put work up every month for a crit and argue our case. There were four or five tutors in each crit; opinions were disparate and we had to fight. Frank never allowed anything or anyone to dominate. No individual would take over. It was a bit colonial – just keep them all fighting.

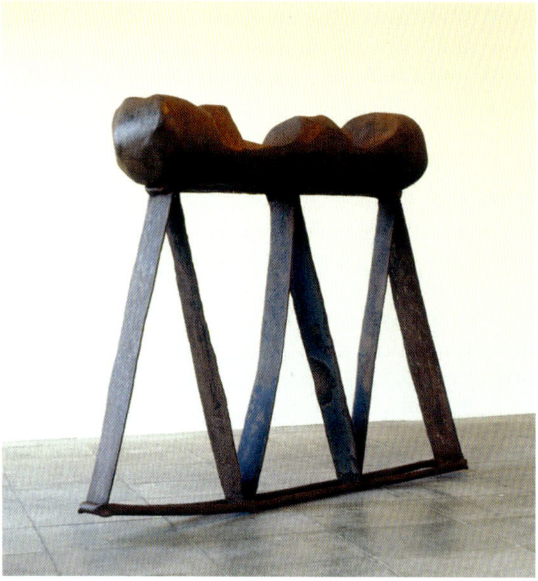

fig. 19

John Gibbons
The Dream (1977–78)
Steel, paint (red oxide wash) and waxed
145 x 32 x 200 cm

JD *You went on to become head of sculpture at Winchester School of Art (WSA). Was it Saint Martin's that influenced your own teaching methodology in the development of the sculpture department?*

JG Absolutely. For me, it was very important that people had individuality, and the freedom and support for that kind of journey. I also wanted to learn and to get something out of every week. I had to get something out of it – it would drive you bonkers otherwise – so it was self-interest as well as education. I needed to be amused by, and intellectually involved in, what was going on. Let's face it, the money in lecturing isn't good enough – it's so poorly paid it's unbelievable. Whichever way it worked, for me it was very important that I was intellectually stimulated and able to see how people dealt with things individually. That is really important. You have to pass things on. Ideas are ideas: you take an idea from someone or somewhere, it doesn't really matter, it's what you do with it. You take ownership of it and you make it work for you. That is how Tony worked; he's a dreadful magpie. A lot of artists are like that. Picasso was.

JD *From my own experience of studying at WSA, I remember the first year projects vividly – they were seminal to my understanding of introducing a practice methodology.*

JG That's the reason I developed and configured those introductory projects. It was to do with allowing people to witness their own individuality. The stick project, for example, was a classic way of doing that – seeing how you could make something larger than you – and students were empowered and delighted by it. Everyone's individuality came out very clearly and it was fascinating to see. The scale, the fun...

it became like a jungle in there; everyone was in it together. Of course, there were a few who didn't, but people could see how different they were: some struggling to get their structure upright, while others were organised and systematic. The students gained a huge number of lessons and insights from that one task. It brings people down to base level: the activity is the grounder and makes people relax and chill out. It allows them to understand that there is no such thing as a mistake or a single way of doing things. Mistake is such a dreadful, moralistic word. There is no such thing as a mistake in art – what we do is not about mistakes. It's a moral term that has no place.

The attitude at Saint Martin's was that we did not do projects, with the exception of being locked in the white room for a week at the end of our first year, which was our introduction to the A course.

JD *I understand you employ assistants in the production of your own work; how do you view the relationship and do you see similarities to your own experience?*

JG Having another eye in the studio is vital – it opens you up, takes you out of your comfort zone. There are a number of people who visit whose eye I trust. As for my assistants: Natuka (Honrubia) cleans down and prepares the work so that I can see the surface and work to a finish. She's very good at resourcing materials and equipment, like various abrasives. For some of the colour work, she will get a range of sprays and materials. I like to do that because then I get a range that I have to react to, and for me it's more interesting. She also has a good eye, which is very important because it allows you to see from another perspective and in another way. She doesn't do any welding or fabrication.

I only ever had someone make my work for me when I was in India, where I directed it. That work was made on a lathe; it was interesting to delegate it. I figured that, from all the guys working there, one was a genius and understood what I was doing and really knew how to make the machine speak. I would do a drawing, work out the measurements, angles and curvature, and he would look and pick stuff up. He didn't speak English, but could read the drawings and do the maths – he really understood and we had a lot of fun.

JD *You touched upon how Nemon and Caro provided you with professionalism; how else did they inform your practice?*

JG When you work with Tony or Nemon you have to train your eye. It actually isolates certain behavioural patterns and you disentangle this from other things. So you could pull that out of something else, out of your own experiences or whatever. We all use our eye and we all use it differently, so when you're with someone like that, a specific part of that becomes even more special, because you have to understand straight away what he is asking you to do. Then you're able to empower that facility and hone it to your advantage.

The business side of things is to do with having a sense that the work has a life outside of you, and you have a responsibility to engage with it, and that's part of your profession. It's not that you were self-indulgent before, but it makes you aware that this has to go into the world and live by itself.

With Nemon I learnt about the nature of monuments and portraiture and commissions. With Tony, it was the gallery systems and museums. You have a sense of what you're in and what your interests are.

JD *Has your own work been affected or influenced by Caro?*

JG You are influenced by people whose work fascinates you. I don't want to know that in a literal way because it destroys things, so I can't be objective. *Early One Morning* is just such a wonderful masterpiece, so sublime... That level of sublimity is extraordinary.

But how does it affect my work? Well, I have no idea. I've been told how much he takes from me, but I can't be objective about how much I take from him. I'm sure I do. I enjoy going to see shows with him: the conversations we have and the range of work we see together opens up all kinds of dialogues. We are so different from each other, in terms of aesthetics, temperament and character, which helps. Sometimes we have huge rows, which are quite intense. It's not very often, but we do have them. That's a privilege; I couldn't have those sorts of conversations with anyone else.

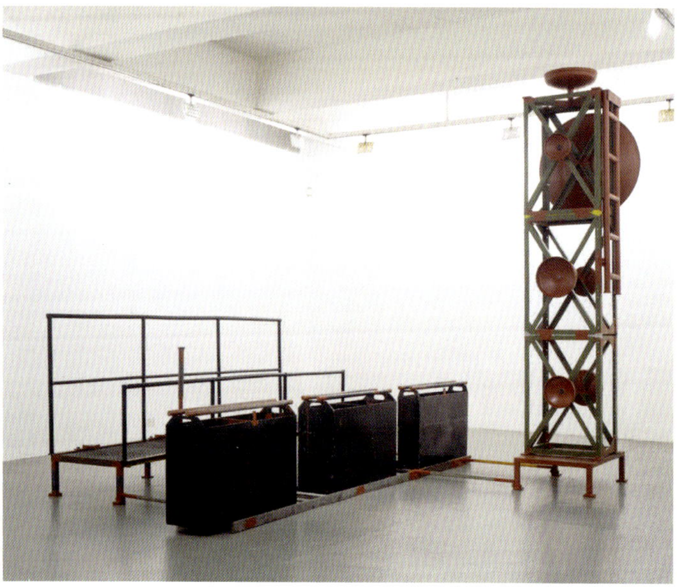

fig. 20

John Gibbons
Exodus (1992–94)
Steel, painted and waxed
320 x 365 x 398 cm

JD *What does this relationship do for an artist?*

JG I saw the Belvedere Torso in the Vatican this year – it's an extraordinary sculpture. It's like a collage because it brings together the best parts of the body, in the best positions they can be in, into a seated figure. It looks like a regular seated figure, but then you realise the chest is in the moment of some physical activity and not sitting on a chair, and it's the same with the thighs and back. You can see how Michelangelo saw this and thought 'Oh yeah, right!' And that's very much how it is... When you look at Tony's work you can see Gonzalez and Smith. That's how it should be. When you look at Cézanne, you can see Titian. When you look at Picasso you can see Cézanne. What's important is that they keep their own voice: a very clear, distinct voice that's part of the continuum that links all work. Nothing is external.

At the 'Matisse Picasso' exhibition at the Tate, Tony asked me, 'Who is the best?' It was a classic Tony question, but this time it sounded wrong. It took me some time to figure out what the right question might be – I wasn't quick enough to think of it at the time. I think the right question is, 'Would these two guys be as good without each other?' I don't think they would be. They pushed each other: Matisse was very cool and laid back; Picasso was noisy. They were working at such a consistently high level right the way through their lives, and they never got distracted by publicity or whatever. They knew and understood it, but were never distracted from their work. It's the same with Cézanne. They never became involved in maintaining an iconic image for commercial purposes.

JD *All of the artists discussed here appear to have an essential attribute – a determined focus to continually push the parameters of a practice.*

JG There are lots of artists who have found a commercial motif and they just manufacture. They run a consistent production line. Everyone recognises their products, and everyone has to have one. In our time, in terms of commerce and business, if you have a consistent look, you can make a lot of money and there are a lot of artists seduced by it. But there are several artists who will intentionally question and challenge their work. Larry Poons is continually challenging. I have time for people like Larry. There are people who are commercially successful, and that's their thing. When I look at art, I expect to be challenged and nourished; I don't expect to think, 'I've seen this before'.

JD *With that in mind, how do you maintain your focus and drive?*

JG I think it's the way I'm wired; I don't think I could be any other way. I was put in a position where I had to make a choice. I had a show at the Serpentine, which did really well. I sold a lot of work (the Tate bought *Desire*, and I made other important sales) but I had no real handle on it. It was just this work I'd made, and I felt I needed to get more under my belt. I decided to work in my studio for two years and just figure it out. I didn't want to remake or make more work like that. I knew I needed more time in the studio so I backed away from dealers.

For me, that was a very important moment. Would I have made a different decision now? No, I wouldn't. It's not the money, it's the curious state of being acknowledged but not recognised.

You make a decision on how you want to be and that's important. If you are happy, and it works, it is recognising self and how self needs to be. Whatever you do, life is challenging, and money doesn't make it easier or simpler. That was a point I recognised – whatever you do it costs, so what do you want to pay for?

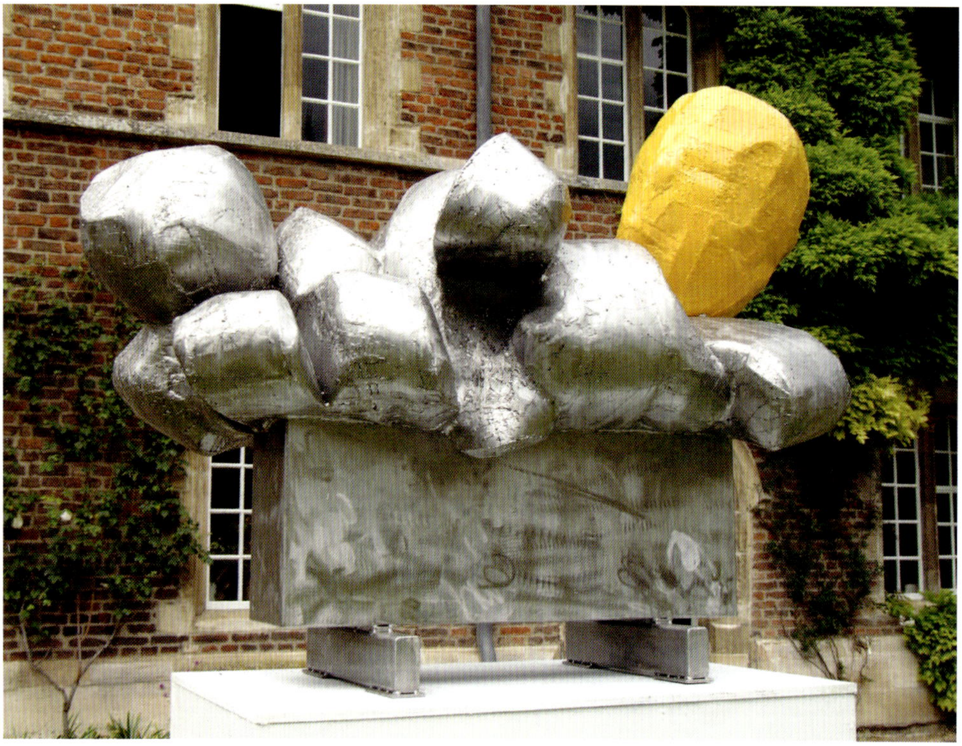

fig. 21

John Gibbons
First Moment (2006–7)
Stainless steel, painted and varnished
128 x 106 x 164 cm

Essay: Making a Show of Yourself

Dr Michael Petry

"As time has moved on, I have become comfortable being ever more distant from 'making' art."

I emigrated from the US to the UK in 1981. It took me a while to get used to British idiosyncrasies, especially the figures of speech that abound in British English. Shortly after I arrived, I remember overhearing a mother chastise her sullen teenage son for dressing as a punk: 'Stop making a show of yourself', she said.

I grew up in El Paso, Texas. I think I might have been the only New Waver, and one of the few artists. I went to great lengths at art school to dress glamorously and apply full make-up (thank you David Bowie). I thought making a show of myself was a good thing, and *de rigueur* in London. Overhearing the mother chastise her son, I was worried I'd got the wrong end of the stick...

But I needn't have worried. Back in the day, London overflowed with people making shows of themselves, not least on the art scene. In fact, relatively speaking, I was something of a traditionalist, having had a fairly orthodox BA art education that focussed, among other things, on 'making' art. My undergraduate studies taught me to stretch a canvas, to weld, to use a blowtorch, to cast bronze using the lost wax method, and to make prints (although I was far too messy to make more than one or two in an edition).

But London was experimenting with more collaborative art production techniques. Installation art (an anachronistic reference, because the label 'installation art' had not then been applied to that art practice) and performance art required contributions from more people than just a lone artist. I threw myself into this scene... I remember making an installation in an abandoned cold-storage warehouse in Vauxhall, which required many friends to help produce and document; and making a video on a tributary of the Thames, which required two naked men to roll about in the mud.

As time has moved on, I have become comfortable being ever more distant from 'making' art. Where appropriate, my work is made by artisans (who have more skill than I could hope or wish to possess), by foundries (which bring more manpower than I possess to the process of working with bronze and glass), or computers and 3D printers (which have greater accuracy than my mind or my hand). I've also learned that what seemed new to me in London in the 1980s is, in fact, very old; that throughout the ages artists have collaborated with others in the production of their work. I think of this as the art of 'not-making'.

Rembrandt (1606–69) is a good example of an artist who practiced not-making. I was taught that Rembrandt's assistants helped him in the studio so that they could learn from the master as he diligently worked away. But, in fact, those assistants did much more than watch and learn – they helped Rembrandt to paint. And not just to paint details in the background or drapery, but to substantially paint the canvas. According to the official Rembrandt Research Project (1968–2011), Rembrandt knowingly signed paintings that, effectively, were not his own. They would have it that he collaborated in making forgeries of his own work.

To protect the unsuspecting public, the Rembrandt Database[1] authenticates 'genuine' Rembrandts. The Database initially whittled down about 700[2] genuine Rembrandts by nearly 300, on the basis that the master only contributed 50–90 per cent of the work. The Database now records just 176 genuine Rembrandts. The rest are described as being of the 'school of Rembrandt'. No-one disputes that all carry Rembrandt's true signature, or that the original buyers would have understood how the studio system worked (i.e. that their Rembrandt would have been a collaborative effort). The Database contests that only those 176 paintings containing sufficient

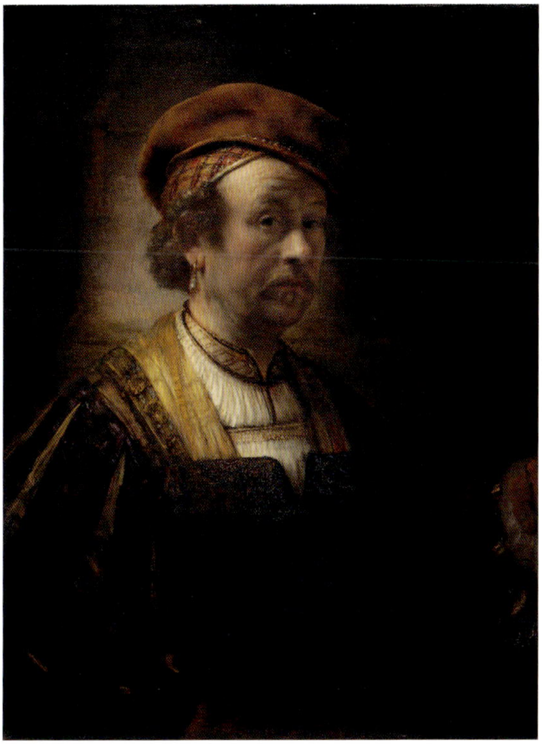

fig. 22

Rembrandt Workshop
Portrait of Rembrandt (1650)
Oil on canvas
125.1 x 107 x 11.4 cm framed

original contribution from Rembrandt should be ascribed to him; in effect, it implies that he should not have signed the others, and that he could not distinguish his own work from Rembrandt-ish imposters.

This would be funny if the motivation was not so fraught with conflicts of interest. Reducing the number of 'real' Rembrandts adds great value to those that are left. If a 100 per cent Rembrandt is worth, say, £20 million, an 80 per cent Rembrandt is worth only £2 million. Authentication boards exist for many other artists, and some have ended up in murky financial water. The Andy Warhol Estate has had to close its own authentication board due to its many contested decisions, which included de-authenticating a painting that Warhol himself chose as the cover for a book of his own work while he, Warhol, was still alive.[3] Perhaps Warhol, like Rembrandt, forged his own work.

The sculptor and architect Gian Lorenzo Bernini (1598–1680), father of the Baroque who designed the sweeping semi-circular arcade for the Piazza San Pietro, understood a thing or two about not-making...

First, and most obviously, even though Bernini designed the Piazza, he did not physically build it – he did not dig the foundation, construct the scaffold, cut, lay and dress the stone... We understand that architecture relies on not-making; that Zaha Hadid, no less than Bernini, did not pour concrete, join wood or plumb toilets (all of which would have been impractical in her fabulous Issey Miyake gowns and Manolo Blahnik shoes).

We also understand that architecture requires collaborations with technical specialists and engineers; that Hadid was assisted by a small army who prepared technical drawings, calculated stresses and loads, and rendered the overall design. But we still think of Hadid as the architect of the London Aquatics Centre in Stratford, just as we think of Bernini as the architect of the Piazza (although presumably the people who maintain the Rembrandt Database would disagree).

Second, setting aside Bernini's work as an architect and focussing on his work as a sculptor, the art historian Guus van den Hout notes that even his most physiologically dramatic sculptures were 'almost always made by assistants and master sculptors either in his employ or hired for specific projects'.[4] Bernini made terracotta models for these works (often much smaller than the final marble copy) and would oversee their production. For example, Bernini oversaw Giuliano Finelli (1601–53) carve his sculptures of *Apollo and Daphne* and *The Rape of Proserpina*, which van den Hout describes as 'wonderful examples of this division between *invenit* (Bernini) and *fecit* (Finelli). Bernini made the model and Finelli executed his ideas in marble.'[5]

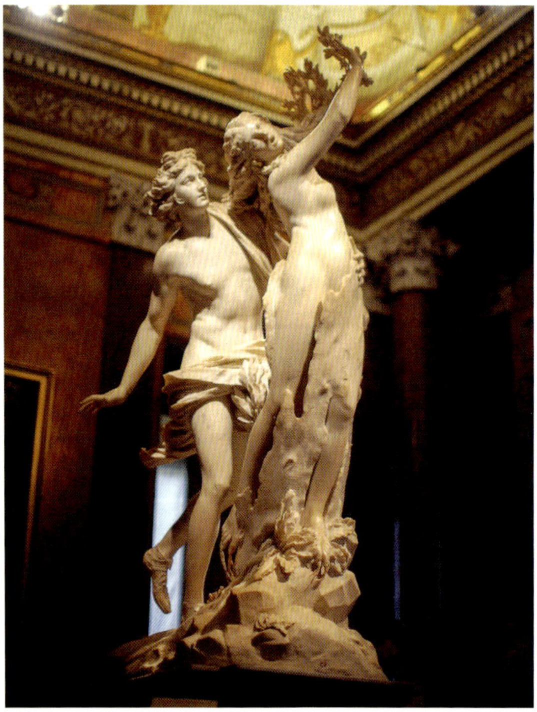

fig. 23

Gian Lorenzo Bernini
Apollo and Daphne (1622–25)
Marble
Height: 243 cm

Finelli eventually quit working for Bernini, annoyed that he did not get enough credit, and subsequently made his own work, but these were never as fluid or dramatic as those he produced for Bernini. People wanted Bernini's vision, not Finelli's craftsmanship, although perhaps were happiest when they got both. They were not bothered if Bernini's sculptural ideas were fulfilled by other master carvers, or put off by his tendency to make a show of himself in front of popes, cardinals or the law – like many Renaissance artists, he was a shocking self-publicist and bad boy.

Joshua Reynolds (1723–92) was one of the founders and the first president of the Royal Academy of Arts (1768) and was a widely sought portrait painter to the nobility and gentry. He was so much in demand that he graced few clients with the honour of painting their entire portrait himself. Reynolds would design the composition and (depending on the sitter's status) would paint the face and hands before passing it over to his assistants to paint the clothes and background. He employed a specialist for velvet dresses and fur capes, for the glister of gold and the sparkle of gems, and if a client wanted his stately home in the background, then Reynolds would arrange for the canvas and an assistant to be carted off to the house, where it would be duly inserted. Given the state of the roads in the eighteenth century and the risk of highway robbery, it is not surprising that Reynolds packed his assistants off on those long journeys. Just like buyers of a Rembrandt, buyers of a Reynolds knew the score – that the end painting was a collaboration but no less genuine for that.

There are even a few contemporary painters who use the hands of others. The two most famous are Damien Hirst and Jeff Koons. They are interesting to contrast because they collaborate differently with their assistants.

Hirst requires his assistants to sign a confidentiality agreement covering their work in his studio, so in theory we ought not to know much about what goes on. But in practice, tongues wag and much has been revealed, including by Hirst himself, who acknowledges that if others can paint dots or pills better then he can, then he would prefer to employ them to do so (although Hirst says that if his work depicts carnage he likes to add the blood himself).[6] When it comes to his sculptures, it is still more obvious that he does not cast the large bronzes that appear under his name any more than Henry Moore did. Moore, like Bernini, provided a small maquette to foundry workers to work from; in Hirst's case the maquette itself is usually an existing or found object, be it a collecting box (*Charity*) or a human medical sculpture (*Hymn*). *Hymn* landed Hirst in a lawsuit with the original manufacturer of the medical sculpture[7] – Hirst settled out of court and donated an undisclosed sum to charity. In the same year, he threatened to sue British Airways for decorating one of their planes with dots. It seems that appropriation is not a two-way street for Hirst.

Koons also employs others to make his paintings and sculptures. His studio is known to be as clean as an operating theatre, where white-coated young artists paint away at large works that Koons has assembled on a computer screen. Once he is happy with an image, his employees toil to replicate a copy that is as flat and perfect as possible.[8] Koons aims to remove any notion of the presence of human touch, as is evident in his sculptures. His large stainless steel balloon dogs have to be perfect, otherwise he requires the work to be discarded and started over again, regardless of cost. Koons was an earlier adopter of appropriation than Hirst – he took an image of a woman and a man holding eight puppies, by the photographer Art Rogers (*Puppies*),[9] and had Italian woodcarvers make it into a three-dimensional sculpture (*String of Puppies*). Rogers sued, and the courts found in his favour: Koons had gone beyond any 'fair use'. Incidentally, if Koons had carved the sculpture himself, he may still have lost the case, as the Belgian artist Luc Tuymans found when he was sued for using a photographer's image as the basis for a painting he himself painted.[10]

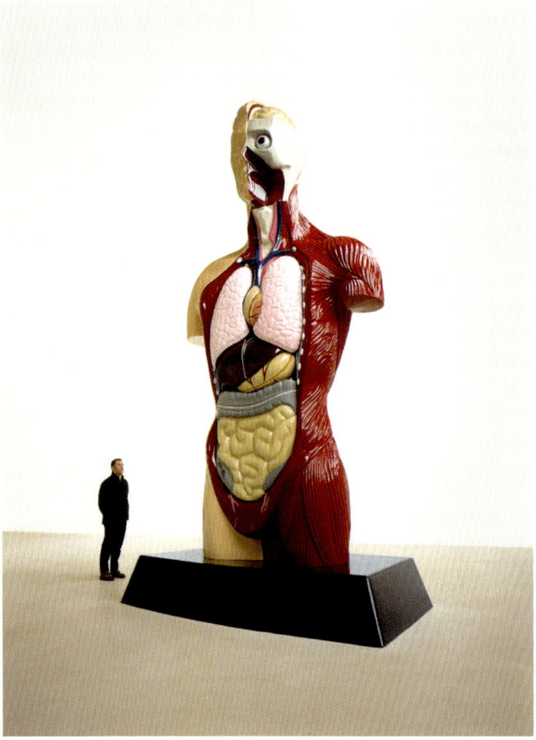

fig. 24

Damien Hirst
Hymn (1999–2005)
Painted bronze
234.37 x 131.5 x 80.98 in

So: a painting by Rembrandt is not a genuine Rembrandt if he didn't paint enough of it; but a sculpture by Bernini is a genuine Bernini despite the fact that he didn't sculpt any of it; and a painting by Tuymans isn't a genuine Tuymans despite the fact that he painted all of it. And it's not just fine art that exhibits this strange relationship with making and not-making – architecture (as described above), music, literature, film and fashion are all similarly impacted.

It is hard to make much sense of this, other than by appealing to the nebulous concept of 'brand'. Yves St Laurent never sewed a stitch of a coat that was bought by even his richest client. If the coat was a hand-made couture item, it would have been stitched in Paris by the *petits mains*; if it was a ready-to-wear item, it would have been made in a factory (most likely in Italy and later in China). If the latter, and the same factory made a few extras on their own account to the same design and from the same material, then what is to distinguish between the original and the fake, other than their brand?

I have been to shopping malls in Thailand where copies of every brand are for sale. China is not only awash with these 'extras' but is also shipping them globally – both in fashion and in fine art. The city of Karamay has just installed a sculpture of a 'big oil bubble' that is strikingly similar to Anish Kapoor's Chicago *Cloud Gate* (2004).[11] An official defended their sculpture, stating that: 'Cloud Gate intends to reflect the sky, but ours reflects the ground'. Kapoor has not sued[12] – perhaps because it is difficult (or near impossible) to win a copyright case under Chinese law. Anyhow, suing is beside the point, because a true collector wants the real thing/brand, not a knock-off, irrespective of how faithful it may be. That's why the UK's Land Rover car manufacturer has not sued the Chinese makers of the *Land Wind,* an astonishingly similar vehicle that is unlikely to be of interest to a true collector and can only be sold in China.[13]

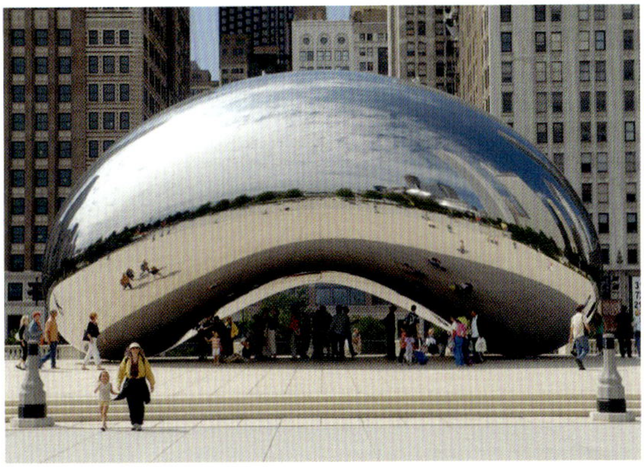

fig. 25

Anish Kapoor
Cloud Gate (2004)
at Millennium Park, Chicago
Stainless steel
10 x 20.1 x 12.8 m

Needless to say, not-making is not just a guy thing, but it is a capital-intensive thing, and therefore fewer women have access to this way of making. But women artists have also collaborated with others to make their work. Barbara Hepworth 'made' huge bronze works in the same way as Moore – by providing maquettes to her assistants. Similarly, at 90 years of age, Louise Bourgeois did not wield a blowtorch to make her famous spiders (*Maman*); she worked with assistants. Ditto the Spanish artist Angela de la Cruz, both before and after ill-health required her to rely on support from assistants, and the Portuguese artist Joana Vasconcelos, who buys pottery and lace from local artisans to fashion into her own signature work. She now employs a small army of makers to construct her large fabric-based sculptures, culminating in a massive installation at Versailles (2012).

It could be argued that any artist who uses a camera, video or computer is partially not-making their work, to the extent that they rely on these machines, their underlying software and peripheral devices such as projectors and screens. But where technology causes fine art to overlap with film, we seem willing to entertain a looser sense of authorship. A film directed by Scorsese is 'a Scorsese' irrespective of his collaboration with actors, script writers, lighting engineers, costume designers, editors and the rest of the many hundreds of names that roll up at the end of a film.

I have made a whole body of work using glass and yet I am neither a glass blower nor a glass caster. I work with artisans in many countries and they all have their own way of making glass, which is something I had to learn along the way. Just as language differs between the USA and the UK, so glass blowing differs between Murano and London. I enjoy a very collaborative approach with artisans. I enjoy the interaction of the conceptualist (*invenit*) and the hands of the maker (*fecit*). I like to be present when the work is fabricated, not least so that I can decide whether manufacturing accidents are lucky (or not). Others – like Koons – prefer to eliminate all makers' marks.

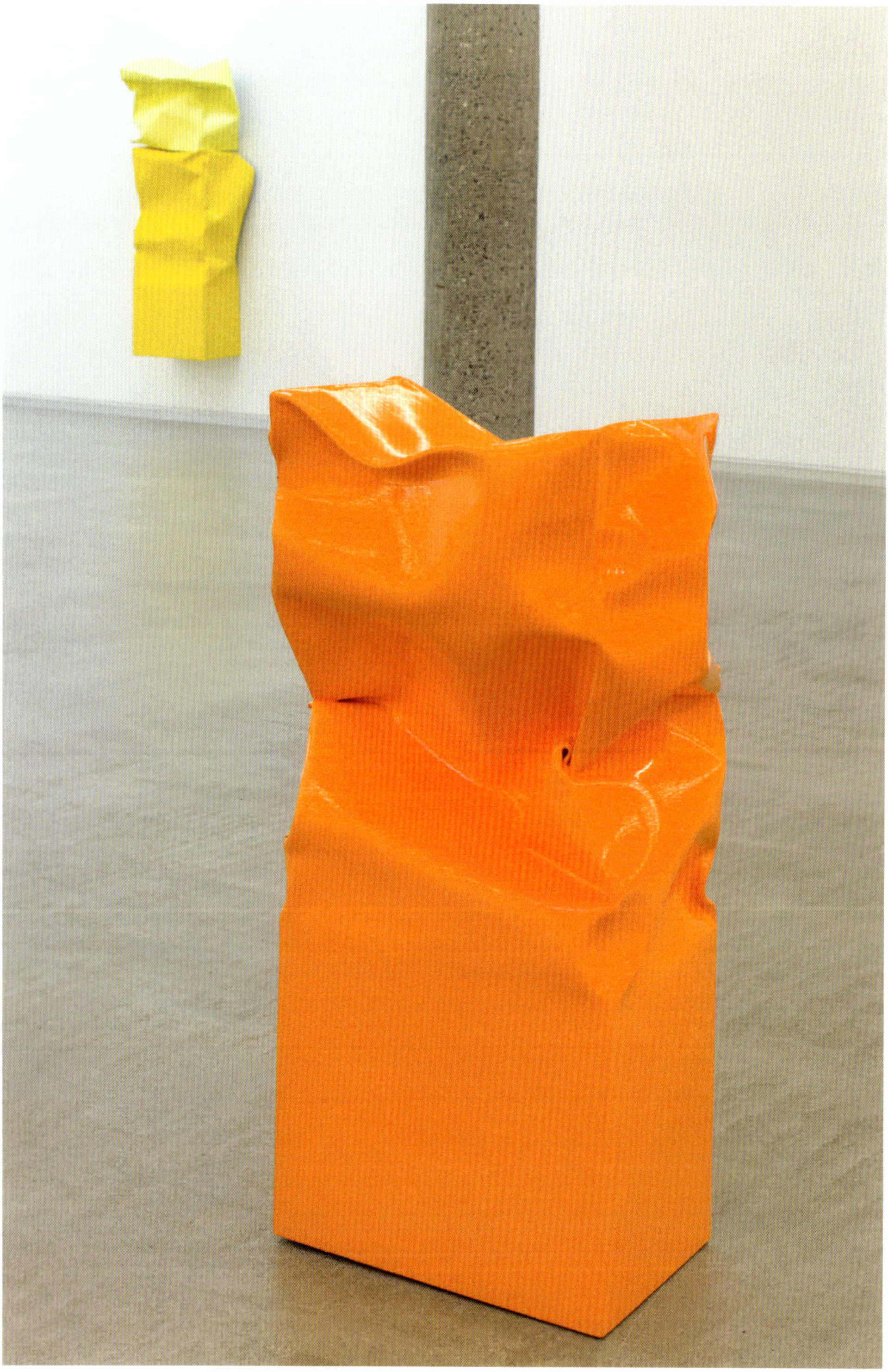

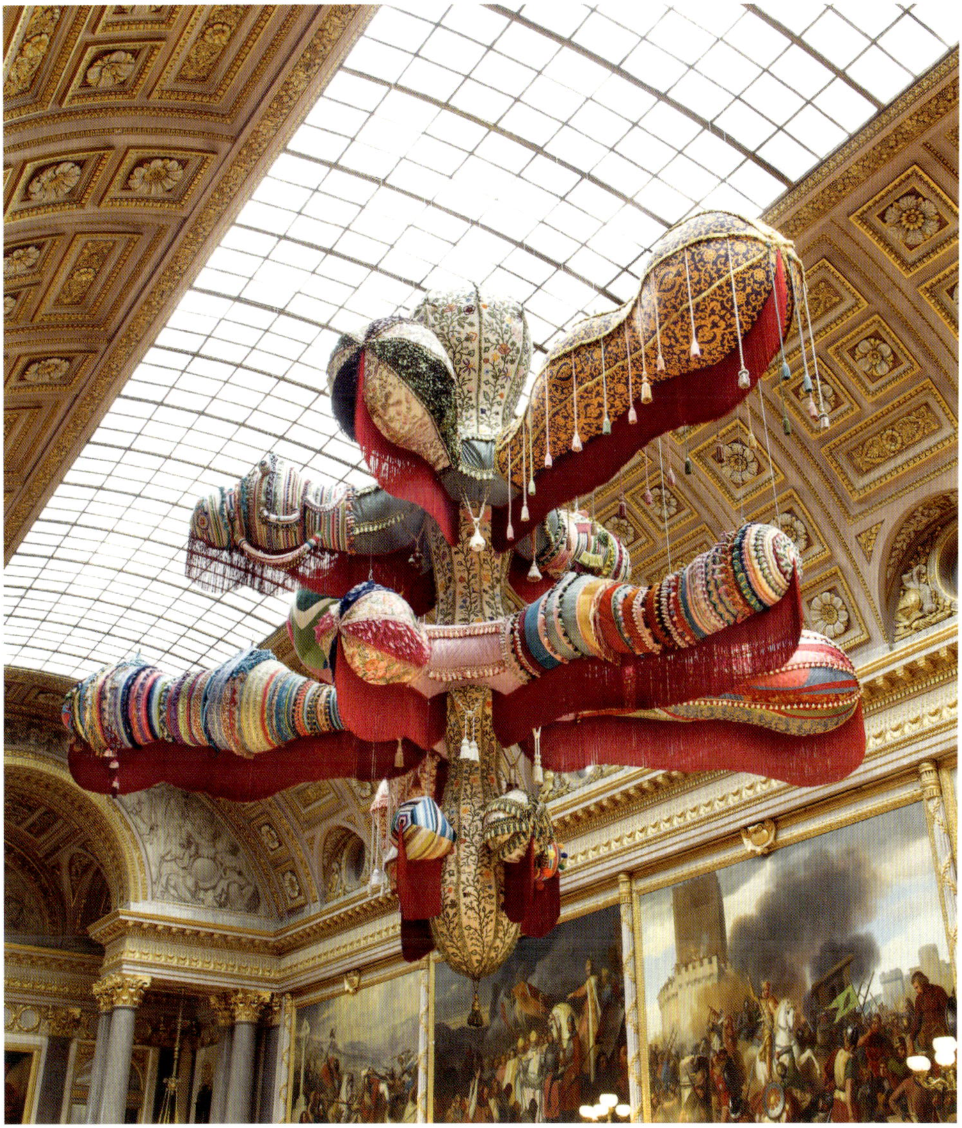

fig. 27

Joana Vasconcelos
Royal Valkyrie (2012)
Galerie des Batailles [The Battle Gallery]
Handmade woollen crochet, felt appliqués, industrial knitted fabric, fabrics, ornaments, polystyrene, polyester and steel cables
Work produced in collaboration with artisans of Nisa and with the support of Manufacture Prelle, Paris
625 x 600 x 900 cm

fig. 26 (left)

Angela de la Cruz
Standing Up Box Large (Light Orange) (2015)
Oil and acrylic on aluminium
and *Box Large with Small Box (Yellow)*
Oil and acrylic on aluminium
Installation shot

The art of not-making is not prescriptive and any ethical method is fine by me.

I recently made an edition of large gold-glazed porcelain libation bowls in Jindezhen, China (or rather, the master throwers made the bowl to my design). We worked over the internet until I was happy with the results, which changed because my original designs proved impossible to realise in porcelain. Even the final designs were so difficult to realise that the makers said they could do no more than the three we eventually got (too many were broken drying and in the kiln). So, unlike Kapoor, I think I will not be seeing any 'extras' on the market. But who knows – perhaps in years to come the makers will relent, and seek to make a show of themselves.

1 The Rembrandt Database ⟨rembrandtdatabase.org/Rembrandt⟩

2 Arthur K. Wheelock Jr., 'Issues of attribution in the Rembrandt workshop', in *Dutch Paintings of the Seventeenth Century*, (Washington: NGA Online Editions, 2014). ⟨nga.gov/content/ngaweb/research/online-editions/17th-century-dutch-paintings/essay-issues-attribution-rembrandt.html⟩

3 Eileen Kinsella, 'The trouble with Warhol', in *ArtNews* (New York, 4 April 2011). ⟨artnews.com/2011/04/01/the-trouble-with-warhol⟩

4 In an email conversation with the author, 8 January 2016.

5 Ibid.

6 Martin Gayford, 'Paint it like it is: what Damien did next' in *Modern Painters*, March 2005, p. 57.

7 Clare Dyer, 'Hirst pays up for Hymn that wasn't his', in *The Guardian* (published online 19 May 2000). ⟨www.theguardian.com/uk/2000/may/19/claredyer1⟩

8 John Powers, 'I was Jeff Koons's studio serf', in *The New York Times Magazine*, (published online 17 August 2012). ⟨nytimes.com/2012/08/19/magazine/i-was-jeff-koonss-studio-serf.html⟩

9 Linda Joy Kattwinkel, 'Jeff Koons and copyright infringement', in *Legalities*, 30 (2007). ⟨owe.com/resources/legalities/30-jeff-koons-copyright-infringement⟩

10 'Luc Tuymans appropriation case settled out of court', *artlyst*, (5 October 2015). ⟨artlyst.com/articles/luc-tuymans-appropriation-case-settled-out-of-court⟩

11 'Anish Kapoor accuses China of copying "bean" sculpture', *BBC News*, (published online 12 August 2015). ⟨bbc.co.uk/news/entertainment-arts-33886678⟩

12 At the time of writing there was no evidence that Kapoor had started legal action.

13 Chris Ebbs, 'Chinese copycat cars', *Auto Express*, (published online 21 April 2015). ⟨autoexpress.co.uk/car-news/87772/chinese-copycat-cars⟩

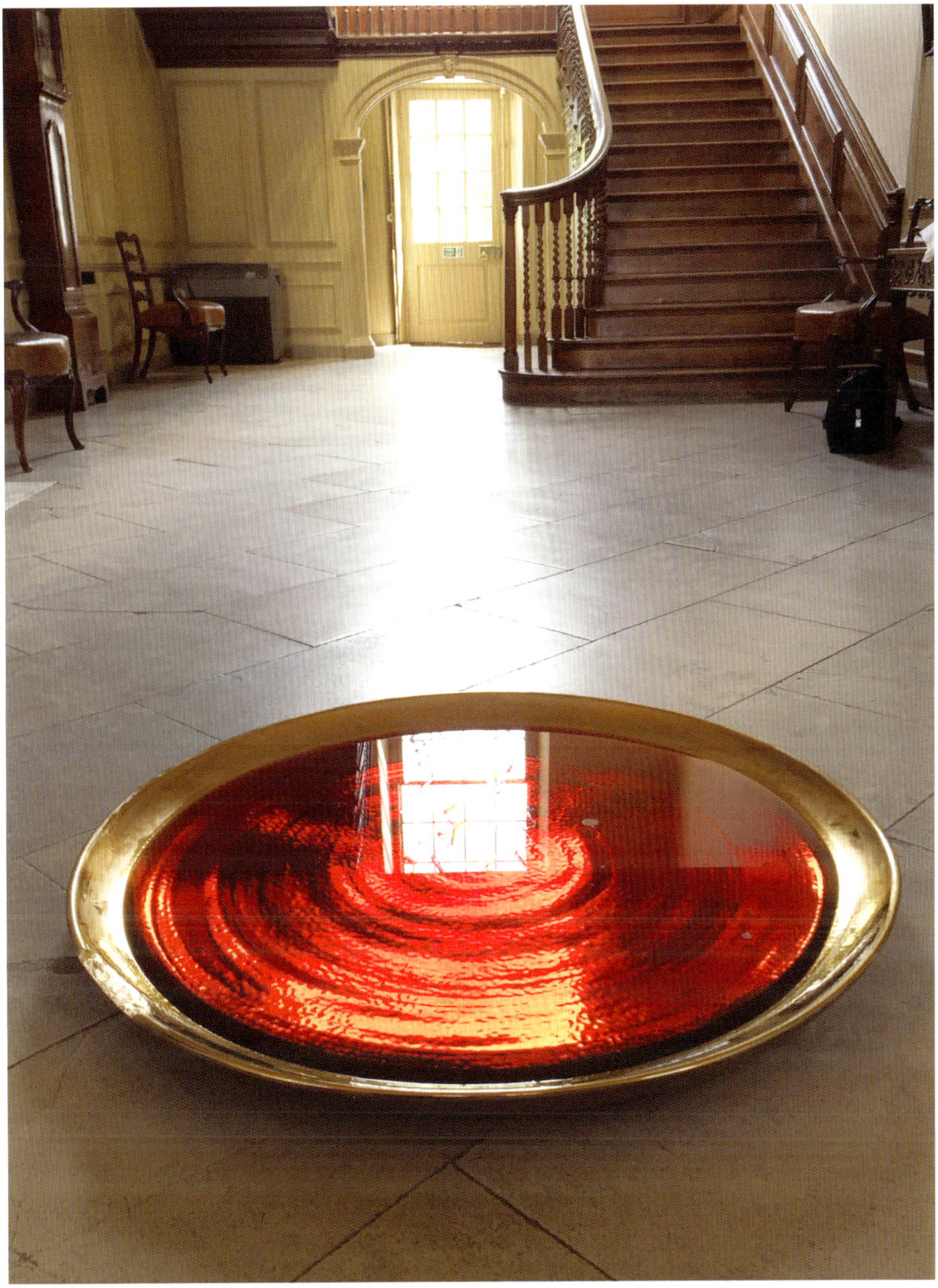

fig. 28

Michael Petry
Libation to Dionysius (2015)
24k gold glazed porcelain bowl filled with red wine

Interview:

JON ISHERWOOD

Studio assistant 1982–95/7

Bennington, USA

Skype interview (June 2015)

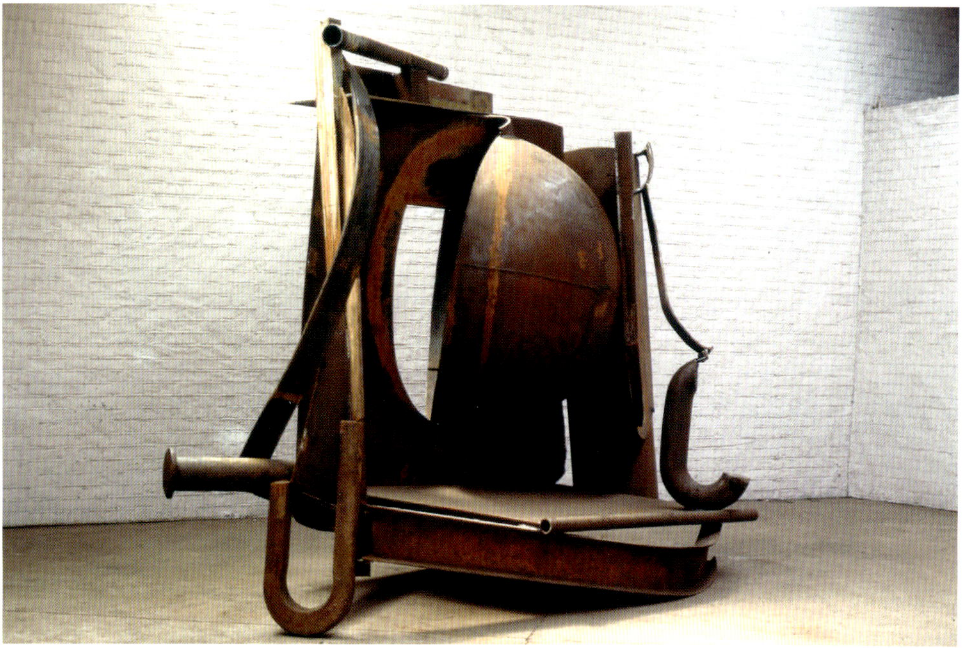

fig. 29

Anthony Caro
Ocean (1982–83)
Steel, rusted
254 x 360.5 x 200.5 cm

JENNY DUNSEATH *I am interested in your experience as a studio assistant to Anthony Caro and what influence, if any, it has had on you as an artist and educator. When did you start working for Caro?*

JON ISHERWOOD It was during my second year at Canterbury [College of Art, UK] and it's a funny story... John Gibbons and the Greenwich group (Jeff Lowe, Geoff Rigden, Mali Morris, Richard Rome, Hamish Black and Mary Shemilt) were teaching down at Canterbury. It was getting close to Christmas, and Gibbons knew I had done a lot of construction, you know, helping people build stuff and working weekends to pay my way through college. And he asked, 'Do you want to help me on this job I've got?' And I said, 'Sure.'

He said, 'You're going to have work over Christmas and through the holiday', and I agreed. I figured I'd make some good money and that would be fine. He didn't tell us where we were going or what we were doing. He told me to meet him at Camden Tube station at 9am the following Saturday morning. Hamish McLennen (who was in the same year as me) and I turned up at the station and Gibbons wasn't there! We waited around for an hour, thinking he'd stood us up and that it was some sort of joke.

Suddenly, a guy who introduced himself as Pat Cunningham showed up. Somehow he recognised us and he took us over to a complex of buildings off Royal College Street, but he didn't tell us where we were going, or whom we were working for. We got taken to this building, and we were instructed to start knocking down some walls, ripping down ceilings and pulling up the floor tiles. We didn't know whose place it was. We never went into any of the other buildings or anything, and we kept walking past this pile of steel, and I thought, 'That looks like sculpture...'

I think it was the second day; I was up a ladder scraping the walls and this grey-haired fellow walked in. And I thought, 'Shoot, I recognise him! I've seen him in a book, on the TV or someplace...' Finally, he said 'Hello' and asked us who we were, how we were, and then invited us for lunch. So we went up to Parkway and suddenly I realised it was this guy that we'd all been studying at college! The great British sculptor Anthony Caro!

We had a wonderful lunch and, in what turned out to be his usual fashion, Tony asked a thousand questions and got us to reveal our anxieties and ambitions. What sculpture we were looking at; what we liked, what we disliked; what questions we were asking in the studio; what we were thinking about and so on and so forth. It was really wonderful.

After we'd finished the building renovation, which took the whole holiday, Tony or Pat asked if I wanted to come up at the weekends and do some welding. So for my whole third year, on Saturdays and Sundays, I would take the train up to London and I had a key to the studio. I hardly ever saw those guys. I would just follow the white lines on the sculpture – cut here, weld, and grind here – so I would just do that. It was crazy! I didn't know if I was doing it right or wrong.

JD *What was it like working there in the early days and what did you learn?*

JI Sometimes Pat would come in and tell me if I'd done something right, but I was mostly on my own at first. I was just working and I wasn't really working with Tony so much. I was going into the studio and being there alone. It was quite incredible because I was touching his material and his process and an aesthetic that I had great admiration for. Back at Canterbury I would emulate it but also try to find a way from that to my own language. It was a really great complement to my education at Canterbury because I was seeing how things could be made.

Probably the biggest revelation was learning his process. In Tony's process, the sculpture was never made in one sitting and then sent out. It was always made and re-made three or four times. His insistence to have, at each interval, the sculpture made in such a way that it would be ready to exhibit was significant, because he would look at it as a finished work in order to see it as clearly as possible. Most often, from that clean take he would make radical changes.

I think that it gave me permission to break from the preciousness that we had as students, and maybe still have as artists. The hardest thing is to go back into a piece when it doesn't feel quite right and Tony had that ability to detach, in a way. Not in a way that was distant from the work, but detached and not being fearful of changing the work. I think that's one of the hardest things to teach, because students have limited budgets, restricted time, limited processes and resources. One invests a lot in making something and I think that it's a struggle to overcome the pressures of that investment when instinct indicates that change and editing are necessary.

Tony used to tell stories about different methods he would employ in his teaching at Saint Martin's to get people to develop form. For example, he would ask the students to use game strategies to make a sculpture. Roll the dice, and whatever number came up you might cut the piece of metal or sculpture that many times. With the next roll if, say, a two came up, you would connect two pieces together, and so forth. A four: chop it in quarters. Make six out of four or whatever. These simple formulaic processes are another example of how not to be precious, and I always think about those methods when I am developing new strategies for my students' projects and sometimes my own work.

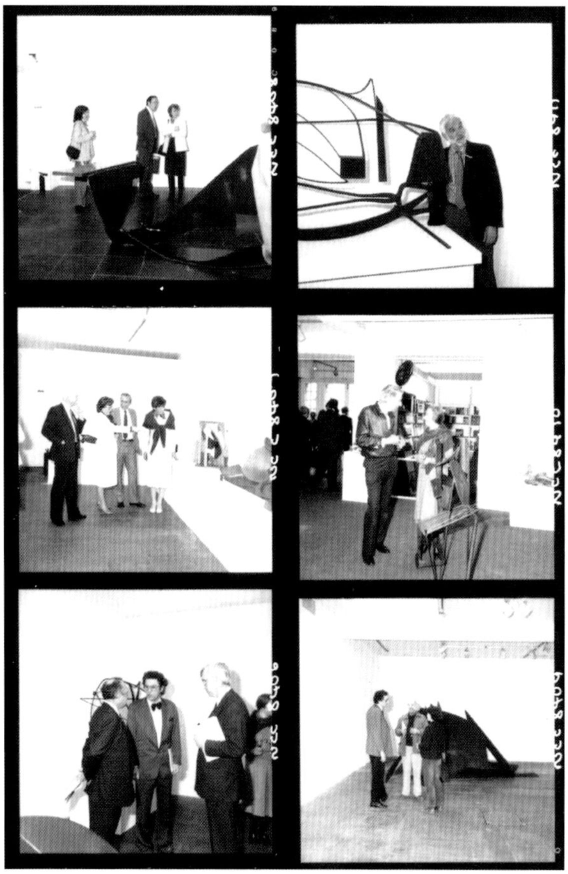

fig. 30

Serpentine opening (1984)

JD *What were the first sculptures you worked on?*

JI Oh... the first show I worked on was the Serpentine show in 1984, I think. The first piece I worked on was a sculpture called *Ocean*. It's now in New Haven, CT, at the Yale Centre of British Art, over here in the States. I think what was so magical was that I went down to Portsmouth (if I remember rightly) to the ship-breaking yards to help select that scrap steel. There were big buoys from the sea, pieces of anchor, and crazy bits and things like that. And what was so interesting about it was that the material had a narrative that I hadn't seen before in Caro's work. Material in Caro's sculpture was material and it was not about its connotation as a narrative. The stuff we selected, because of its origins (it was from the naval yard) held something thematic about it and that made the sculptures the way they were. Tony had always denied the titles had anything to do with anything, but these were called *Ocean*, or *Soldier's Tale*.

For me it indicated that there was a way to get narrative content into one's work and that is what's so interesting about that first group. In retrospect I think it was a significant turning point for Tony.

JD *And by that stage were you working full-time?*

JI Transitioning from weekends, I think I started to work full-time just after the Serpentine show opened.

It was an interesting time because that's when I met Mike Bolus: he was working at the studio as well. Mike was just a treasure to be around, he was a big personality in a way; a beautiful person and he cared for things. He had a great sense of humour about it all. I was about twenty-one or twenty-two and he would have been probably sixty. There was something very humbling about him finding his way working for Tony: he had been a very prominent artist in the 1960s and 1970s. The instances where he would share stuff about his own work were pretty spectacular.

So in some ways the studio wasn't just about Tony, it was the people who were there too. Like Guy Martin, who worked on the wood and lead sculptures.

It was also the exposure to critics, writers, historians and even the gallerists... Seeing their behaviour and how Tony would engage collectors and so forth.

JD *How do you describe your role with Tony: assistant or fabricator? Do you feel you influenced his work in any way, or is that too grand a proposition?*

JI I would say I was an assistant. Tony always asked my opinion, but it took some time for him to trust it and therefore to allow my opinion to influence the work. Confidence and influence comes out of a shared dialogue. I think I would bring ideas that were references. So if at the weekend I'd been to see an exhibition at the British Museum or the Tate or wherever I'd share that experience. Sometimes we'd jump in the car and check the show out. The discussions would always begin with what we had seen and then take the form of a proposition like, 'Could a sculpture be a doorway that was a void, or could a sculpture turn in on itself?' I guess the dialogues were always about how one rethinks the properties of a sculpture in a way, or the conditions a sculpture is working in.

I assisted for two years in London and then I sort of escaped and went to the States. But Tony was influential in that. He introduced me to Rodger Mack, who was the Dean at Syracuse University, and Tony was absolutely encouraging of me going to grad school. When I made that move, I was then to be responsible for his shows that came to New York. When I first came over to the USA he had sculptures stored in Millbrook and he then built a studio in upstate New York. So I sort of became indirectly responsible for that. I would drive down to the Ancram studio from Syracuse at the weekend and repair something or show some visitors around or something like that.

It wasn't until I finished my masters degree that he suggested I work three days a week and run the US studio. So that's what I did and it was very convenient, in all honesty, because it could be more like a job. I could go three days a week and he would come over for a week or two every three or four months. We would develop a set of work and I would make them ready for him to look at, and then work on them. Like the London studio, he'd change them radically and then I'd work on them again, and backwards and forwards.

JD *Can you tell me more about his time in the US?*

JI The draw for him was also the Triangle Artists' Workshop; we would work there together as well. It was around that time that he moved towards working from the figure. I think he was fascinated by the figure because he saw something there that [art critic and historian] Mike Fried was beginning to talk about. Mike had moved into a more historical perspective on art in terms of his own research and when he would come to the studio he would talk about it. Whether it was Manet or Caravaggio, I think Tony wanted some kind of revision of what the figure could express. And I was sort of responsible for that whole series, so when he came to the States we would work with the figure, hire a model, work life-size with clay. I guess in some ways I was responsible for the deviations in the work. The studio in London was serious, making the steel and the bronzes, and in the States, it was mirrors and figures, architecture and stainless steel!

It was kind of the alternate space or something, and I think that's what we liked about each other. It would allow for that kind of conversation and deviation. I had stopped working in steel and started working in concrete and wood, making installations. It helped me to have some distance from his work and process, and also for the pair of us to have dialogue as I was becoming slightly more independent... It was bridging the gap between being a student assistant and a full-time assistant in a slightly more professional role.

JD *Was it the shift in your own material use that enabled you to keep a distance between your own work and Tony's?*

JI I think so. I think it was a combination of definitely wanting to try to find some personal identity. I think we learned together.

It was 1987; we met Frank Gehry, and Peter Palumbo had put some money up for an artist and architect collaboration at the Triangle Artists' Workshop. There was a wonderful meeting with Frank Gehry in New York and Tony had me drag this heavy bronze sculpture to the hotel. He put this bronze sculpture on the table, and we had a beer. Tony turned to Frank and said, 'Let's turn this into a building!' Frank was brilliant: he said, 'If you want to turn this into a building, you should do just that!' Gehry's response said something really interesting about collaboration, which I've held onto. He said that collaboration is about bringing your own to the collective in some way. Frank indicated this by suggesting to Tony that he pick one part of a sculpture that he really liked and he said, 'I'll pick one part of my building that I really like, and Jon, you pick one part of your sculpture,' and similarly to the others involved in the collaboration. So we all just picked parts, had them enlarged to a monumental scale, and brought them together to see whether we could make something from them. That was a big moment: in a way it gave Tony a way to think about the 'Sculpitecture' pieces, as we called them, and it gave me a way of merging modelled form with a sort of rigidity. I didn't want to go the figure and yet I wanted plasticity in the work. Gehry's 'soft architecture', let's call it, somehow brought the body in for me but not in a representational way.

I think those moments with Tony were really the moments when we kind of began to collaborate rather than me just being simply the assistant. And it opened up a different way of dialogue. I never felt as though my name should be on any of the sculptures and I knew very clearly that I was getting paid to collaborate, to bring my ideas forward. That's how I saw it, as clearly as I could, to keep my own sanity and understand the division between my work and his. If I hadn't been paid it would have been a very different dynamic. Payment kept it clear, and in a way it kept my own work moving where it had to move to.

JD *Considering that dynamic, what were the challenges?*

JI One of the most challenging things of working for Tony was that he could move a lot faster on an idea than those around him. So if you came stumbling in with something that you'd seen on the back of a truck or something, or some set of drawers had fallen over and it was a great image, he would be able to make it that afternoon and just trust that that was something to try.

So influences from other artists, whether historical or contemporary, was something he could move on, and I think in a way, that was his method of learning. He was in some ways like the traditional artist from the Academy; he would study through making. He wasn't copying; he would work through it, to learn what it was about.

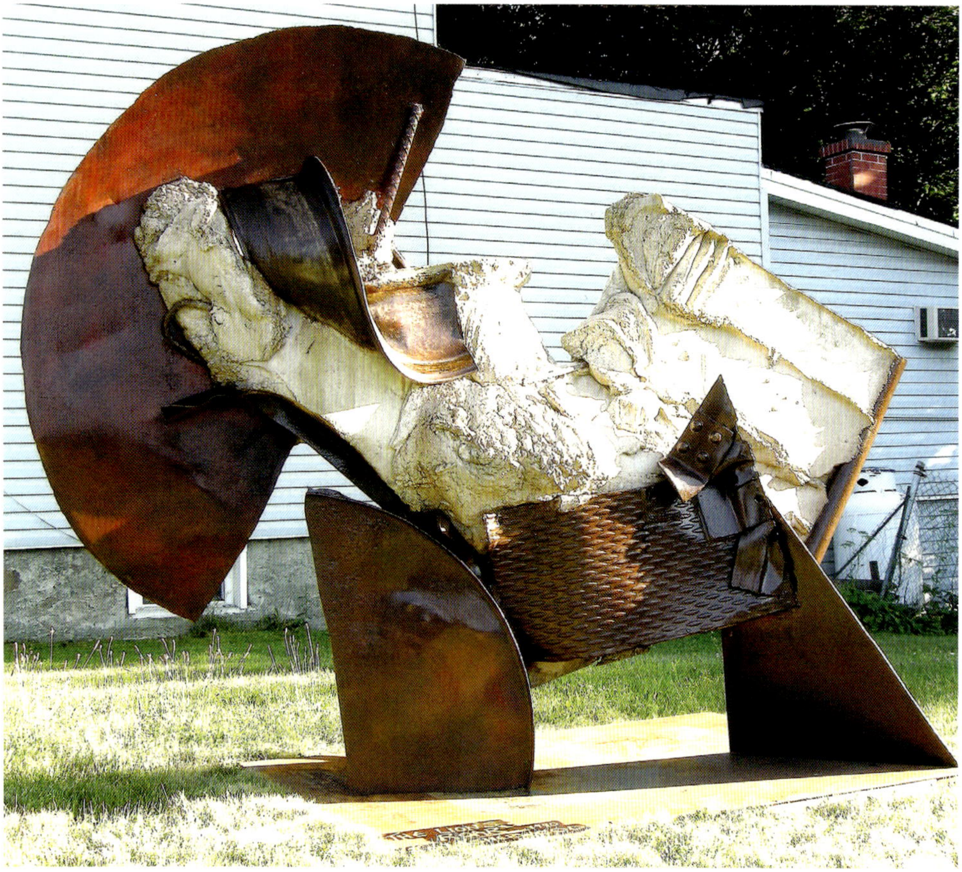

fig. 31

Jon Isherwood
The Lion's Roar (1990)
Steel and concrete
152 x 91 x 238 cm

I think that's something in relation to teaching that is hard, because we struggle with originality in one's work, and in the students' work and in the ambition to be original. With Tony I developed some ideas. It was in relationship to the 'Encounters' show at the National Portrait Gallery. They'd asked artists to respond to paintings in the collection. It was a very interesting practice that I've sort of adopted with students, which is to introduce 'encounters'. I choose groups of artists that the students have to encounter very directly, not copying, but imitating the style and process to learn from it, analyse it through making and then to move to the next step, which is how do you then respond and make the next move, to the advancement of the aesthetic.

I would use Tony's process to work out my teaching methodologies in some ways, because he was doing that. I think he used structured methodologies that would keep him on track. He would always have the book open with the picture in it, and somehow be checking the image against his work – wanting it to be like it but not. For me that was the transition, and it felt more collaborative.

JD *The element of collaboration is fascinating; this project looks exclusively at studio assistants as opposed to those he collaborated with, such as architects, ceramists, artists or craftspeople. When does being in the studio become a collaborative, reciprocal and shared experience?*

JI When you're visiting another artist's studio, it tends to be about you and them, and that dynamic – trying to read the tea leaves and help the person see the future. I think in retrospect, when you're talking about a working relationship between one artist and another, one can hopefully give the other some kind of perspective. I've thought about this a little, because working for Tony influenced me: he influenced my teaching and approach. I think that many texts have been about Tony's aesthetic and few, if any at all, have reflected on how he has allowed other people to contribute to that lineage.

And I think that's always the big dilemma when we are teaching: do we teach the past, the future, the present? Is it process, technique; are we requesting a contribution, are we progressing? How and where do we position ourselves when we are learning and teaching simultaneously?

It's a very interesting dilemma right now with teaching in general and particularly because of the way we are so influenced by commerce and the popularity of art making.

There was a recent article in *The Wall Street Journal* that talked about student preparation for life after college. It was suggesting how different it is now; how previously it was very much about the solitary studio activity, whereas now, and this is maybe more specific to the States, graduate students in their final year take classes in business, PR and legalities, all in preparation for a professional career. Careerism has kind of taken over studio activity. So how to navigate this is a big question for us as teachers. What is our role and responsibility? Should we be complementing our studio practice with promotional practices rather than art historical learning?

JD *It's a very similar situation here in the UK...*

JI I think it's important that artists have some sense of how to move into the world. I know I had no sense of the world when I left art school. It was working for Tony that enabled me to cobble together some sense of what those strategies should be.

JD *Do you discuss your experience of working for Tony with your students? How aware are they of his work and legacy?*

JI I think that it comes out in experiential dialogues, if that makes any sense, in the moments we just talked about, like how do you move a work on, how do you further develop the language, how do you have the confidence to change it and so forth. I talk about Tony's methodologies in my intro to sculpture class; he gets put into the historic survey that I take the students through. I choose, however, to do it in reverse – contemporary to historical – and I guess my instinct there is to bring people back through the influences that then had been influenced, so you can see where it came from rather than propose where things are going. Tony's sculpture is helpful in that the work is a bridge from abstraction to figuration. I use him like that.

There is a piece of Tony's on the campus, an early piece called *Radix* from the 1970s – students are baffled by it. They don't quite know what it is or what it is doing sculpturally. It's a great teaching aid because we can look at it and try to unpack it; I get them to analyse and simply describe it before we put it in context. I use it as almost an obscurity, because I find that most of the students I teach are very much about an imaged world, a contemporary world, and they are less comfortable with an abstract dialogue. I use his work as a way through to that. He gets to be seen next to sculptors from a younger generation, so Cragg, Woodrow, Whiteread, Quinn, Hirst, etc. He also gets to be shown as the radical and antagonist of Moore, and yet he worked for Moore, so that comes into play for them too.

It's funny, I met Henry Moore a couple of times and he is the reason I became an artist, but that's another story. Anyway, a group of us from Canterbury went to see Moore in 1981. We asked him about Tony Caro and he said, 'Oh yeah, he was a pretty average young student until he worked for me...' I told Tony this. And it's interesting because Tony had a lot of respect for Moore in the end, but as a young sculptor, he acknowledged he had to revolt against him and find a way forward.

JD *Thinking about the lineage of artists working for artists and the professionalisation of art education mentioned before, do you recommend your students seek that experience?*

JI I do encourage my students and we are lucky here at Bennington College because we have something called fieldwork term. It was established years ago and it means that students have to go and get a job or internship with a professional between December and the end of February every year they are in college. The college has over 800 internships that students can select from, and we have agreements with artists and galleries, museums, curators, etc. Often those positions lead to employment again in the summer. It puts them in the workplace and it places them as an assistant to an artist.

When they come back they have stronger work ethics and they seem to have a better sense of studio behaviour and that works for us. I would say that, of the students who graduate, in sculpture at least, fifty to sixty per cent first try to get jobs as assistants or they go to galleries or whatever.

Often that is down to their experience of fieldwork term. I totally encourage it, and raise it as an opportunity. They don't necessarily get paid.

JD *Do you use assistants in the production of your own work?*

JI Ummm… On occasion. I sort of don't in the end and there's a couple of reasons why. One, I like being alone in the studio and I'm not a performer in the studio. I think Tony could perform. I mean, it wasn't falsified, but in a way he was like the conductor. He could arrange people, manage and oversee. He wasn't the maker and he wasn't invested in the physical connecting of materials, of welding or fabricating.

I think my experience of working for Tony made it very apparent to me that I have to make the work. The work has to be the result of my activity even though I use a lot of technologies and computer-aided equipment. There are people I employ for certain jobs and companies that I use, but I don't like to employ people just to keep them busy.

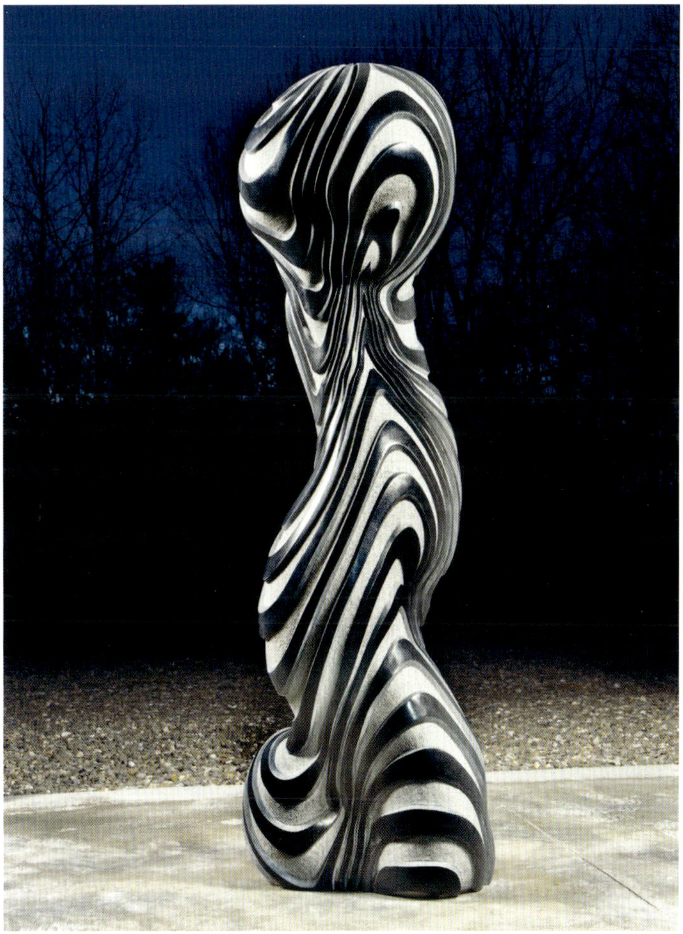

fig. 32

Jon Isherwood
The Move's On (2010–13)
Black granite
221 x 91 x 71 cm

JD *Does the use of technology in your own work allow you a freedom from physically making and enable you to think about the work in another way?*

JI I think so; there is a moment when you let go. When you've modelled something in clay and you've scanned it, suddenly it is within the computer and you're able to model it and change it, duplicate it, rescale and so forth.

Suddenly the freedom occurs from the restraint of the hand, and then it comes back because you have to shape it and carve it somehow. There are similarities, I would say. I tried to get Tony to work with some CAD programing but he couldn't see it, he couldn't feel it, couldn't walk around it. I think he could have got there but I don't know. I think he liked to conduct.

JD *When you were an assistant and running the studio, how did your contemporaries receive your role as an assistant?*

JI When I was working for Tony at Canterbury, many of my peers felt that it was something I shouldn't be doing.

JD *Why was that?*

JI I think it had to do with helping the contemporary master and the advantages he had as a famous artist... I don't know whether one would call it jealousy, but they inferred a sort of positioning. Not everyone got invited to work there and some people did and didn't last very long. Some felt or assumed that I wanted to work for him because I wanted my work to be like his.

After college, it could in some ways feel as though it was hindering my artistic presence, in that I would be seen to be primarily Tony's assistant and an artist second. People wanted to know, which are you? I think that it would cause confusion with people professionally. Some were able to see it clearly and others were not. It was complex.

JD *Is it in part about serving someone, and what that position does? Are you perpetually in their shadow and does it negate your own position?*

JI I don't think it would have worked if I had stayed in England. I was away, in the States. Interestingly, my peers in the US were in some ways no different because they were working for Serra, di Suvero, Schnabel, etc. Any place, it's the dilemma of how you support yourself, where you make your money, and how you bring and apply your given skills. And balancing the freedom to be in a creative environment was a compromise you needed to make to survive.

JD *When did you get into teaching?*

JI I didn't think of teaching until around 2000. The teaching came out of feeling less prejudice in a weird sort of way and that took time.

The closeness of working for an artist, and being in that close relationship and dialogue, and then one's own dialogue – one has to create parameters that one can work within. When moving into teaching you've got to be able to deal with the highly conceptual, highly formal, figurative, etc. Students are working with a full range of approaches, and when you are trying to find yourself, and working for another artist, that's a lot without contending with reading the tea leaves of the students, as we call it.

JD *You mentioned peers who worked for other practitioners and discussed their experiences; what were the similarities or differences?*

JI I think that Tony's studio process was the most community-driven. People who were working for Serra et al. would work from the artists' designs and ideas would be executed. Artists' processes tend to be very different. The artist Mark di Suvero is a welder and he operates the crane. He insists that he flame-cuts the steel sections. So assistants are more involved in the lifting, placing and moving the pieces. Those artists' assistants wouldn't be witness to the range, or the changes in the work that I was. Similarly, people who worked for Joel Shapiro were basically casting his work.

The assistants for some of the painters of Tony's generation over here in the US would be there to stretch the canvas and make sure the buckets are clean at the end of day, with little dialogue about process.

JD *Certainly the emphasis of having people around seems vital to his approach to conduct and orchestrate. The Triangle Workshops are a prime example of collective activity; can you tell us how you were involved with them?*

JI I didn't attend the first one; I did the second, 1983–84. I was on the board of directors and I organised a couple. Then we moved to the World Trade Centre and I decided I would resign. Others will disagree, but I think it sort of exhausted itself and there is a time for certain structures.

It seemed there was a time when Tony saw a disconnect between peers and people thinking similarly and we all tried, through the Triangle Workshops, to create a dialogue around that. After many of those artists, second and third generations of artists, had attended, it became more about who might be an interesting participant and in some ways that agenda sort of adjusted its dynamic.

The Workshops moved to the city, and moving to Manhattan meant that everyone was very conscious of the NY scene. When you're in the woods, there's nothing but groundhogs to worry about. I felt it was moving towards a sort of commercialisation, so I resigned and I think Tony moved away at the same time because I think he felt that he was on show, that people were seeing him as an art camp leader, and I don't think he really wanted that.

I have continued to run other projects. I organise a workshop for professional artists, architects, and graduate students in Italy called Carving with Robots, at Garfagnana Innovazione. It involves visual thinkers developing 3D models that they then CNC mill in marble with seven axis robots. Everyone shows up and learns how to carve marble for a month.

JD *Is there anything else you want to add about your relationship to Tony?*

JI I think it's a delicate, difficult thing, when you've had any kind of relationship with somebody and then you are asked to reflect on it. Tony was unique in that he never considered art making in relationship to careerism. Art making was always a passionate pursuit. He gave little credibility to the theorists whose rhetoric attempted to justify the absence of making.

He was one of the most significant visual intellectuals I have ever met; his interest in how the eye and brain have made – and continue to make – sense of our world was central to his every living day. He was the best mentor you could ever wish for... The type that makes it almost impossible to live up to.

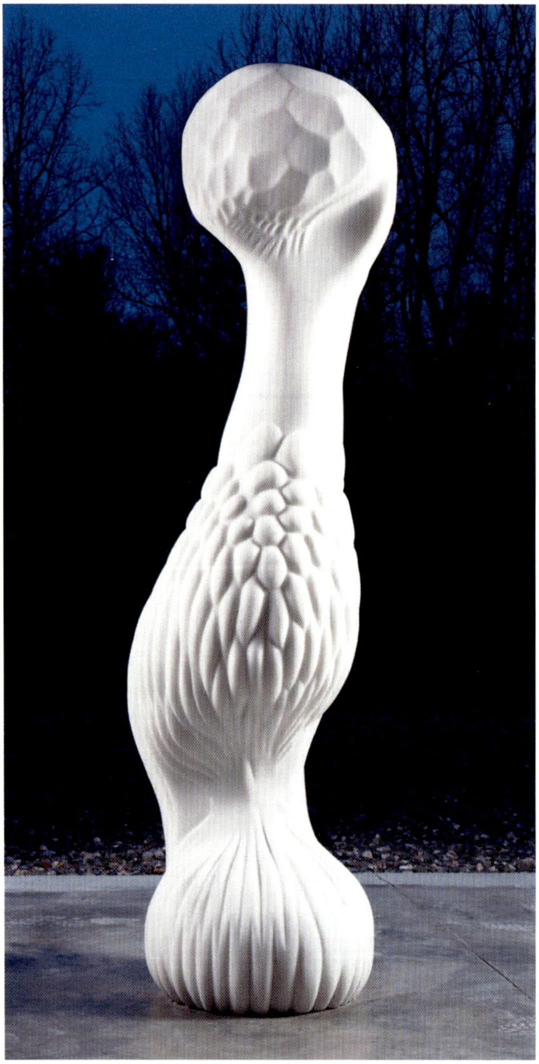

fig. 33

Jon Isherwood
Siren (2010–13)
White marble
200 x 73 x 61 cm

Interview:

SHAUN CASSIDY

Studio assistant 1989–91

Winthrop University, USA

Email correspondence (February 2011 to December 2015)

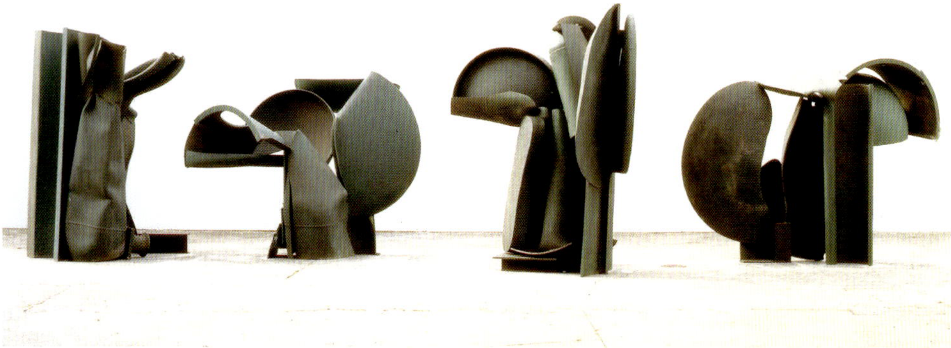

fig. 34

Anthony Caro
Night Movements (1987/90)
Steel, stained green, varnished and waxed
275.5 x 1077 x 335 cm

Did you have an art school education?
Yes. I completed my foundation course at West Surrey College of Art and Design. I received a first class BA (Hons) from Norwich School of Art, and an MFA from the University of Alberta, Canada.

When did you work for Tony?
Full-time from 1989, and then on and off during holidays from grad school.

How did the job come about?
I met Tony when I was a participant at the Hardingham sculpture workshop run by the sculptor John Foster. After meeting Tony, I wrote him a letter asking if he needed help.

Why did you want to work for him?
I wanted a job in the arts, to see how a great artist functions on a daily, practical level and to get connected in London.

Which sculptures did you work on? And what was involved in the making?
I worked on *Descent from the Cross*, *Night Movements*, the Cascades series, both *Dejeuner sur l'herbe* corner sculptures, the Mint series and *Medusa*. I was welding, grinding, moving shapes, selecting shapes, preparing for photography and assisting the photographer.

Who else worked there? Are you still in touch?
Michael Bolus (a totally wonderful artist and human being), Derek

Haworth, Pat, Sue in the office. It was a small team when I first started, then it increased to include Simon Black, Shap McDonald and others.

Have you worked as an artist's assistant to anyone else?
I worked on several projects for Ken Noland in Vermont, and lived in Jules Olitski's studio in Bennington, where I made two small sculptures of his a year in lieu of rent – a very sweet deal!

Do you believe that a pedagogic relationship existed between you and Tony?
Yes, I really believe Tony was aware of how much we were learning and in that respect his total inclusiveness of us in the process of thinking and making was very generous. Both he and Pat were very supportive and showed me the discipline needed to be a successful artist.

How has – or has – working for Tony influenced you?
He influenced me in many ways, mainly my thinking about the process of making art. He showed me the courage that's needed to make innovative work – the willingness to change and cut apart work when it looked almost done. Creativity feeds creativity, and Tony's use of other artists as a springboard (the Matisse cut-outs, for example) was an eye opener for me.

He always wanted to hear people's opinion of his work so he could filter out the good stuff. He was interested in discovery as opposed to sustaining an ideal vision. And he was willing to trust his initial gesture and let it sit for a while before making qualitative judgements.

How was your role of assistant received by your contemporaries?
I think my peers were rather envious of my position, failing to realise the sheer hard work of my role.

Do you still make work?
Yes. I make a good amount of sculpture, public art, drawing and paintings. I use students as assistants because it's an extension of my teaching. I try to be open and inclusive like Tony was.

Have you taught in art schools?
I have taught at the Kansas City Art Institute, Missouri, and now coordinate the sculpture program at Winthrop University in South Carolina. I very much try to teach students to obtain a range of skills, both practical and creative.

Has being an assistant informed your teaching methods in any way?
Yes, it has. I try to insist that students don't edit themselves too soon in the process, have courage and be willing to try something that extends their capabilities both technical and creatively.

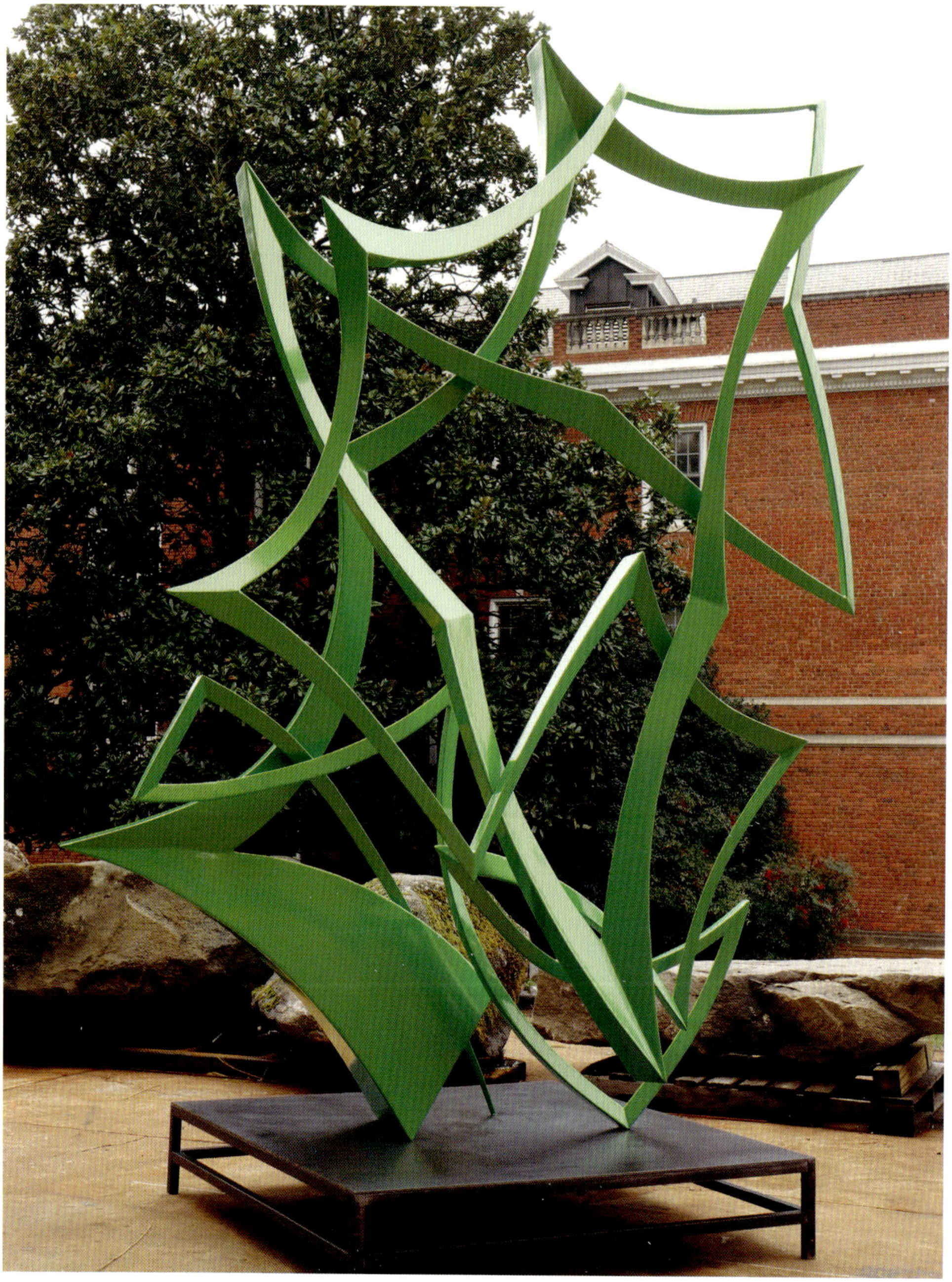

fig. 35

Shaun Cassidy
The Sound of Everything, Slicing Clean (2015)
Powder coated steel
320 x 122 x 78 cm

Interview:

IAN DAWSON

Studio assistant 1991–94

South East London, UK

Interview (April 2015)

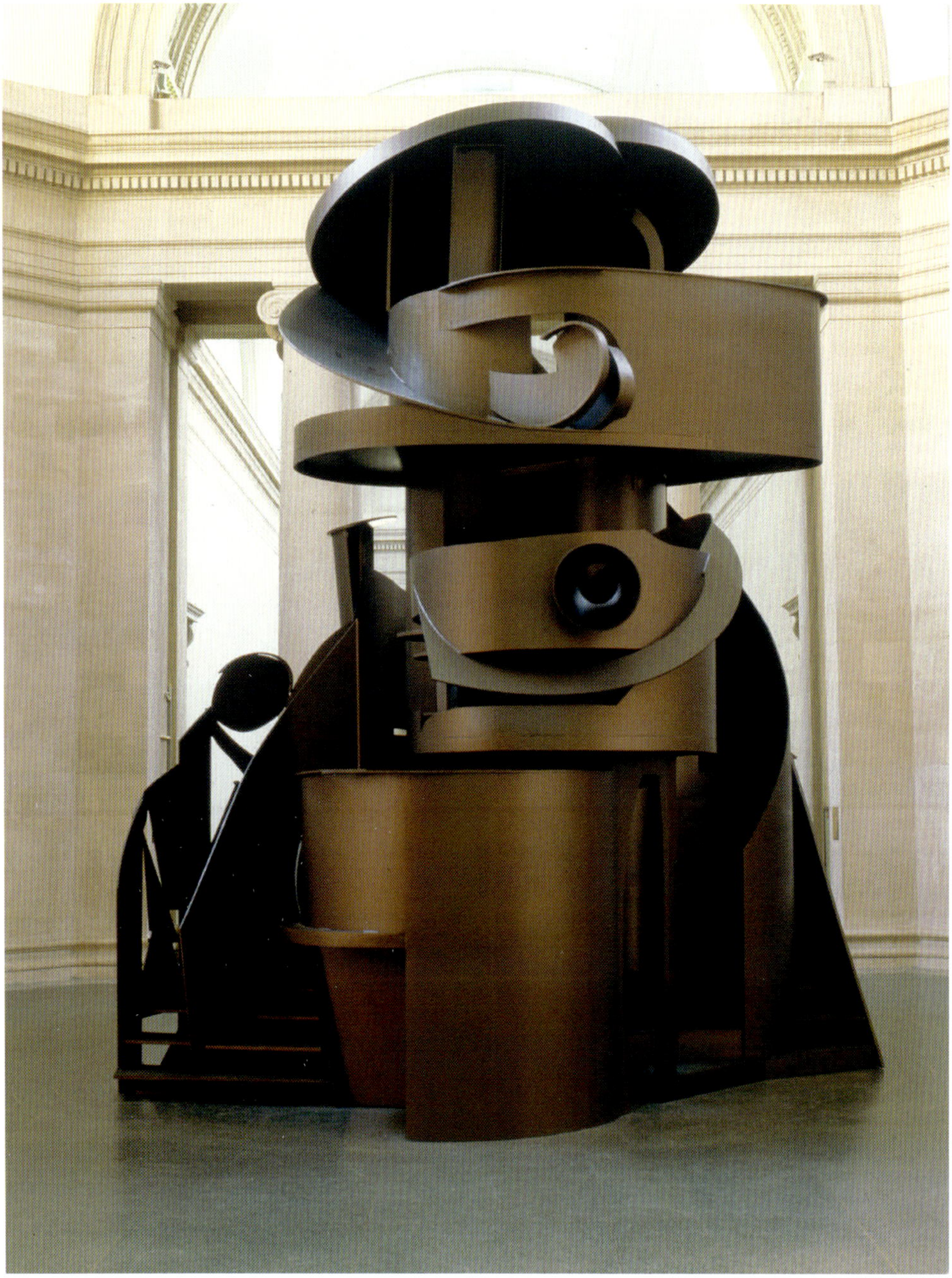

fig. 36

Anthony Caro
Tower of Discovery (1991)
Steel, painted bronze
670.5 x 553.5 x 553.5 cm

JENNY DUNSEATH *I am interested in your experience as a studio assistant to Anthony Caro and what influence, if any, it has had on you as an artist and educator. My first question; when did you work for Caro?*

IAN DAWSON 1991–93/4. Not long at all really. The first stint was on *The Tower of Discovery* project, one of the earliest Duveen Gallery commissions at the Tate. I was one of a whole swathe of students to come out of Winchester School of Art [WSA] having been taught by John Gibbons. Somehow John would put in the call to Tony or Pat – I presume Pat – and you'd go up there to meet them both and see if you cut the mustard. So I spent a summer embroiled in making this full-on 'Sculpitecture' piece; there must have been about twenty of us working on it – the scale of it was incredible.

JD *Who else was working there?*

ID Shap McDonald had also come from Winchester. Derek Haworth came down from Manchester, Elizabeth Wright and Giorgio Sadotti were there very briefly, and Mike Bolus was there too.

When I arrived they had a third-scale model of *The Tower* on a table-top and Mike and Shap would be there with hardboard, scaling up all of the sections, and we'd be there fabricating. This was a level of engineering that was so incredibly precise to get straight into: my learning curve went through the roof in terms of engineering and fabrication.

JD *With that level of fabrication, I assume there were demands outside of your own practice. What impact did it have on your own practice?*

ID It all went into the evolution of my own work at the time, because I was still studying at the Royal College of Art. I would work some weekends and the holidays, but I was lucky enough to have whole blocks of time when I was just experimenting in the new RCA Battersea studios (Howie Street was very similar to Georgiana Street: a converted light-industrial A-framed building) utilising and assimilating these incredible technical and practical skills and applying them.

JD *Did you see your role there as a fabricator?*

ID Umm, yeah... I guess I did.

JD *Could you tell me about the relationship between you and Tony?*

ID Yeah... Well, I remember once that he gave me some wax and said 'Just mess around with it', and then after about three days decided that it just wasn't right for me. And from that we ended up going back into steel. We would drive up to collect *Table* pieces he had been welding at his Frognal studio, taking them back to Georgina Street. I would work on them, completely dismantling them, bit by bit, using tack bars to ensure every relationship was maintained before putting them back together as completely clean, coherent sculptures.

JD *Was there much dialogue between studio assistants and Tony about your own practices?*

ID We did a couple of things, which I thought might have been like Henry Moore's relationship to him, where he would want to do studio visits. So you'd get into the old clapped-out Range Rover with him, and Derek – or someone – would be driving and we'd do five or six studio visits in a day. One of them was all the way down to Bristol and so you would do a really big day and your conversations would continue for these journeys. I remember one of them was bantering about Picasso and Matisse or whatever.

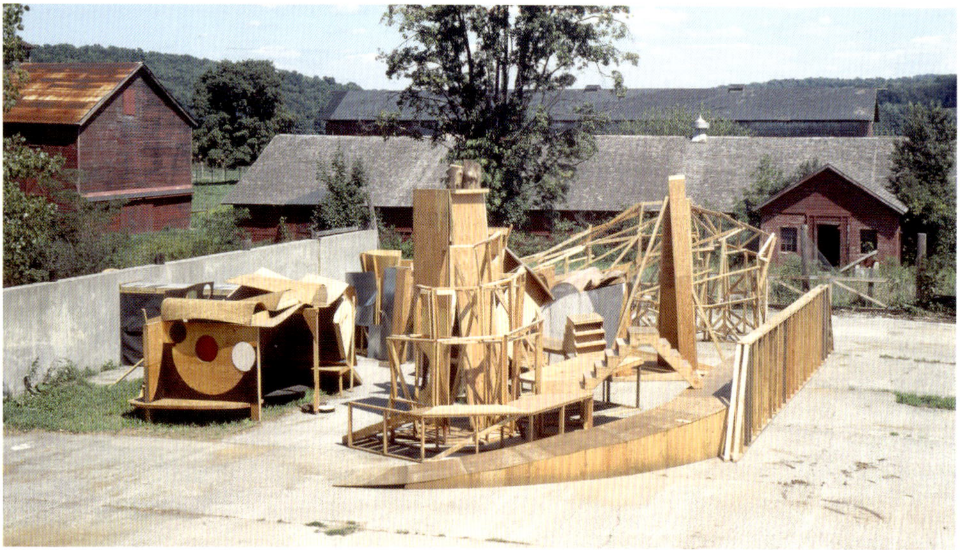

fig. 37

Anthony Caro
Sculptural Village (1988)
Wood
Variable dimensions

JD *Would you describe it as a pedagogic relationship?*

ID Just an artist's relationship. Because studio banter is very different isn't it? Well, I always think it is. You throw up ideas in a freer way, without them being tethered to things. I think it was like that.

Tony would take the studio visits really seriously; there was a real investment from him in them. It was something you could see he was really into.

I had also remained close to John Gibbons. He wouldn't let Tony into his studio, and our conversations would offer a different perspective. I never really knew what his relationship with Tony was like, but he was a lot more antagonistic. He would always speak about another side, of young artists whose creativity was bled dry by Tony, and I found that interesting.

JD *So you were very mindful of the potential negative effect of being an assistant?*

ID Yes.

JD *As a result of that, how do you define the relationship?*

ID I remember at the time being very interested in why the legacy of Caro wasn't as well cemented as I thought it should have been. I remember the times in the studio when Tony would go home; there would be this period where you would work into the evening and natter with whoever was working. Mike Bolus would come in at midday and leave at midnight if he had the chance, when it had quietened down.

And the talk would be about why, from those great works like *Early One Morning* and *Prairie*, there wasn't a more powerful movement. Because when you look at those, and look at the lineage from them, there wasn't the sense that the magic of those had been sufficiently manifested in future generations.

JD *Did it become a tangible problem for you to fight with or against?*

ID When I was working there I had the opinion that the work after a certain period wasn't as powerful, and that it relied on a set pattern of arranging to keep it alive. And the question would be: is that enough?

JD *A recurrent question Tony would ask was, 'Is it sculpture?', affirming but questioning the definition of sculpture. Do you subscribe to that?*

ID No, not at all. I found that a troubling aspect because to me it doesn't matter. It just doesn't. But this question, 'Is it sculpture?', seems to matter to a lot of people who are dogmatic in their belief structures about what sculpture is and isn't. That it is one thing and not another seemed to me to be a narrow-minded position.

Was Caro as dogmatic as that? Not in my opinion, but why did the legacy of such amazing artworks end up within this narrow debate?

JD *We have talked a little about the influence of John Gibbons, being at Winchester and working as an assistant. You now run the sculpture department at WSA. Could we talk a little about the relationship between learning, teaching and being an assistant? Has being an assistant affected how you teach or how you think about teaching? Perhaps you could start by explaining how and why you got into teaching?*

ID Originally I had denied its importance; it was only after having kids that I realised its importance. So much of my early teaching was a horrendous experience. The problem was going back to where I was taught, where John had embedded much of the Caro and Saint Martin's culture, like the crit structure. It was only after structural change that my teaching at Winchester opened up.

In setting up a more collaborative approach one could say, 'That's come out of my experience of making something together,' like making *The Tower of Discovery*. Whereby in actual fact, you subsume your role as author completely and you are just one of a whole load of people making this thing, and you all come together and pool your resources and skills to a common goal. For me that's become quite a pervasive method of teaching. I remember thinking that about my degree show: the whole thing is bigger than the constituent parts.

JD *With collaborative projects in mind, you orchestrated a student project to replicate* Early One Morning *at WSA. Could you tell us about this, and the agenda for these activities?*

ID Well that was the first one. I got a bit tired of this single tutorial situation. The idea that you go into a student's workspace, you sit there and they show you what they've been making and you give them some artists that they should see that they haven't seen and suggest a few things. And there was this moment, when I was sitting there – the studio space is the size of a desk, with shelves on the wall – and I was looking at something the size of this water bottle, something on a desk, but I was looking through their sketchbooks and they're looking at Ernesto Neto, Phyllida Barlow or whatever. And, all of a sudden, I'm thinking the difference between what they perceive the work to be and their practice is so dramatically different. The chasm is so huge – how do you go about dealing with that?

I realised that something wasn't working; that it doesn't matter how long you can spend in that tutorial, the practice is wrong for what they are perceiving their activity to be. The only way to deal with that was to open up the workshops again to try to make it so that the technicians, the academics and the workshop activities all start to interlink again. And the interlinking became a key thing – to instil practice via a set of technical challenges. You can stand in the studio and talk about context, but to instil practical matters becomes this really hazardous thing because there is a barrier between the two things – the academic and the technical.

I figured the way to address this was to make something collectively in the studio and workshops, and to don overalls and be there as one of them, I guess. As simple as that.

It felt good because it brought back all this stuff from making *The Tower of Discovery* in a way, and being there in Tony's studio.

The piece was chosen because of the workshop size. *Early One Morning* fitted into our workshop in the same way – or with a similar relation to how one imagined – as the original came out of Caro's Frognal studio. The workshop space was the same dimensions as *Early One Morning*, so we were working to the absolute confines of the space, opening up the dialogue with how it was first made.

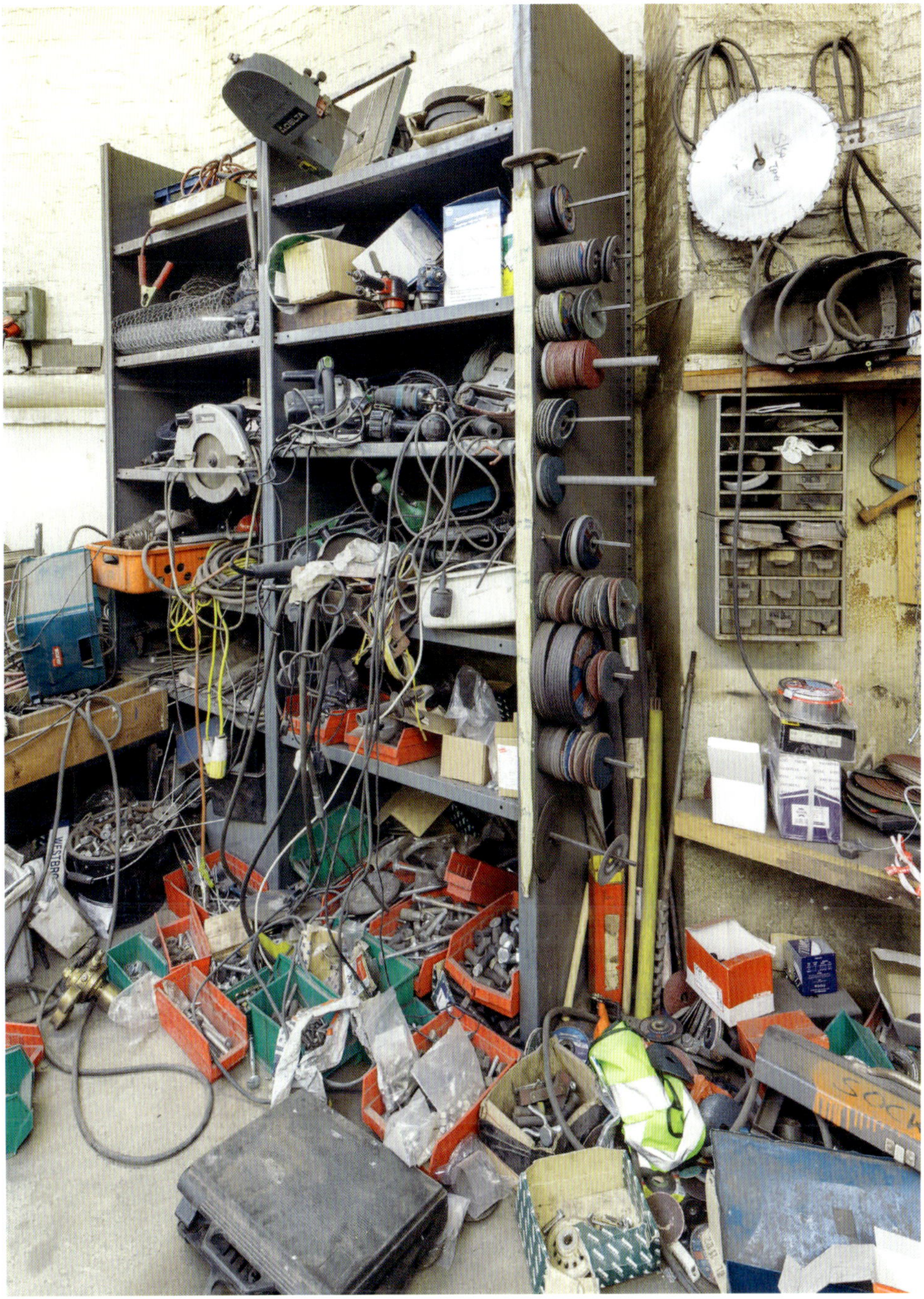

fig. 38

Grinding discs, Camden studio (2013)

JD *Did Tony know about the project? What did he think of it?*

ID No, we made it without Tony knowing, we just did it. But I promised the students that if we did a good job on it, I'd get in touch with Tony. So I wrote him a letter once we'd made it and photographed it, and wrote that I had wanted to make a difference and decided to do this as a method to deal with something. I was on a bus when I got a call from Tony saying what an amazing project and to bring the students to the studio for tea.

So we all went up to see Tony, and we had an amazing afternoon with him. It was quite stunning the way he reminisced about the making of the original. There were the usual nuggets about how it was originally green and Sheila looked out the next morning and said, 'Try it red'; these amazing insights. You recognise that, whenever anyone talks in that way about the way a piece of work is made, the process of creating such a masterpiece is based upon paying attention.

And there were other ones, you know, of Clement Greenberg saying, 'If you want to change your art, change your habits', and of the things he put into place to change his habits: the simple things of working with a new material. Tony saying these things held huge sway – it was quite remarkable. It was something else to have him on a roll. My jaw was on the ground and I was so dumbstruck by what was coming out in terms of the power of those comments.

JD *It must have been an amazing experience for the students. Did it influence how they worked?*

ID Its success created the momentum to develop the project further. Other iterations have been Jean Tinguley's *Homage to New York* (1960), and the Independent Group's *This is Tomorrow* from the Whitechapel Gallery, 1956. We've recently remade *The Raft of the Medusa* as a physical structure, and François Willème's photo-sculpture production device from the 1870s. I'm not answering your question directly, but what's been interesting is that it has tried to embed a different form of practice-based teaching and learning. To help to define where we are now with things.

I was taught in a particular environment and you probably had three or four choices – painting, sculpture or printmaking would be it. And then within that you would have your subdivisions of abstraction or figuration, and within that there would be then construction, carving or whatever. So you would find that what you were basing your choices on were so dramatically small. And now it's not like that at all; the field is so vast and the context for making the work is so great as well.

JD *If that has changed and you recognised it through teaching, what about your practice? Do you have assistants?*

ID No. I did use them some years ago. It was kind of fun because you realise the beauty of having assistants is that they can do the stuff that... Well, they can drive something to a different place, and this is what I found Tony had a real handle on. They can accelerate the making of mistakes, in a funny sort of way. It's interesting, because you can have them do something that you don't know is going to work. It enables your decision-making to be much more varied. You can take a punt with something just by asking someone else to do it and by taking it out of your control. When you are making your own decisions, a lot of the time you are trying to short-circuit what you think you want to do; using assistants can mean that you can naturally short-circuit things anyway.

I remember Tony telling us about a time when he'd just come back from Hans Spinner's (the ceramist who also worked for Eduardo Chillida). The first thing Spinner said to Tony was: 'What do you want me to do with the clay?' And Tony said, 'I don't know, just throw it and see.' The first action is done without any prerequisite, so that you're getting someone else to begin in the expressive position without you having to make that decision, and that's really neat. When that happens it's exciting. You're not controlling it, it's being controlled by something else; most of the time when you're working by yourself you're trying to eradicate that element anyway, because the excitement happens when it's outside your control. So the short-circuits can happen that much quicker. And that's the magnificent bit about it and Tony would always do that.

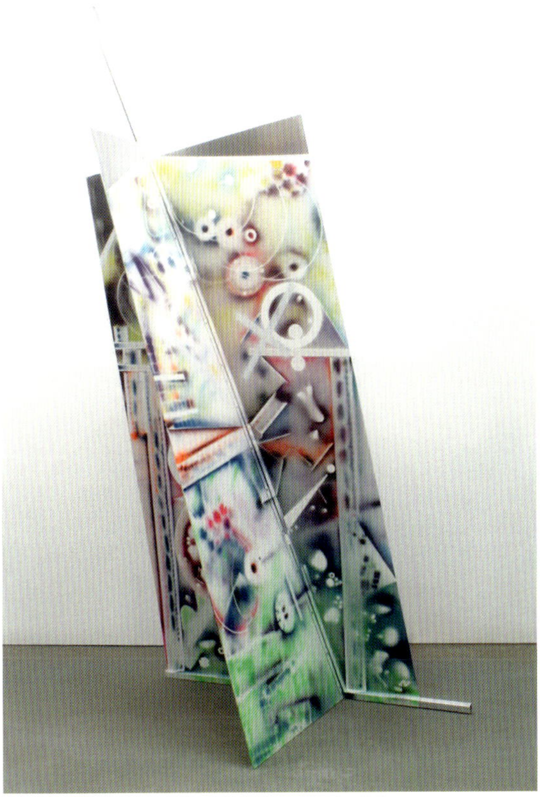

fig. 39

Ian Dawson
POV0002 (2015)
Aluminium and enamel
240 x 120 x 60 cm

I often thought it was how a musician or composer might work. Like the Miles Davis sessions of the early 1970s, where the musicians would get the call and come into the recording studio and they would just start playing with the tape running from the word go, without any prompting from Davis. He would never play back any of the recordings to the musicians either, so that they would always be within this live improvisational format, and I often thought Tony had an equally key way of keeping it fresh.

Now, I'm realising the importance of that. I will always remember the conversations: Spinner saying, 'You need to tell me something to do with it,' and Tony forcefully saying, 'No, let's just see how you do it and let's go with that.' Tony would ensure that that starting point was open, and the openness when you use assistants is not to demand it be done in a particular way.

JD *Almost handing over responsibility... But within that is a freedom to orchestrate and compose. How does that relate to your use of machines – the 3D printers that require orchestration and planning – within your own practice?*

ID Having this conversation with you makes me aware of how 3D printing and scanning is very much like leaving it to the mercy of someone else. What comes back can be different to a grotesque degree, and that's what I find interesting. That, and how you subsume the demands of that responsibility, and I guess if you're thinking about the positive elements I took from Caro, they would be how to position yourself as an open person with whatever is required to make the work, whether that's machinery or people.

JD *Were there any works of Tony's on which you could see your 'hand', your touch or your influence?*

ID No, I don't think so. I would never... Working on the *Table* pieces was just this beautiful thing, and I've always enjoyed them because they're like little sketches, aren't they? They're just these beautiful things that were done in the work of a moment, and then they were forensically taken apart to be cleaned up and finished. I've really loved that activity; to have, on the one hand, say, this pile of polystyrene [points to polystyrene in studio] and to think, 'What do you do to take this to being finished?' And with those pieces of Tony's, when they're frozen in that moment, you then go through taking them apart bit by bit to ensure that they're finished enough to be finished in the terms that Tony's after. Ok, so they were Tony's terms, but it makes you aware of what that circuitous route is, and that has always fascinated me.

I always enjoy starting work myself, and it made me aware of the focus that's required to finish works. When you don't have the focus to finish work it's horrendous, but it's brilliant when you do.

JD *How did your fellow staff, students, and peers perceive your role and relationship?*

ID I think there was a bit of kudos, but not much, because it was changing dramatically at that time – there were other assistant experiences. Someone was Antony Gormley's assistant, so we'd swap stories. But another route into the art world was opening up: the route via the gallery, like being a gallery assistant. Darren Almond was working at Anthony d'Offay's gallery, and had started to get experience of the art object through this other route, which was becoming much more fashionable.

JD *You felt the artist assistant role was less well regarded?*

ID Yeah, perhaps it was wiped out by the Hirst/YBA thing… It wasn't necessarily cool to be an artist assistant, it was much more cool to be a gallery assistant installing works at one of the galleries that were on the up at the time. Saatchi was purchasing on an ever-increasing scale, and it must have appeared much more interesting to be installing something that was going to be part of Saatchi's Boundary Road space.

JD *What about now: where do your students work? Do they work for artists, or steer toward the gallery?*

ID That's interesting… It has kind of levelled out a little bit. The urge to get jobs appears much greater. What I find interesting is that we probably have fewer art students with aspirations to be singular fine artists. They quite probably see themselves working across the creative industries in a less boundaried way.

When I was a student, there was a core group whose aspiration once they'd left studying was clearly to have a studio and try to make art – whether they've maintained it or not is another question. And your output in that instance was through the gallery system. But now there isn't the same aspiration; the museums and galleries have become brands within a global industry.

Museums and galleries are completely different institutions, and I don't think art students aspire to a single path; they are much more open-minded about where their creativity lies, where they can access it, and what those outcomes are going to be.

JD *Many assistants define their time at Tony's by the work, series or commission they were assisting on, and how the role gave them far more than just a wage. What happens when you leave the safety and security of the workplace?*

ID My formative years were in shared studios, and we would end up helping each other out because, at that point, we had time but no-one could afford to pay for assistants. So I remember Richard Woods and Keith Tyson shows where they would be helping each other at those frantic moments when things needed finishing.

I recognised that what we took from Tony's was sharing… You were sharing so much in that relationship, because you were picking up on how Tyson finished works, or how Woods dealt with surface – the work, its meaning, is being laid bare to you in this way that is fundamental to the way your own work is developing as well. At Tony's we often talked about the Triangle Workshops in relation to that, because he described the sharing of time and the intense periods of making as kind of similar.

JD *Your projects at WSA are doing precisely that – sharing, collaborating. Would you ever do a project replicating your own work with the students?*

ID Maybe that's happening already.

JD *How is the sharing manifested?*

ID I always remember back to the moments after my degree show… You've invested so heavily in something, and I remember the recognition that it's made up of everybody's work. It's not yours – it never is anyway. It's only in this fake way that it's labelled as someone's.

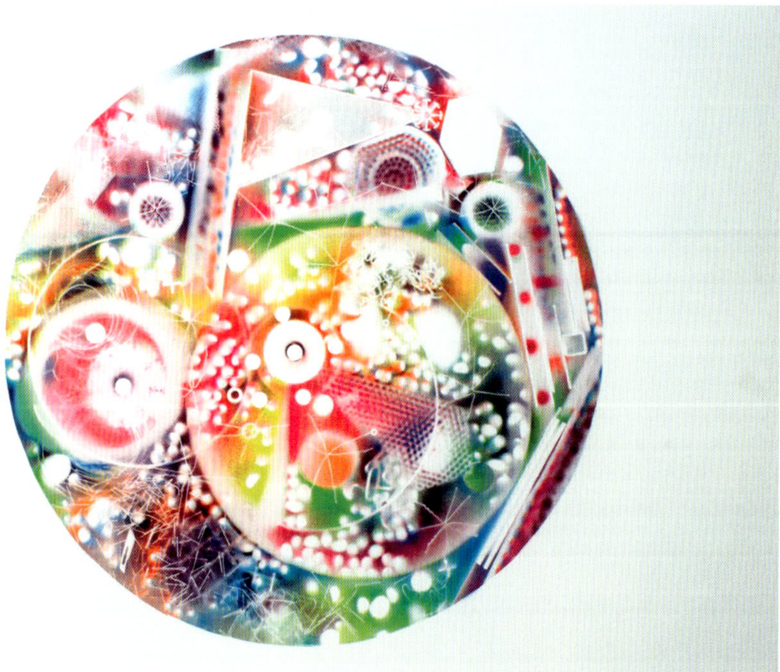

fig. 40

Ian Dawson
POV2.1 (2015)
Aluminium and enamel
150 x 80 cm

Essay: Omnivorous, Restless, Decisive: Caro in Context

Sam Cornish

"Considering Caro as engaged in an ongoing dialogue with his former students, peers and lesser-known contemporaries allows us to create a richer picture of the development of his sculpture."

The first line of William Rubin's catalogue to Anthony Caro's 1975 retrospective at the Museum of Modern Art declared: 'It takes only one great artist to keep a tradition alive.'[1] The exclusions implicit in Rubin's statement were made explicit in surveys of sculpture by Rosalind Krauss in 1977 and Lynne Cook in 1987. Krauss presented the New Generation of sculptors taught by Caro at Saint Martin's in the late 1950s and early 1960s as simply continuing, in attenuated form, limited aspects of his art; Cooke dismissed all the abstract sculptors at Saint Martin's as Caro's 'epigones'.[2]

In this note I will argue against the image of Caro as an isolated generator of sculptural ideas, with those around him as mere receivers – or lesser imitators – of these ideas. There are obvious problems with marginalising at least two generations of artists in this way, both for understanding their art on its own terms, and for understanding the broader context of abstract sculpture at Saint Martin's. Here, though, I want to suggest that it may also lessen our understanding of Caro's *oeuvre* and of how his creativity functioned.

I'll point to a number of sculptures by Caro that I think drew upon, were prompted by, responded to, or incorporated ideas or structures found in the work of other sculptors associated with Saint Martin's. My examples are speculative, based upon similarities I've found by comparing his contemporaries' sculptures to those in Dieter Blume's XIV volume *catalogue raisonné*. It could be that some of the resemblances are coincidences (perhaps inevitably arising from the vast spread of Caro's production) rather than proof of an actual link; or they may be examples of a period style, or imply the existence of a third model that both sculptors were looking to. Perhaps, most importantly, they could suggest the building or exploration of a common language, an interlinked series of answers to the question of what modern sculpture was or could or should be. Yet even with these possibilities in mind, most of the examples that follow seem to me to be fairly direct, to imply Caro consciously approaching or unconsciously following the work of the sculptors in his circle. I hope it is clear that this is not an attempt to downgrade Caro's importance, or to suggest he was not the most influential sculptor at Saint Martin's.

Mutual simulation between artists is often suppressed by art history's monographic tendency. There are almost certainly more books on Caro than on all the other Saint Martin's sculptors combined, and not one that surveys the abstract sculpture at Saint Martin's as a whole. This asymmetry and lack of a proper overview has likely amplified the common trope of reducing the features of a particular field to the attributes of a central figure in it. A monograph will typically confine discussions of influence – though this shorthand seems too passive for the phenomenon I'm trying to discuss – to early stages of a career. If it appears later, 'influence' is generally restricted to suitably illustrious contemporaries or to masters from art history. Outlines of Caro's career fit this scheme neatly. The father figures of Henry Moore and David Smith dominate discussion of his early career and breakthrough to abstraction; in the 1960s and 1970s there is a dialogue with American abstract painting; in the 1980s come his works after artists including Duccio, Rubens, Rembrandt, Manet, and Matisse. The point is not to dismiss these interactions, but to add to them. For example, the sculptures Caro made at Emma Lake, Saskatoon, Canada, in 1977 are generally discussed in relation to Picasso's maquettes for his unrealised *Monument to Apollinaire*, seminal works in the history of open-constructed metal sculpture. But couldn't the Emma Lake sculpture also be considered alongside William Tucker's *Cat's Cradle* and *Beulah* series, made five or so years earlier, and themselves partly indebted to Caro's 1960s sculptures? Even if Caro did not consciously have Tucker's sculptures on his mind while he was working at Emma Lake, a comparison of their improvised, enclosed architectural spaces would certainly be fruitful, and in many ways in these sculptures Tucker and Caro are much closer to each other than Caro was to his admitted model of Picasso.

As I've said, the examples that follow are speculative, and really this note is the beginning of a piece of research rather than a conclusion. But even if specific examples can be doubted, I think raising the possibility of their existence is a useful exercise. In a general sense it counters the biases of an art history based upon the monograph. More specifically, and more importantly, the sculptural exchanges they describe can help open up the complexity of Caro's work, which too often is restricted by the recycling of overly familiar anecdotes. These exchanges add to our understanding of Caro and the context that he shaped and which shaped him.

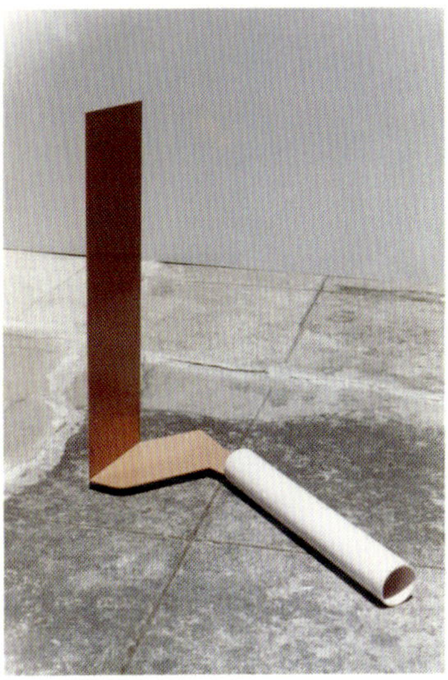

fig. 41

Michael Bolus
Sculpture Three (1963)
Painted mild steel
40.5 x 274 x 396 cm

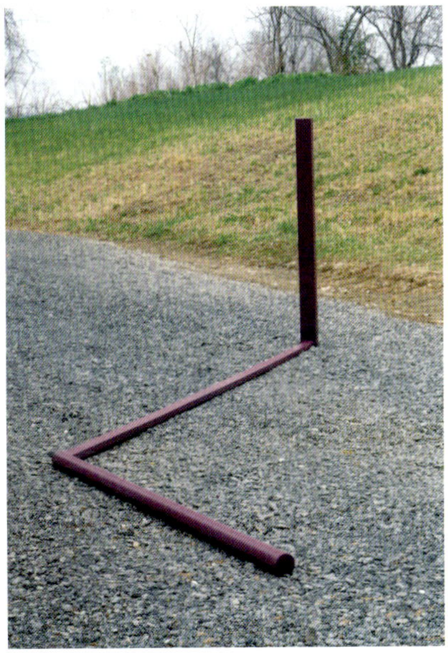

fig. 42

Anthony Caro
Smoulder (1965)
Steel, painted purple
106.5 x 465 x 84 cm

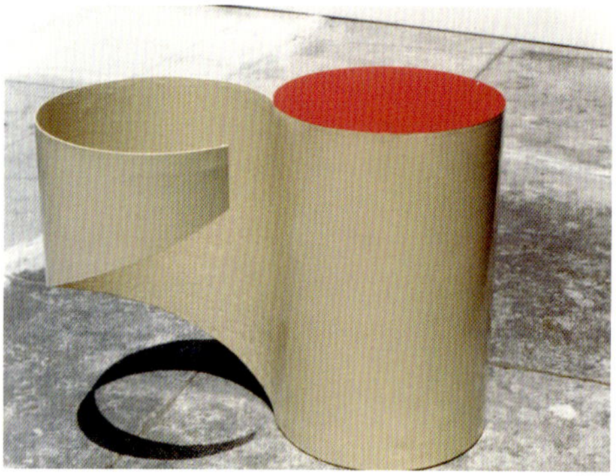

fig. 43

Michael Bolus
Sculpture Five (1963)
Painted steel
60.5 x 81.5 x 41 cm

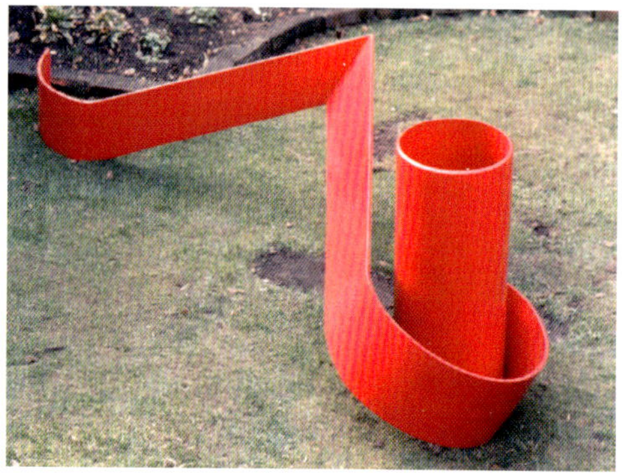

fig. 44

Anthony Caro
Reel (1964)
Steel, painted burgundy
86.5 x 101.5 x 267 cm

Smoulder, which Caro made at Bennington College, Vermont in 1965, and *Reel*, made in London in 1964 after his first sojourn in Bennington, stand in clear relation to two sculptures by Michael Bolus from 1963, *Sculpture Three* and *Sculpture Five*. Caro saw the sculptures he made at Bennington as stemming from a loosening up, encouraged by the painters Kenneth Noland and Jules Olitski, and, more broadly, by the atmosphere of America itself. Looking at these sculptures by Bolus adds another dimension to this explanation. The visual similarities are quite apparent, so it is reasonable to wonder whether Caro had them on – or at least at the back of – his mind during these early Bennington years. Bolus's approach also provides an image of simplicity that precedes the simplicity of Caro's Bennington sculptures. Yet the general comparison – and the isolated specific similarities between *Smoulder* and *Sculpture Three*, and *Reel* and *Sculpture Five* – point to pronounced differences in sensibility that re-emphasise the sense of freedom and quickly developing experiment Caro associated with America. Where Caro's Bennington sculptures are dynamic, fluid, speedily assembled and primarily visual, Bolus's approach is deliberate, refined, almost contrived, and bound up with a peculiar sensitivity to the handling of materials.

Resemblances to David Evison's work can be seen in a handful of Caro's 1970s sculptures. *Up Front* and *Octave* from 1971 relate, perhaps coincidently, to the upright room or cage-like sculptures Evison made during the late 1960s. More concretely, Caro's *Joy Ride* (1977–80) appears a condensed counterpart to the space-cupping curves and struts of Evison's sculptures from the middle of the decade, such as *Sculpture IV* (1975). Most compelling is the comparison between Caro's *Inset* (1972–74) and the sculptures from Evison's first solo exhibition at Kasmin's in 1970 (also Caro's gallery from the mid 1960s to the early 1970s). The resemblance is strong enough to suggest *Inset* was a direct paraphrase of sculptures by Evison, such as *Three Levels*.

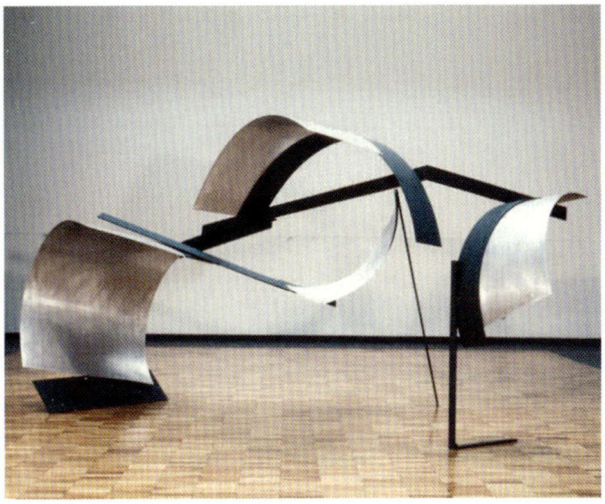

fig. 45

David Evison
Sculpture IV (1975)
Steel and aluminium
222 x 490 x 270 cm

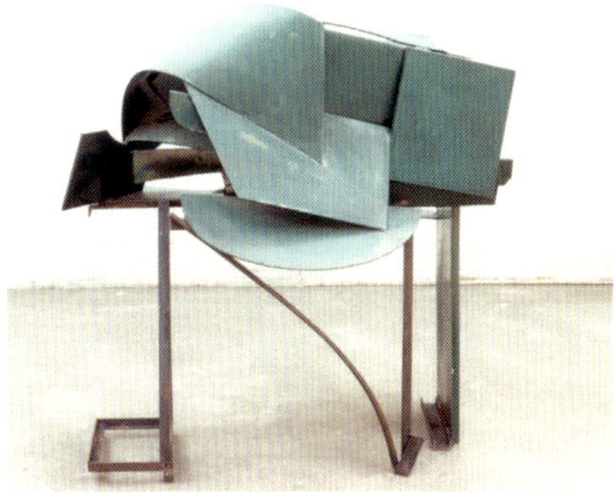

fig. 46

Anthony Caro
Joy Ride (1977–80)
Steel, varnished and painted green
145 x 145 x 100.5 cm

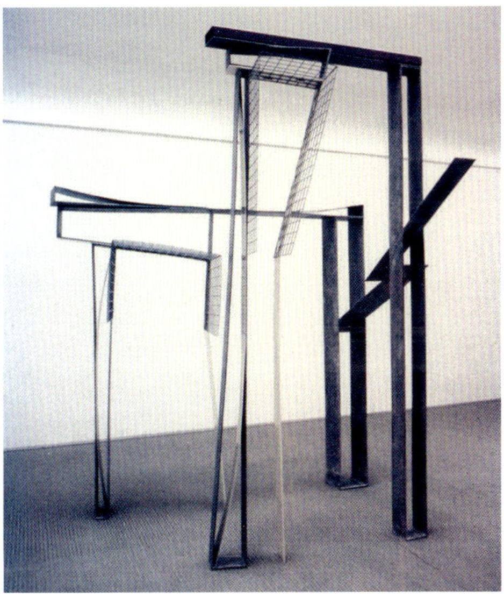

fig. 47

David Evison
Three Levels (1970)
Painted and galvanised steel
Height: 320 cm

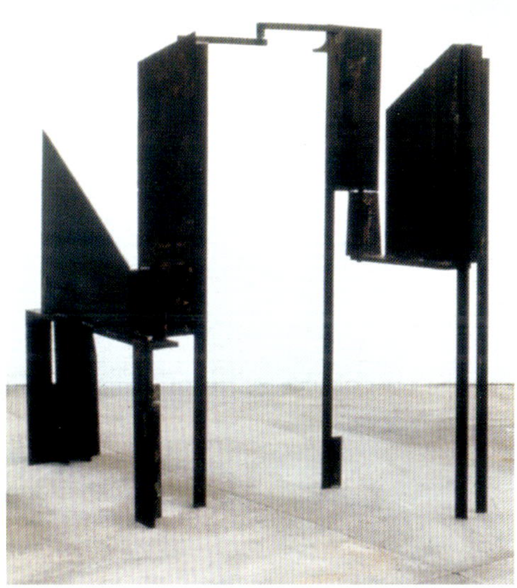

fig. 48

Anthony Caro
Inset (1972–74)
Steel, rusted and varnished
203 x 165 x 180.5 cm

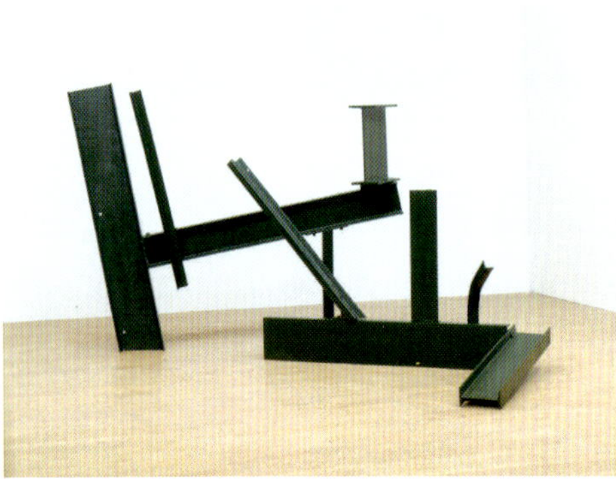

fig. 49

Anthony Caro
Sculpture Two (1962)
Steel, painted green
208.5 x 361 x 259 cm

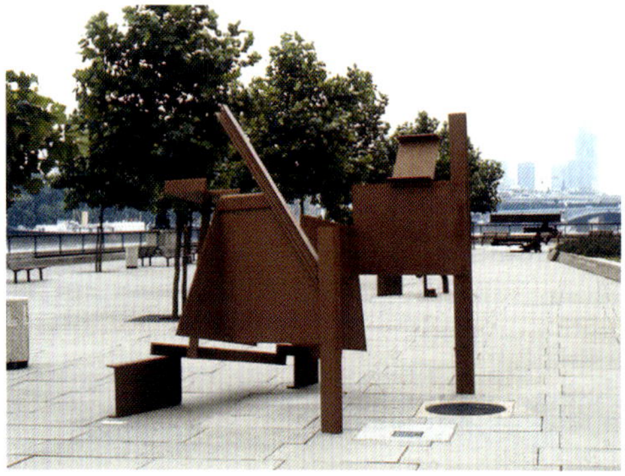

fig. 50

David Evison
Untitled (1977)
Steel, painted
Height: 280 cm

It is as if Caro decided to try to understand how these sculptures functioned by seeing if he could make one himself, a hypothesis lent weight by the relatively isolated appearance of *Inset* in his work of the 1970s. Intriguingly, while *Inset* follows Evison's 1970s sculptures, its solid, sharply angled planes could be seen, in turn, to presage the sculptures Evison made in 1976 and 1977. That these sculptures also recall Caro's seminal *Sculpture Two* (1962) gives some sense of the possible complexity of mutual influence in the British sculpture of the 1970s.

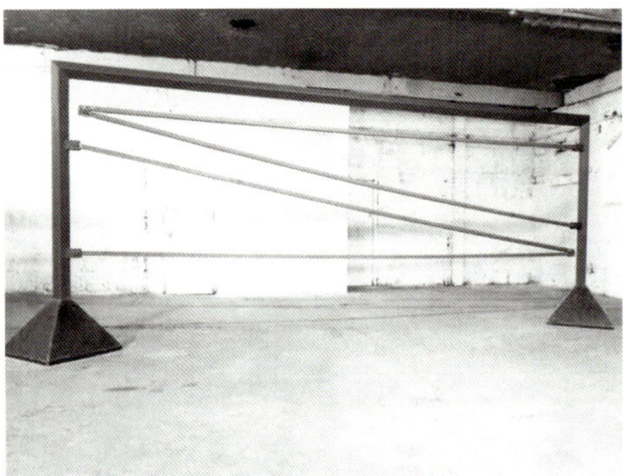

fig. 51

Peter Hide
Sculpture Number 3 (1971)
Painted mild steel, concrete
260 x 650 x 80 cm

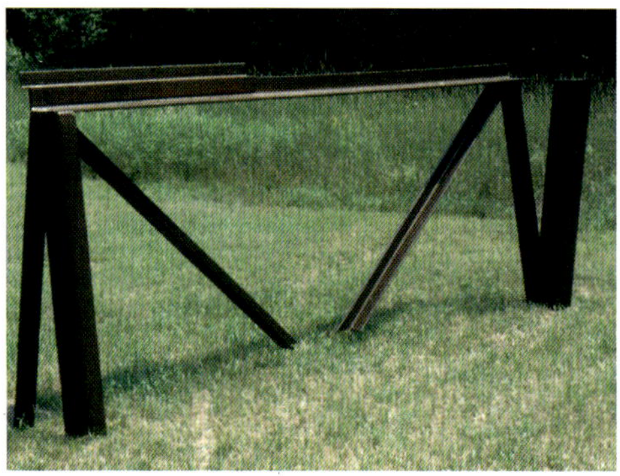

fig. 52

Anthony Caro
On Duty (1971–74)
Steel, rusted and varnished
154 x 375 x 60 cm

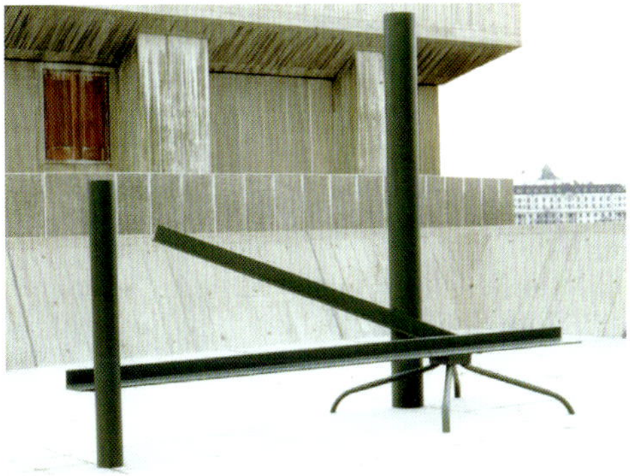

fig. 53

Anthony Caro
Shore (1968)
Steel, painted green
262 x 386 x 223.5 cm

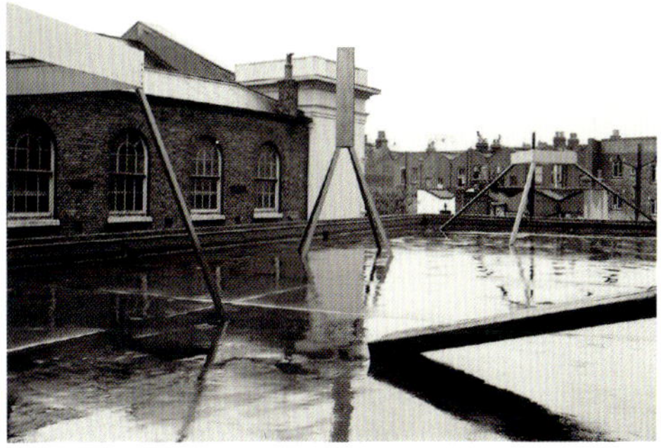

fig. 54

Peter Hide
Tower (1969–70)
Installation view at Stockwell Depot (1970)

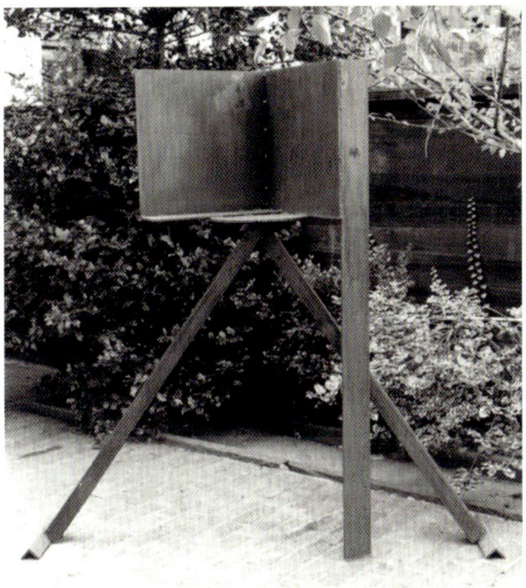

fig. 55

Anthony Caro
The Box (1971)
Steel, varnished
179 x 55 x 180 cm

As Peter Hide has said, his *Tower* of 1969 was, in part, based on Caro's *Shore* of 1968. Hide isolated *Shore's* vertical element, stripped it down to a basic form and made it monumental. Caro's *Box*, created a couple of years later, could be seen as an improvised response to Hide's simplification, opening up and re-complicating the closed box of *Tower*. There is, perhaps, a similar relation between the group of emphatic horizontal sculptures Hide made at the beginning of the 1970s and Caro's *Rack* series. Hide's sculptures reduce and monumentalise the horizontality Caro had developed through the 1960s; Caro, in turn, seems to use Hide's sculptures as a basic framework from which he develops a more improvised and elegant approach to creating structure. For his part, Hide thinks that the links are less evidence of Caro responding to his sculpture and more evidence of a common period style.

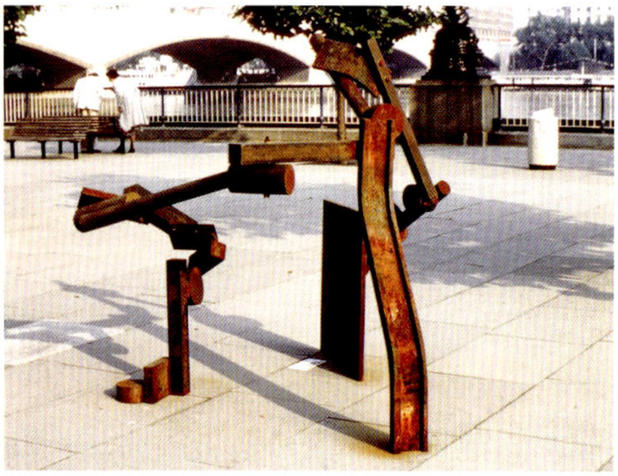

fig. 56

Tim Scott
Nataraja V (1975)
Steel, cut, welded and forged
154 x 170 x 134 cm

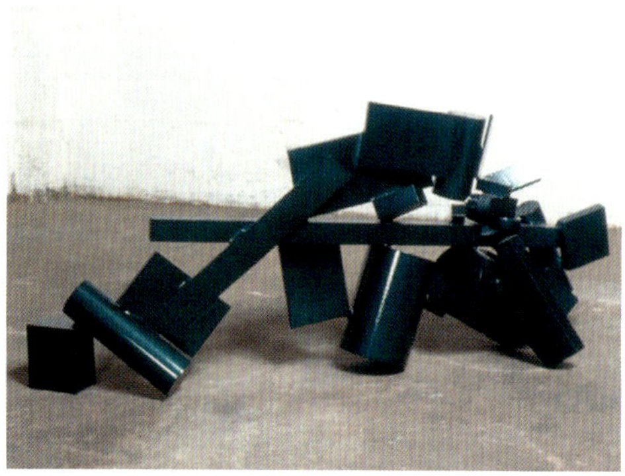

fig. 57

Anthony Caro
Dumbfound (1976)
Steel, sprayed green and varnished
53.5 x 127 x 38 cm

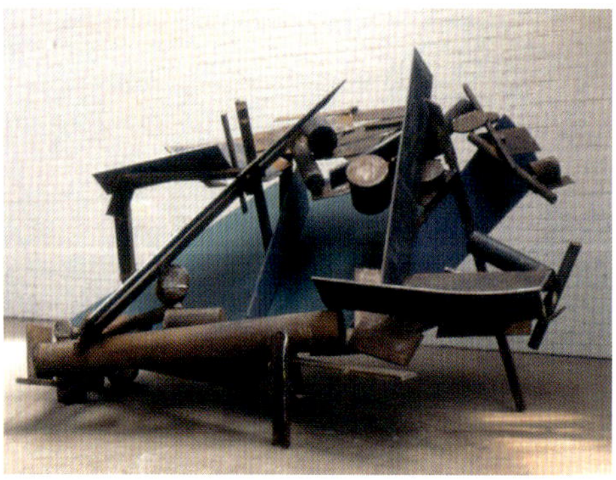

fig. 58

Anthony Caro
Midnight Gap (1976-78)
Steel, varnished and painted green
180.5 x 361 x 279 cm

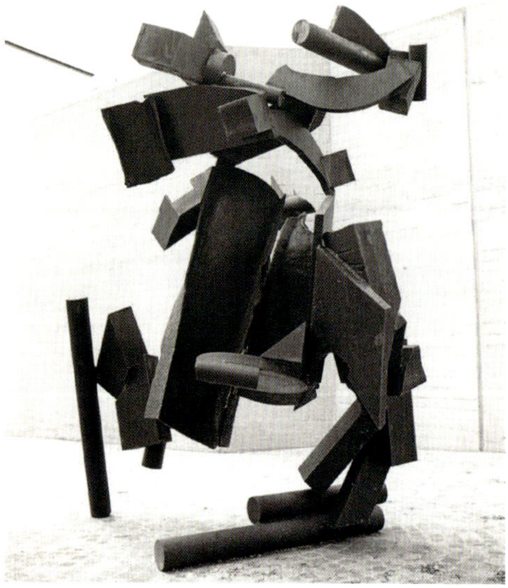

fig. 59

Tim Scott
Khajuraho II (1979)
Steel
264 x 205 x 155 cm

As with *Inset*, I would argue that *Dumbfound* (1976) shows Caro developing an understanding of a fellow artist's work. In *Dumbfound* – and the related sculptures *Slide Left* and *Teepee* – Caro appears to grapple with the complex structures based upon suspended truncated cylinders that Tim Scott had been exploring in his *Mudra* and *Natajara* series since 1974. The experiment apparent in *Dumbfound* found larger expression in the important sculpture *Midnight Gap*, at a scale which was then itself matched by Scott's *Khajuraho II* (1979). Scott intended that his sculptures from the mid 1970s would challenge what he saw as an over-reliance of Caro's sculpture on a 'pictorial' mode of organisation, and wanted them spread out and occupy space in way that he felt was more specifically sculptural. *Dumbfound* takes Scott's elements but argues against the use Scott put them to, arranging them along a single – and so pictorial – axis. *Midnight Gap* takes this further, and in 1984 Caro spoke of it in terms which reveal that it must have been formed in direct response to the anti-pictorial stance of Scott and others:

> It's a very frontal piece because the whole thing is acting against this screen – dancing around the screen really. I think if there was no screen there it wouldn't work at all... Some of my recent sculpture is to do with a datum, a flat datum, and making that volume work against something. That is what makes it different from 'sculptural' sculpture, which always informs itself against the interior of a person, the standing person with an interior axis. This sculpture of mine is working against what you see out there with your eyes.[3]

Considering Caro as engaged in an ongoing dialogue with his former students, peers and lesser-known contemporaries allows us to create a richer picture of the development of his sculpture. It draws attention to his sculpture's great diversity, the myriad pathways he went down. Alongside his dedication to teaching and his use of assistants, it shows how much of a 'social' artist he was. Rather than establishing a style early and then working through its implications for the rest of his career, Caro constantly sought ways to change his art, and the challenges or possibilities offered by sculptors in his orbit were an important part of this. He thought through making, and had a well-developed competitive streak. Instead of the singular focus implied by Rubin's one-man-sustaining-a-tradition, we can imagine that Caro thought of himself as a universal artist, wanting to push his sculpture into new territory, even if this entailed small acts of annexation. He was an omnivorous artist, at once restless and decisive, who sought inspiration in a great number of places and was able to turn it to his advantage.

1 William Rubin, *Anthony Caro*, (New York: The Museum of Modern Art, 1975), p. 15.
2 Rosalind Krauss, *Passages in Modern Sculpture*, (Cambridge, Massachusetts: MIT Press, 1977; 1981 paperback edition), p. 195-200; Lynne Cook, 'Between image and object: the "new British sculpture"', in Terry A. Neff (ed.), *A Quiet Revolution: British Sculpture Since 1965* (London: Thames & Hudson, 1987), p. 39.
3 Anthony Caro, extract from an interview with Melvyn Bragg for the *South Bank Show*, 1984, quoted in Ian Barker, *Anthony Caro: Quest for the New Sculpture* (Aldershot: Lund Humphries, 2004), p. 263.

Interview:

BETH CULLEN-KERRIDGE

Studio assistant 1996–2004

Marlow, UK

Email correspondence (January 2011 to December 2015)

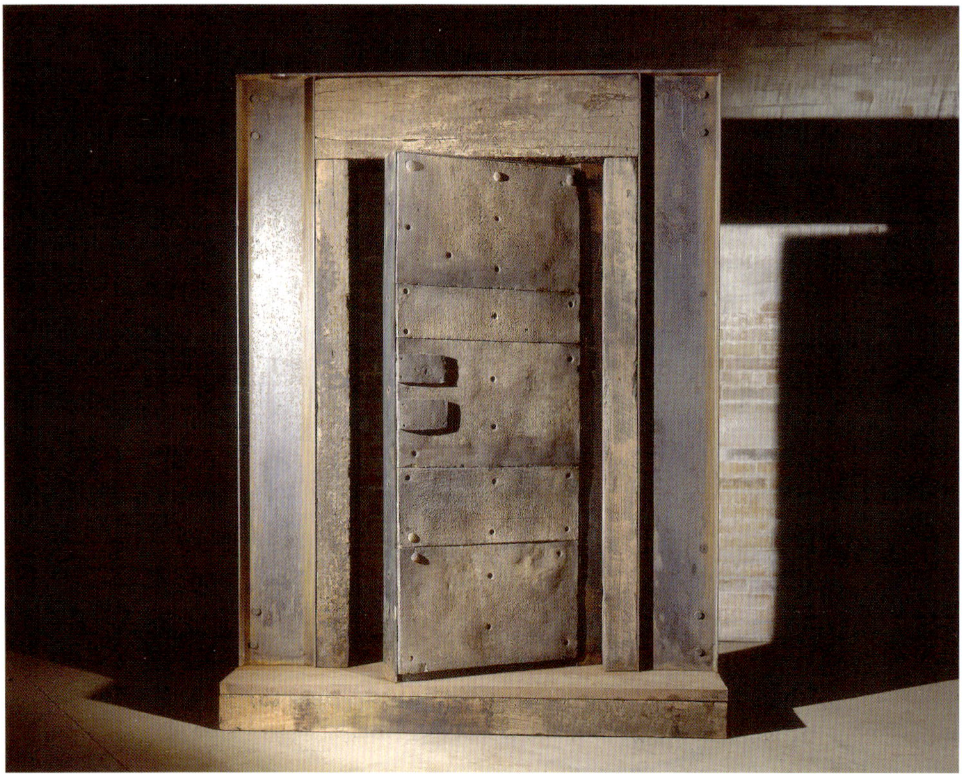

fig. 60

Anthony Caro
Gate of Heaven (The Last Judgement)
(1996–99)
Stoneware, steel and jarrah wood
237.5 x 185.5 x 69 cm

I was his tig welder, driver, painter, model-maker and friend. I suppose this may give you an insight into what skills were required... Loads and all of them, and a bit more to boot!

I started my career in 1991 at Liverpool John Moore's University, where I learned how to think, and the skills I learned were not necessarily physical ones. I was a self-taught chippie really. The technicians were the key to success; I came out with a first, raring to go. Thirsting for some new skills I got into the Royal College of Art's bronze-casting course. It was brilliant – I had barely mixed a bowl of plaster before then, but left with skills that I had only dreamed of. Richard Rome was great teacher and technician.

Caro's studio, Barford [Sculptures], needed a tig welder, so they rang the Royal College of Art [RCA] to get in touch with students who were nearly finished, and off I went. My friend Gavin Morris, also RCA, joined at the same time. It was brilliant – we were sculptors who could pay the rent.

Mike Bolus taught me loads more. He was an assistant for forty years and an amazing sculptor in his own right, but had lost his mojo. From him I learned patience, simplicity and lots more technical skills that I hadn't tried before. From Pat I learned business sense and balls.

From Tony I learnt that thank you letters and correspondence are a huge part of being a real full-time sculptor. Also, because he isn't too hands on, he asks the materials to do more. I only ever had to say no once in eight years, which I was disappointed by, and it still bugs me today. I do think there was an apprenticeship atmosphere and I am privileged to have worked with them all.

I wanted to work for Tony because he is a legend, and later because I love him and Sheila dearly. It was a very special time, but I don't want to do it again because I give 110 per cent – I was drained and for ages afterward could only make Caro-esque sculptures. I had to stop for a while, because I was sculpturally exhausted.

Since then I have embarked on new projects. Last year's was to learn stone carving, which I found I love – I went to Carrera to learn from the artisans. I'm working on a couple of new shows, too, and I also own and run the Hand and Flowers pub, which holds two Michelin stars, with my chef-husband, Tom.

I'm now 45, and have recently spoken to some students who asked for my opinion on their work. They have superb verve, and they reminded me of the feeling of excitement you get from learning new techniques. But I was thanking my stars that I am now so skilled that I don't even think about working out the methods, or justifying them. I just do it, and indulge myself in the ideas and the form. I have worked hard to be this lucky!

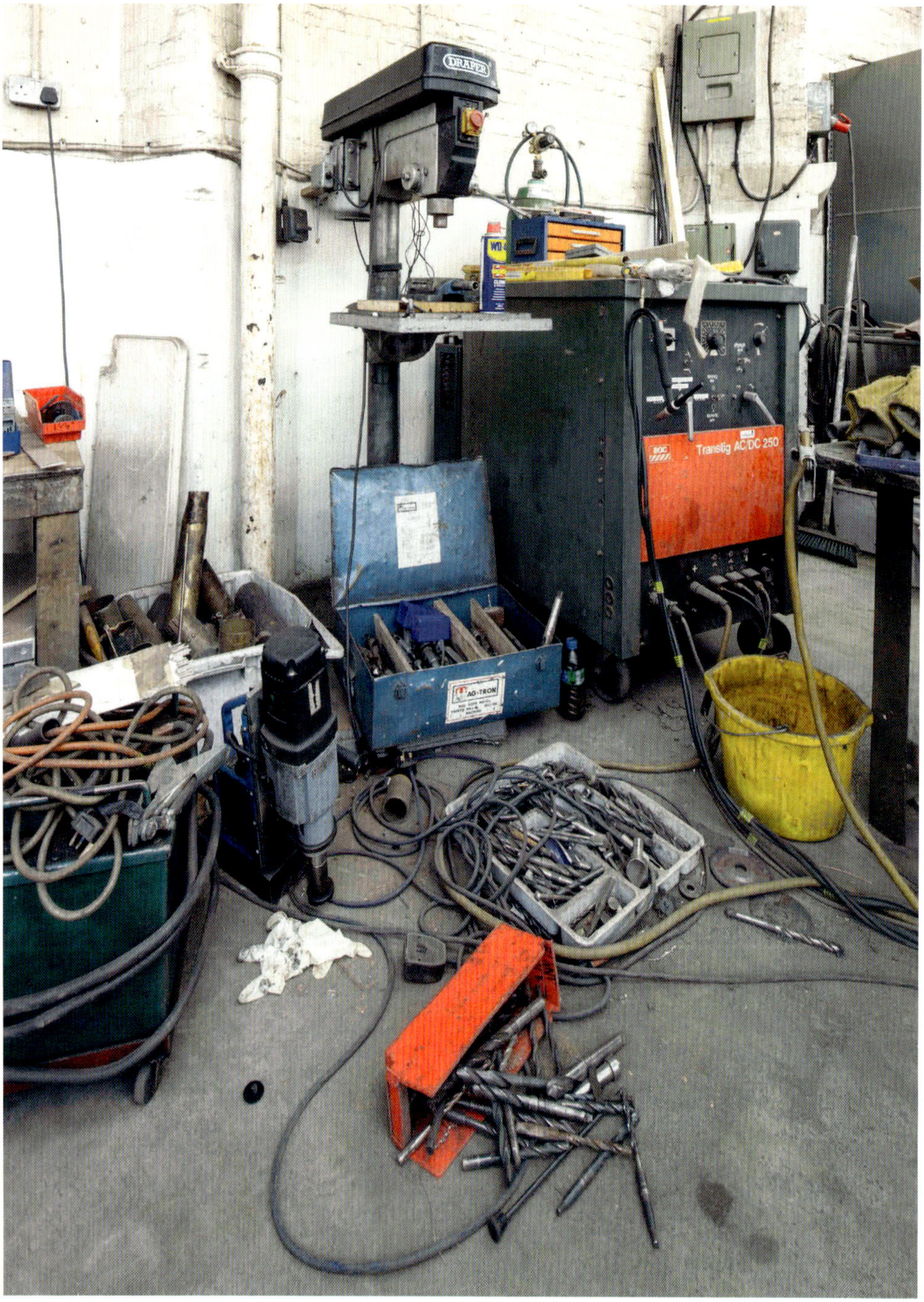

fig. 61

Camden studio (2013)

Interview:

GAVIN MORRIS
Studio assistant 1996–2003
Devon, UK
Telephone interview (January 2011)

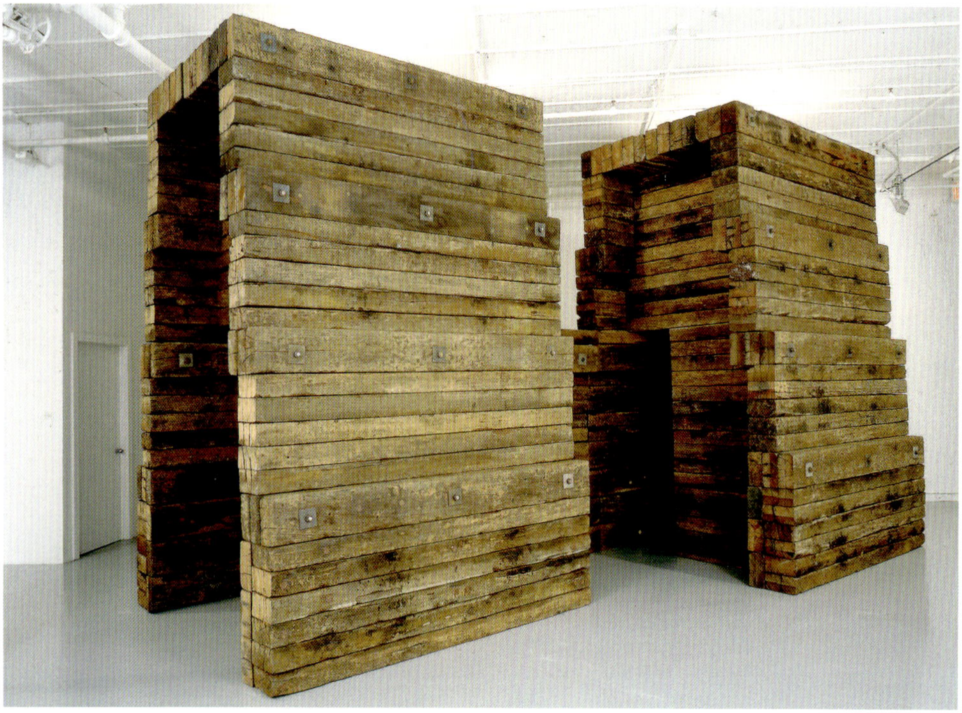

fig. 62

Anthony Caro
Chelsea Ziggurats (1997)
Jarrah wood railroad ties, spiked and bolted together
366 x 625 x 437 cm

JENNY DUNSEATH *I am interested in your experience as a studio assistant to Anthony Caro and what influence, if any, it has had on you as an artist and educator. How did the job come about and why were you interested in working for him?*

GAVIN MORRIS I suppose the main thing for me was his being iconic. I knew about him and I knew about his work. I studied sculpture at Winchester School of Art [WSA] and our head of department was John Gibbons. So there was a bit of a history there – of Tony working for Moore, John Gibbons working for Tony, and ultimately me working for Tony and also for John. I was aware that this kind of thing happened, although oddly, when I was at WSA, I was very, very definite about the fact that I wasn't going to do that! It seemed like a finishing school for people that made that kind of art. You know, big stuff and large object-based work and I was kind of dead against it. Then I finished at WSA, worked for a year and went to the Royal College. After completing my RCA MA, I got this phone call from Tony's studio, and because they made the first move I suppose I could justify it. I worked there for five years or more. For me there was very much a sense of this tradition that I didn't want to be part of, but I did actually feel part of because of the kind of work I was making. There was this weird push/pull thing.

JD *What did you learn from working there?*

GM The big thing that I took from it was a massive sense of feeling humbled by Tony's hard work. It's something I took from Winchester as well. John Gibbons had a similar hard line and relentless work ethic and Tony was exactly the same. I remember having conversations with him (Tony) after everyone had knocked off and over tea breaks with colleagues, thinking, 'This guy's in his seventies and he's still walking from Hampstead up to the studio.' Sometimes he didn't make it all the way and we'd have to pick him up, but five days a week he was in the studio and if he wasn't in the studio in Camden he was working at home. It was a very humbling experience.

I suppose technically I learnt a lot as well, but that's not something I took from Tony the man. I'm sure he wouldn't mind me saying, but his welds were awful and his craftsmanship in terms of sticking one bit of metal to another was rudimentary, but the important thing is that it did what it had to do. It had to hold until somebody else could do it, and he was always aware that he had technicians who would take care of that. That is by no means a criticism of his work. I don't think Tony needs to be able to weld to work with steel, and that side of things I learnt from him.

I was self-taught in many ways. I remember one piece of work that I made for the *Duccio Variations* series that was exhibited at the National Gallery. I worked on a sculpture made of brass, which I worked on solely for nine months. By the end of it I was brilliant at welding brass! That's not because anyone taught me, but because it was a means to an end. In many ways that was the way he worked with a lot of things there; we were given the space to learn those things.

JD *Who else was working there?*

GM Beth Cullen-Kerridge, a friend from the RCA; Tim Peacock, a friend from WSA; Doug Burton, the second generation of Winchester students at the time I was working there… Another guy called Giles Corby and another guy who was pivotal and so inspirational – I can't think why I haven't mentioned him before – Michael Bolus. He was earth-shatteringly inspirational, a truly remarkable man and I can remember thinking what a crime it was for the art world that he didn't keep pushing away at it. I know he had a faltering start and he had some awful experiences with galleries. He made some great works of art and as a character he was just amazing.

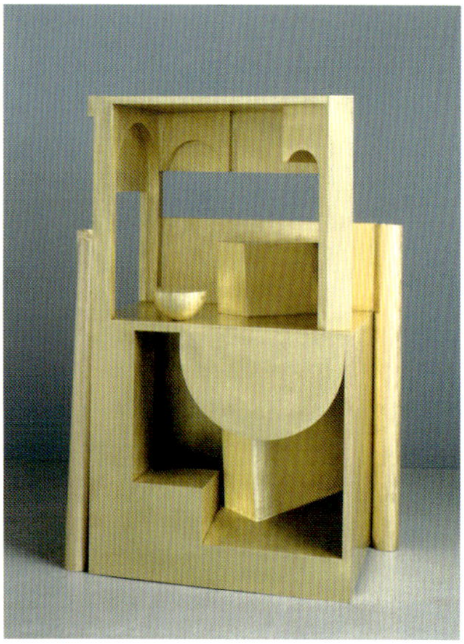

fig. 63

Anthony Caro
Duccio Variations No.2 (1999–2000)
Brass
164 x 119 x 64 cm

One of the massive projects that was under way when I was there was *The Last Judgement*. Mike was working with copper, making some trumpets, and he needed a tool to be able to do a certain job. The tool didn't exist, so he spent what must have been at least two weeks making it. I think that it's quite incredible, not only that Mike was single-minded enough to spend that amount of time making it, but also that Tony would be able to finance it – it's expensive to pay someone for a fortnight! When I left Caro's I went to Mike Smith Studio; everything there was all about time and motion and making things for a price and there was no budging on that. We had a budget for a job and I became acutely aware of how expensive an operation Tony was running; how financially unviable it was. You would have instances like that where Mike would spend two weeks making the tool to do a job that would take him another six weeks. That's incredibly unusual.

JD *At Mike Smith Studio, were you dealing directly with the artists?*
GM Yes we were. Artists would come in with a drawing on the back of a proverbial fag packet and say, 'I want to make this.' For example, I was project manager on Michael Landy's project *Semi-Detached*, which went to Tate Britain. Literally he came in with a drawing on the back of a fag packet and said, 'I've got this notion I want to make my mum and dad's house where they still live.' So we had to work out how to do it, how to make this one-to-one scale facsimile of a house that looked and smelt and sounded real.

JD *How do you describe Tony's set-up?*
GM It seems to me that Tony's set-up is quite old-fashioned. I paused before

I said that because I don't want to give the wrong impression. It's not backward looking in any way, but it's from a different era, because I think we are so capitalist in every walk of life now, much to our detriment. I think everything's got to stack up; we've always got to be able to make things make sense financially, art included. So to be able to have relative freedom from that, I suppose a fair degree of financial success, has allowed Tony that kind of freedom.

In terms of art practice, I can't imagine there are many places that can exist and can afford that level of financial support. I don't know how many assistants he has at the moment, but he had a regular core of four or five people (excluding secretarial staff), and there were times when he had about fifteen people working for him. That's a very costly enterprise, so I can't imagine there are many places like it on earth. It was very, very old-fashioned. It was like an apprenticeship.

JD *Is it possible to return to that? Would we even want to?*

GM I would say no. As soon as you have undone something like that, I think it's inevitable. This goes back to a conversation I had with Tony about Duchamp's *Fountain*. I can remember him getting really, really upset about Duchamp; Tony's perception was of the damage Duchamp had done, and how he had unravelled art. I suppose there seems to be this notional image of art being something else and that *Fountain* damaged the stuff of art so hugely that the damage could never be undone.

JD *What about your own practice; do you still make work?*

GM Yes, I do still make work, although it's not big object-based sculpture anymore and that's partly because I've moved to Devon. I used to have a studio in Peckham, and I became increasingly depressed just because I am rubbish at working in isolation; that's I suppose why I thrived at the Royal College and at Tony's. I started my own business and I was working on my own and then in my studio on my own. Quite frankly, I hated it and so stopped altogether. Most recently I've been doing a lot of printmaking and photography. In a sense I haven't got an artist's career in that I am not making art to pay the bills.

I'm a secondary school teacher, so in a way I am making art pay the bills, but by trying to excite a load of young individuals to make art. I currently teach 11–18 year olds fine art, graphics and photography. I have also in the past taught at university and college. The greatest amount was at Central School of Speech and Drama, which seems weird and unrelated, but I got quite heavily involved in theatre, and as a result ended up teaching sets, props and scenic construction courses for a while as a visiting lecturer. In fact it was through a collaboration between Caro and the theatre company Northern Broadsides on a production of Milton's *Samson Agonistes* that I met my wife Jane. But I retrained four years ago and became a secondary school teacher and that's what I've been doing ever since – teaching art and photography, although that comes under the umbrella of art, but in terms of GCSEs and A Levels you can specialise in a photography or a general art and design paper, so I'm currently teaching both of those.

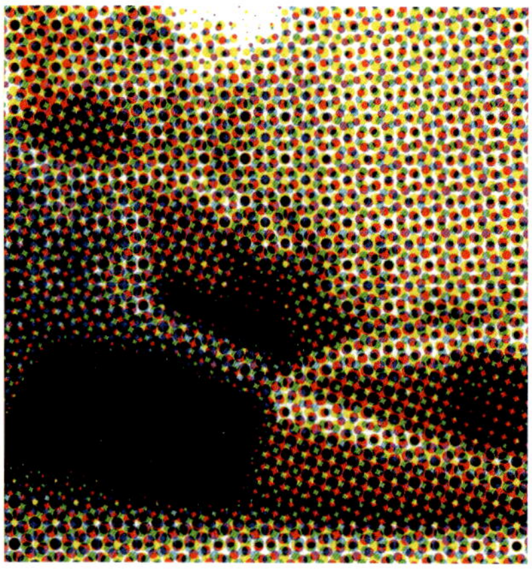

fig. 64

Gavin Morris
Stan (2014)
Photograph

JD *It's interesting to learn that you are a teacher. Did working for Tony have any impact on your teaching methodology?*

GM Funnily enough, it's not something I've really sat down and thought about, but I suppose it must do because all my art training has been done with people who are related to this lineage. With regard to the curriculum, it is incredibly broad. I think the common perception is that it is a very narrow one and we're quite restricted, but actually in terms of subject, I think we get off quite lightly. We have got a very broad curriculum – or broad in the sense that there is no prescription about what you teach or how you deliver the basics. We are expected to teach the formal elements, but the vehicle that we use to get there is not prescribed. I might choose to look at Michael Craig-Martin or Patrick Caulfield, which is what I am doing with my Year 7s at the moment, and my Year 11s are currently looking at animation. The medium is basically just a vehicle, as long as you are teaching those basic formal elements. It gives the practitioner the opportunity to teach what they know. My expertise is sculpture, so I do talk about sculpture quite a lot.

JD *Do you talk to your students about your experience as an assistant?*

GM Yeah, I have done. After I finished at Tony's studio I worked at Mike Smith Studio with Damien Hirst, Rachel Whiteread, Catherine Yass, Keith Tyson and all sorts of contemporary artists. So I try to make my art teaching as culturally relevant as possible. For instance, this morning I talked about Damien Hirst. I talked about Hirst because we were looking at Michael Craig-Martin. We went off on a bit of a tangent and we talked about how many had heard of Hirst, which is quite unusual for us, I think, but for an eleven-year-old boy it is particularly engaging. That's what my job is; it's about exciting people about the stuff of art. Getting back to Tony and John Gibbons, I think both of those certainly had that by the bucketful. Neither was narrow in their artistic interests. Tony's interests were really, really broad.

For me, my significant fond memory of working for Tony was being in the car and driving him. We used to natter, sometimes over long distances like to Yorkshire and back. You'd cover quite a lot of ground during those conversations – some were fascinating and some were really quite heated. I can remember talking about the slum clearances that happened as a by-product of the Blitz and Tony being very cross and sad about the whole thing. I suppose I had a more optimistic view of it, although I wasn't directly involved.

We drove past the fourth plinth in Trafalgar Square and saw Mark Wallinger's *Ecce Homo*, which I thought was one of the strongest fourth plinth works. I was singing its praises, and Tony was dead against it. We had this huge row about scale; I was saying that the whole point of *Ecce Homo* was it was out of scale and Tony was saying no, the whole point was that he [Wallinger] didn't understand scale! We had this big row about it and I can remember the conversation, so quite clearly he influenced me, or at least provoked me.

JD *Would you recommend your students do work experience with an artist?*

GM I suppose at this stage in their artistic life they are a bit young for that. I always make a point of trying to be a human being and I think that, regardless of what subjects you teach, to be able to teach you have to relate to, believe in and trust, so the more human you make yourself the better. I often talk about my family and, towards the end of their academic career, show a group my portfolio and talk about my work – trying to make art real. It might seem like name-dropping to those in my class, but I've met and worked with a lot of artists during my career. I don't have a problem with name-dropping and trying to make it as tangible as possible.

JD *It's making it real and accessible?*

GM That's something that has come up very recently. I'm now teaching in Devon – people are far more removed from the arts here than they were in South London. My previous school was in Streatham, and people in Streatham knew about contemporary art, which always surprised me. Often they regarded going to Tate Modern as a massive day out, even though it was actually only four or five miles away as the crow flies, but they were at least familiar with it and felt confident about what it contained, but it was still 'going out to London'. They felt that Streatham wasn't London – that's a young person's typically narrow view of the world – but they were still aware of the cultural thing that was happening, whereas in South Devon that's far more challenging: I'm trying to instil in them that there are other careers besides the armed forces, working in shops or surfing!

I've been reading around the subject because I've had several conversations in which kids will say, 'What's the point of art? It doesn't mean anything', so I needed some ammunition to back up my arguments. Apart from the fact that it's good for you to learn to use your eyes, and to learn about yourself and others, it's also important to say how much value art – and the arts more broadly – adds to the economy. The fact that last year more people visited art galleries and museums than visited football matches means something to a fourteen-year-old boy. Forty-one million people went to museums and art galleries last year – that's a lot of people! Six per cent of GDP is generated from the arts, which is more than banking, though newspaper column inches might suggest otherwise.

JD *You mentioned how working at Tony's was like an apprenticeship. What does the role of an assistant do for the development of a career?*

GM I feel like I'm in the second half right now. The first half was all that sort of stuff and now I'm doing something quite different, but it's still inextricably linked. My dream is to infect as many people as possible with this brilliant stuff called art that I've had the joy of working with all my professional life. Clearly that's the job of any educator, and that's the same whether you're in secondary or tertiary education. You're trying to excite and encourage interest in knowledge. I suppose that's what an artist does: works really, really hard at making stuff and learns from their mistakes along the way. Generally, as a group, I suppose artists are quite accepting of mistakes. We recognise that they are a necessary means to an end; it's important to inform young people that mistakes are acceptable and an essential part of the process of art making, and that art is democratic and their voices count for something.

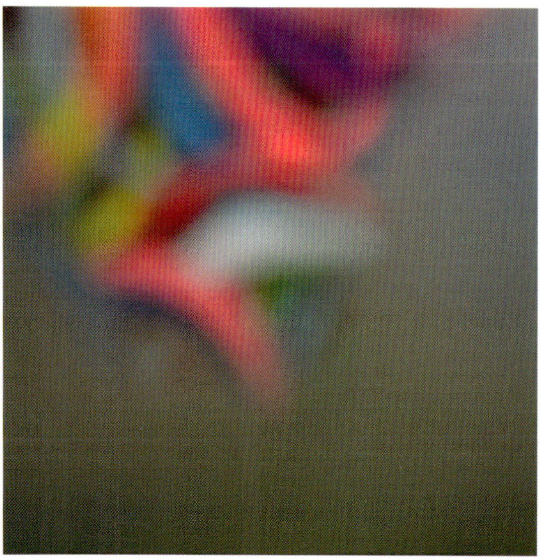

fig. 65

Gavin Morris
Bands (2014)
Photograph

Interview:

TIM PEACOCK

Studio assistant 1996–2001 (full-time); 2001–5 (part-time)

London, UK

Email correspondence (July to December 2015)

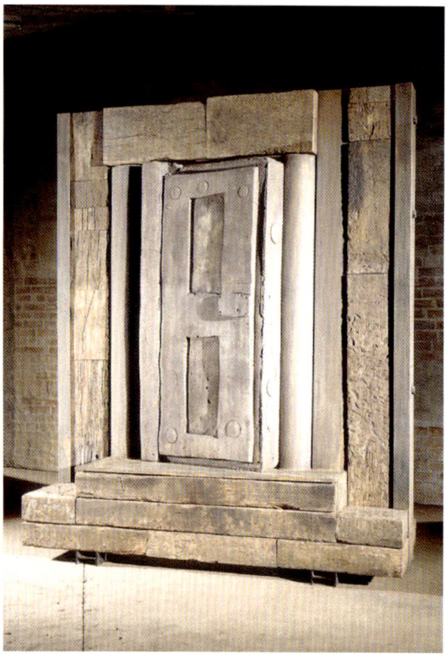

fig. 66

Anthony Caro
The Door of Death (The Last Judgement)
(1996–99)
Stoneware, jarrah wood and steel
222 x 183 x 71 cm

I started working for Tony in 1996. A good friend of mine, Gavin Morris, had been at Barford Sculptures for a couple of months and was kind enough to give me a call when it was decided they needed another pair of hands in the studio.

At the time I was living seventy miles away in Cambridgeshire and working on a building site, but despite my reluctance to have anything to do with London (I was very much a country boy back then) it was just too good an opportunity to ignore and I arranged to take a Friday afternoon train to meet Pat and Tony. After a very informal chat with them and a full guided tour, I was offered a two-week trial... By the Monday morning I'd found somewhere to stay, and I've been living in London ever since.

I'd finished my BA at Winchester College three years before and consequently was out of the habit of working with steel, so the whole place seemed a bit daunting at first. I remember relying on Gav and Pat to talk me through several unfamiliar bits of machinery during the evenings of that first week, but because I'd decided very early on that I wanted to stay, I made damn sure I knew how to do everything that was expected of me before the two-week trial period was up!

As well as Gavin Morris, both Giles Corby and Beth Cullen were there full-time when I started. Beth helped me settle in and quickly learn the ropes, and myself, Beth and Gav all remain excellent friends to this day.

I got the distinct impression quite early on that, before the three of us started, the norm was for studio assistants to work for Tony for a year then move on, their experience helping further their own art practice somewhere else. Tony actively encouraged this to happen and didn't want to stand in the way of anyone producing their own work.

We just had such a good time, though. Pat, Tony and all of us clicked so well with each other, that one year turned into two, two turned into three... Before we knew it, Beth, Gav and myself became the Barford Sculptures in-house team, working full-time while others came and went. It was a situation that carried on after we left, with a close-knit core of two or three assistants remaining with Tony for several years, rather than moving on annually.

Working there was a pleasure, but it certainly helped that there was a continuous flow of very interesting and talented visitors to the studio. Aside from some of Tony's more notable collaborations (Norman Foster and the Millennium Bridge, David Pelham's *Leaf Pool*, *Samson Agonistes* for Barrie Rutter and a piece that Gavin and myself made for John Hoyland all spring to mind) there were also friends, colleagues and assistants from Tony's past such as John Gibbons, Hamish Black and Jon Isherwood dropping in for an impromptu visit, or coming to advise and work on a specific project. Regular specialists in their own fields like Jaana Fowler, Jolyon Oliver, Garry Doherty and John Riddy would also come in and work on a more frequent basis, whenever their particular skill set was required. Someone whom I do feel very privileged to have worked alongside while at Tony's studio was Mike Bolus. He was the man who seemed capable of making anything – beautiful objects that only someone with a vast knowledge of materials and processes would be capable of producing. I learned a lot from just watching the methodical, meticulous way he worked and I shall always remember him extremely fondly.

I'm not sure how it was after I left, but during my time there was a tendency for us (the studio assistants) to work on our individual sculptures from conception all the way through to completion. Tony would naturally be involved with every single aesthetic decision along the way (nothing, however seemingly insignificant, went unnoticed) but one of the particular joys for me were the occasions that my opinion was asked for. Both of us standing back from the piece of work; together we would look at, discuss and resolve any issues Tony thought there might have been.

I saw this as a particular privilege, because I was in the unusual position of being a Caro assistant who didn't make his own sculpture. Tony was aware from the beginning of my time there that I had no intention of getting a studio of my own in order to produce my own work, but I think he made an exception and didn't try to persuade me into doing so because he could see the enthusiasm I had for making his sculpture. This was, indeed, very much the case... His passion and love for what he did almost instantly rubbed off on me and – although this may be a naive thing to say – while I was working on those sculptures I genuinely did treat them with the same care and attention I would've done had they been my own work. Other studio assistants used to regularly comment about how difficult it was to leave Tony's at 6pm and put his work behind them so that they could fully concentrate on their own sculpture... But I never needed to clear my head of his work; for me it wasn't a distraction.

I feel fortunate to have worked on dozens of sculptures with Tony over what was nearly ten years, but some of the more memorable ones are *Chelsea Ziggurats* (1997), the *Van Gogh Chairs* (1997), and the *Door of Death* and *Gate of Heaven* from *The Last Judgement* (1996–99) and sculptures like *French Horn* and *Double Bass* from the series of brass instrument/wooden sculptures (1999–2000). I also had to clamber inside *Requiem* armed with an oxyacetylene torch to separate the top section from the bottom because it was too heavy for the Annely Juda gallery's hoist to lift in one piece from the street... But that's not such a fond memory! In the end I was sorry to leave Barford Sculptures, but it was time to move on. Tony, as always, was hugely supportive and encouraging, and we stayed in contact. Alister Warman gave me the opportunity to breathe new life into the sculpture workshops at Byam Shaw School of Art, and I had seven happy years there teaching students how to bring their sculptural ideas to fruition. It was through Byam Shaw that I also ended up teaching both adults' and children's short courses, so I soon found myself passing on to them some of the things I'd learned from people like John Gibbons, Mike Bolus and Tony Caro!

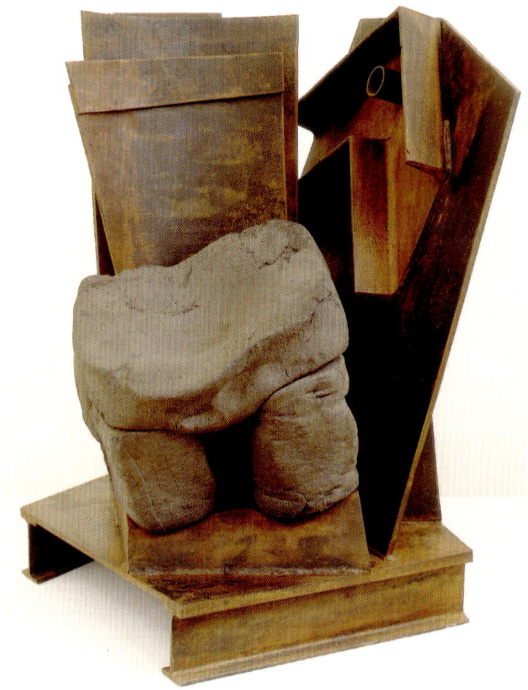

fig. 67

Anthony Caro
Van Gogh Chair IV (1997)
Stoneware and steel, waxed
89 x 67 x 61 cm

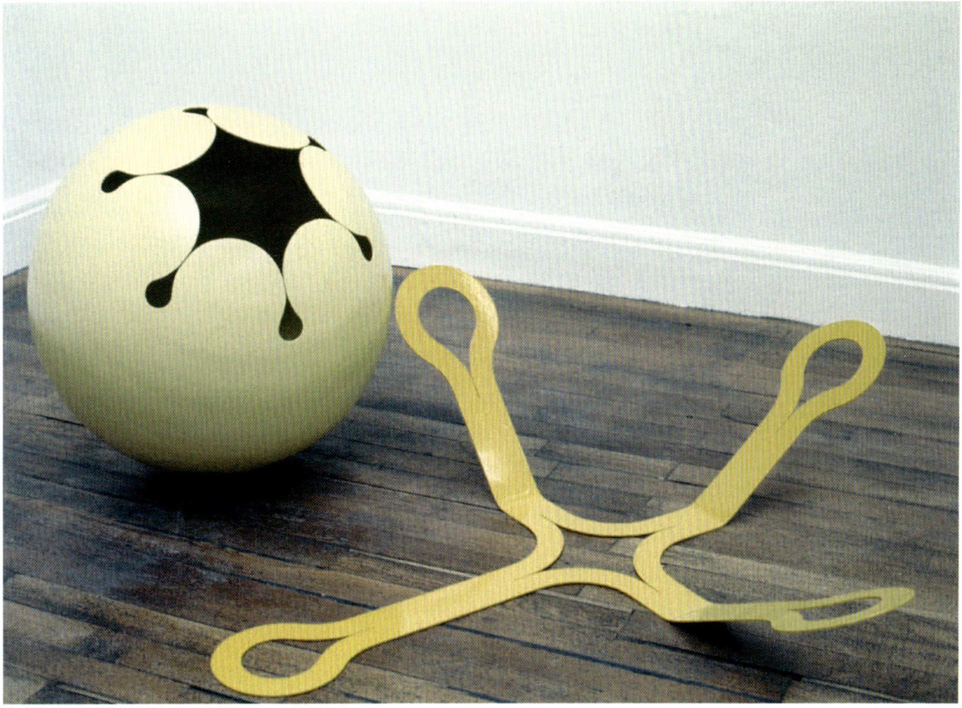

fig. 68

Michael Bolus
Sculpture 7 (1965)
Painted steel
76.8 x 183.5 x 120.6 cm

While at Byam Shaw I was approached by Kalliopi Lemos, a Greek artist based in London, who asked me if I'd establish and manage a sculpture studio for her. I took all my experience from working at Tony's (largely Pat's studio management skills!) and set up KCL Fine Arts in Kilburn. The best thing about that particular situation was that I found myself in a position to hand-pick talented and enthusiastic students who I thought might be interested in helping me produce Kalliopi's work after their graduation from Byam. Many of them, I'm pleased and a little proud to say, went on to become successful artists in their own right.

Regardless of the fact that I don't make my own work, Tony was still a huge influence on me. He taught me how to stand back and really look at sculpture. He instilled in me the appreciation of both controlled detail and carefree spontaneity. He showed me when to walk away and say, 'That's finished', which is not always as easy as it sounds, and when to roll up one's sleeves and persevere with something that seemingly can't be resolved. He was a great man and I cared about him very much.

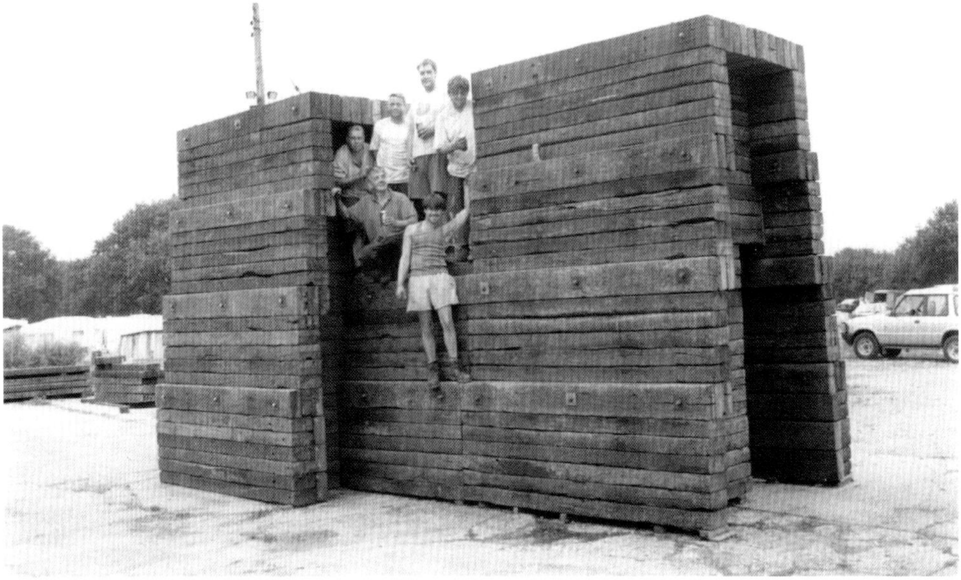

fig. 69

Making of *Ziggurats* (1997)

Essay: Why Learning Communities? Why Now?

Professor K. Patricia Cross

"Knowledge requires language, and people construct knowledge out of the language available to them in their community."

The stimulus for today's high interest in learning communities is coming from many sources, which often have differing motivations that nevertheless complement and reinforce one another. Most people are interested in learning communities because they offer hope of making college a more holistic, integrated learning experience for students. But learning communities can range all the way from loosely structured programs that offer students the opportunity to take a set of courses in common, to heavily structured programs of integrated courses that are team-taught by faculty from different disciplines, to a cohort of students who may even live together in residence halls. Understandably, there is thus considerable debate over the definition of 'learning communities'. For the purposes of this article I shall simply define them as 'groups of people engaged in intellectual interaction for the purpose of learning'.

Why is there so much interest in learning communities? I think the reasons can be divided into three broad categories: philosophical (because learning communities fit into a changing philosophy of knowledge), research based (because learning communities fit with what research tells us about learning), and pragmatic (because learning communities work).

The most radical – and some would say most coherent – concept of learning communities is based in the concept of collaborative learning. The term 'collaborative learning' has been captured by its advocates as something of a brand name and has become associated with a distinctive epistemology for learning communities. Kenneth Bruffee, a professor of English at Brooklyn College, bases his advocacy of collaborative learning in the concept of 'non-foundational social construction', which to my mind is a rather awkward term for the belief that knowledge is socially constructed rather than discovered. 'We construct and maintain knowledge', Bruffee says, 'not by examining the world but by negotiating with one another in communities of knowledgeable peers.'[1] Knowledge requires language, and people construct knowledge out of the language available to them in their community. Knowledge, says Bruffee, is 'therefore not universal and absolute. It is local and historically changing. We construct it and reconstruct it, time after time, and build it up in layers.'[2]

In contrast, the traditional view of knowledge as foundational contends that there is a reality 'out there', a foundation on which all knowledge is built. It is the task of learners to discover the external reality that exists. This might be done in groups, of course, but students would work together cooperatively to find the best or 'correct' answer. The argument for group work from the knowledge-as-foundational viewpoint is that two heads (or more) are better than one. So even in this traditional view of knowledge as reality waiting to be discovered, group learning may prove advantageous.

In the non-foundational view of knowledge, however, a community of learners is not only advantageous, it is also necessary, because people construct knowledge by working together, not just cooperatively but interdependently. The fundamental assumption of constructivism is that knowledge is actively built by learners as they shape and build mental frameworks to make sense of their environments.

As William Whipple argues, the strengths of social construction for learning communities are several. First and foremost, social construction conceives of knowledge not as something that is transferred in an authoritarian structure from teacher to student but rather as something that teachers and students work interdependently to develop. Thus it fosters active learning over passive learning, cooperation over competition, and community over isolation. The passive learning presumably encouraged or at least permitted by lectures, the competition engendered by grades and test scores, and the isolation that exists for large numbers of commuting, part-time students are some of the major criticisms of the pedagogies of our time. A nonfoundational view of knowledge may be one way to correct these faults.

It does not take a whole lot of looking to see how much of the scholarly work on learning today is questioning, in one way or another, our dependence on the authority of the scientific method to discover knowledge. The late Donald Schön, for example, contended that the professions are in the midst of a crisis of confidence and legitimacy because professional knowledge is mismatched to the conditions of practice. Education is a perfect example of the mismatch between research and practice. The problems we have to solve in education are complex and ill-formed. It is nowhere near as simple as we pretend when we talk earnestly about improving learning and assessing learning outcomes. The currently popular distillations of research findings with implications for practice rely largely on what Schön calls 'technical rationality', which he defines as 'instrumental problem solving made rigorous by the application of scientific theory and technique'.[3] He describes the process this way: 'Researchers are supposed to provide the basic and applied science from which to derive techniques for diagnosing and solving the problems of practice. Practitioners are supposed to furnish researchers with problems for study and with tests of the utility of research results. The researcher's role is distinct from, and usually considered superior to, the role of the practitioner'.[4]

This view not only results in the hierarchical model and the separation of research and practice, but it also calls into question the epistemology upon which current education is based: specifically, the discovery of knowledge through a rigorous application of the 'scientific method'. Schön puts the dilemma this way:

> There is a high, hard ground where practitioners can make effective use of research-based theory and technique, and there is a swampy lowland where situations are confusing 'messes' incapable of technical solution. The difficulty is that the problems of the high ground, however great their technical interest, are often relatively unimportant to clients or to the larger society, while in the swamp are the problems of greatest human concern. Shall the practitioner stay on the high, hard ground where he can practice rigorously, as he understands rigor, but where he is constrained to deal with problems of relatively little social importance? Or shall he descend into the swamp where he can engage the most important and challenging problems if he is willing to forsake technical rigor?[5]

Schön recommends that practitioners engage in a search for knowledge by asking themselves what 'kinds of knowing are already embedded in competent practice'.[6] Such a search calls for communities of practitioners to generate relevant knowledge about the practice of their profession. Such communities, it seems to me, would include college teachers and college students working collaboratively to learn chemistry or history or political science or any other subject matter that is part of the higher education curriculum. The practice of scholarship, many would say, is embedded in learning communities.

Another strong sign of a radical shift in our view of how knowledge is generated and of its implications for learning is found in work on ethnic minorities and women. Mary Field Belenky and her colleagues sparked a strong strain of sympathetic recognition among women teachers and students when they demonstrated that many women display 'ways of knowing' that differ from those of the male model that has dominated academe for so many years. The male model is characterised by 'separate knowing' – a way of learning that is impersonal and objective, involving detachment, critical argument, analysis, and other descriptors that we associate with the scientific method. Many women, however, are 'connected learners'.[7]

Blythe Clinchy describes a connected learner's search for knowledge: 'She does not ask whether it is right; she asks what it means. When she says, "Why do you think that?" she doesn't mean, "What evidence do you have to back that up?" She means, "What in your experience led you to that position?"'.[8] This student's search for knowledge, argues Clinchy, is best accomplished through connected conversations 'in which each person serves as midwife to each other person's thoughts, and each builds on the other's ideas'.[9] At heart, then, a connected conversation is a learning community at its best, and it is also a reflection of changing ideas about the source of knowledge and learning.

My point is that this changing view of the nature of knowledge is more than an academic diversion. It is providing an alternative view for some of the most prevalent criticisms of our educational systems – egalitarianism versus hierarchies, collaboration versus competitiveness, and active participation versus passive absorption. The current wave of interest in learning communities is not, I think, just nostalgia for the human touch, or just research about the efficacy of small-group learning, but a fundamental revolution in epistemology.

A longer version of this essay was first published in *About Campus*, 3:3, (July–August 1998), p. 4–11.

1 Kenneth Bruffee, *Collaborative Learning: Higher Education, Interdependence, and the Authority of Knowledge* (Baltimore: Johns Hopkins University Press, 1995), p. 9.

2 Ibid. p. 222.

3 Donald Schön, *The Reflective Practitioner* (New York: Basic Books, 1983), p. 21.

4 Ibid. p. 26.

5 Ibid. p. 42.

6 Ibid. p. 29.

7 Mary Field Belenky, Blythe McVicker Clinchy, Nancy Rule Goldberger, Jill Mattuck Tarule (eds), *Women's Ways of Knowing: The Development of Self, Voice, and Mind* (New York: Basic Books, 1986).

8 Blythe Clinchy, 'Issues of gender in teaching and learning', *Journal on Excellence in College Teaching*, 1 (1990). Reprinted in Kenneth A. Feldman and Michael B. Paulsen (eds), *Teaching and Learning in the College Classroom: ASHE Reader* (New York: Ginn Press, 1994), p. 122.

9 Ibid. p. 123.

Interview:

HYWEL LIVINGSTONE

Studio assistant 2003–6 (full-time); 2006–present day (part-time)

Cheltenham, UK

Email correspondence (June 2014 to December 2015)

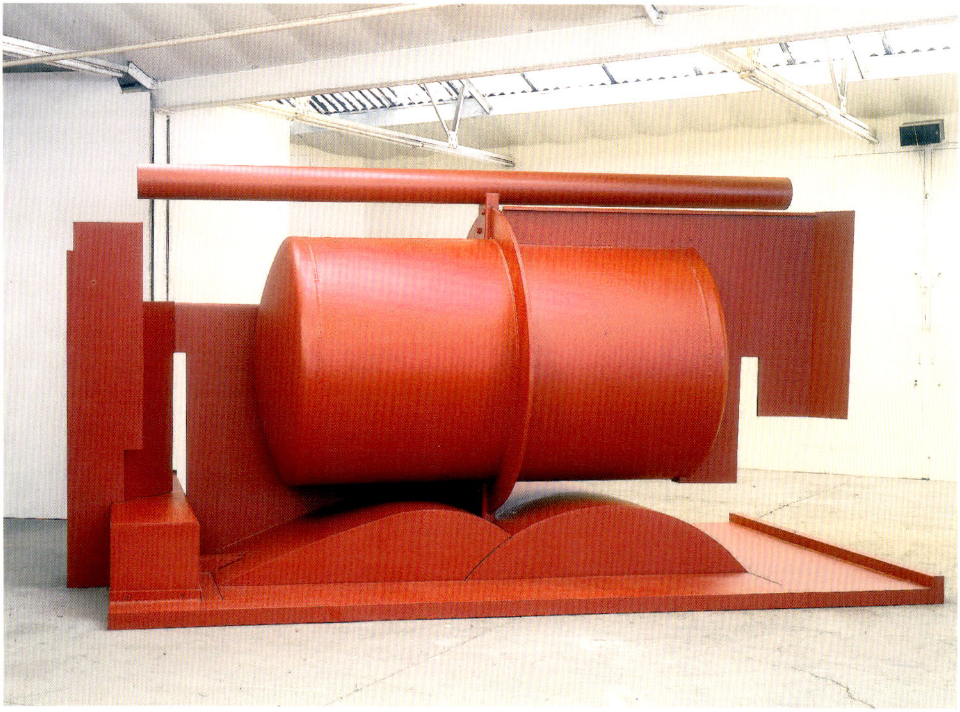

fig. 70

Anthony Caro
Aurora (2000-03)
Steel, painted red
265 x 523 x 308 cm

Did you have an art school education?
Yes, I have a BA (Hons) Fine Art Sculpture from Winchester School of Art, and an MA Art History (Histories and Interpretations) from Bristol University.

When did you work for Tony?
I started doing one day a week during my last year of undergrad (2003) and went full-time when I graduated. I worked full-time in the studio for three years, and have been part-time since.

How did the job come about?
I was put forward for the role by my professor at Winchester, John Gibbons.

Why did you want to work for him?
First and foremost it was the offer of a job in London before I'd even graduated! Also, it meant continuing and building on what I'd learnt at university, in a field that I loved.

Which sculptures did you work on? And what was involved in the making? There have been too many to remember them all... The first one I worked on was *Aurora*, and other sculptures that I found particularly engaging and informative to work on were the Kenwood House series (2003–4) and the series of galvanised works, begun around 2004.

Working on the sculptures involved two main approaches, the first being 'tuning in' to Tony's way of thinking and understanding his instructions – which sometimes meant sharing the source materials informing the work, usually paintings, but also newspaper or magazine clippings – and then engineering the sculptures in such a way as to be discreet enough not to detract from the content of the works themselves. This latter point was particularly challenging and rewarding when Tony combined more than one material, such as the terracotta and steel in the sculptures shown at Kenwood House (*A Life in Sculpture: The Kenwood Series*).

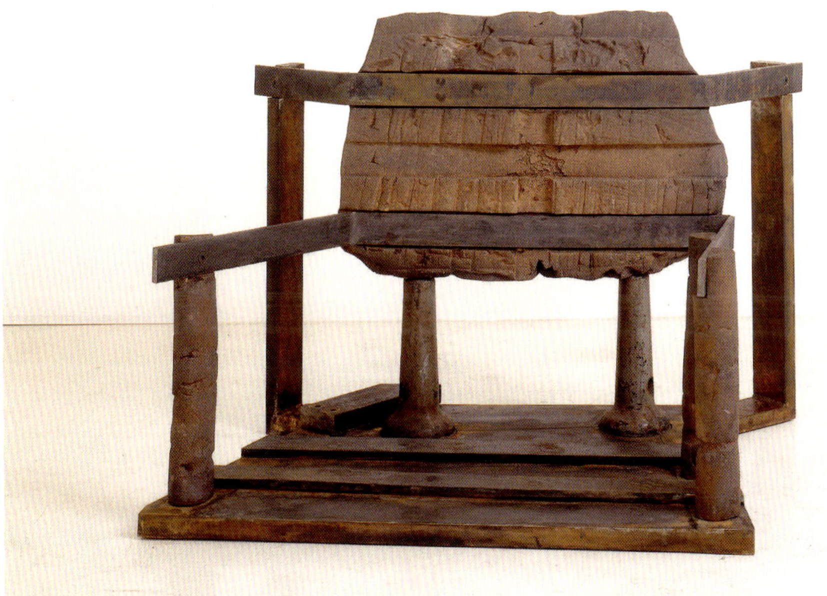

fig. 71

Anthony Caro
Messages (The Kenwood Series) (2003-4)
Stoneware and steel
108 x 143.5 x 108 cm

Who else worked there?
Ed Goolden started working at the studio in Camden soon after I began there full-time. Since then I have worked with many others, latterly Olivia Bax, Neil Ayling and John Wallbank. We are all very much still in touch, and often work together.

Have you worked as an artist's assistant to anyone else?
In my second year at Winchester, and before working for Tony, I worked at the weekends as an assistant to Jim Unsworth in his studio in Bow, East London. The process of working was very similar, and I learnt a lot about manipulating material (steel) to effectively convey counter-intuitive qualities – the flow of fabric, balance, counterbalance, weight, lightness and so on. It was a steep and brilliant learning curve, and prepared me very well for going on to work for Tony.

Do you believe that a pedagogic relationship existed between Caro and his assistants?
Yes, but only as an ancillary. There was no formal learning (other than in a practical sense), and we had to intuit quickly to keep up with Tony's thought processes. He wasn't there to teach us, but we had to learn from him quickly. I think that's why the footfall of assistants through the studio was so high: some simply couldn't gel, and instead of working with Tony they worked against him.

However, it became easier as time went on and you began to understand what he was looking for in his sculptures, and what he didn't want to see. Eventually the working relationship became very fluid, and we were able to almost pre-empt his thoughts, which meant a much quicker, efficient and therefore prolific output. The downside of this almost osmotic working relationship was that it was very hard to shake off this (his) approach to looking and making, especially when trying to make my own work. It took me a long time to get out of his mode of thinking and develop my own.

How has – or has – working for Tony influenced you?
It has given me a strong critical framework, and an ability to assess the merits and/or failings of my own sculptures during my personal studio process. In a broader sense, working for Tony has put me in contact with a large group of friends and colleagues, whom I value greatly.

How was your role of assistant received by your contemporaries?
Mostly positively – but not all were compatible, hence the high studio footfall.

Do you still make work? If so, do you employ assistants in the making of your own work?
I still make sculpture, but do not employ assistants. I would find it extremely

difficult to have other people around while I work in my studio, and would only ever contemplate assistants for practical reasons.

Have you taught in art schools? If so, has being an assistant informed your teaching methods in any way?
I teach in an art school. The studio as a concept is something that is very difficult for undergrads (and graduate students) to grasp, and being a former assistant has informed my methods in so far as I am able to convey the importance of organising an efficient studio (both practically and psychologically) as being conducive to producing work. The clarity of critical understanding that was demanded by Tony in his studio has been a very useful tool in an art school environment, as is the confidence to express it.

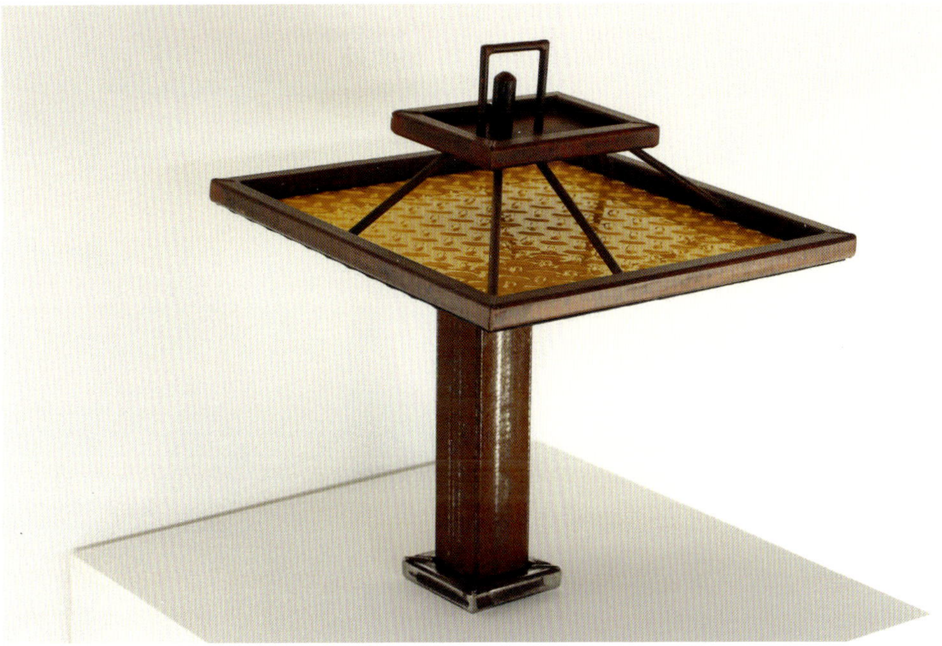

fig. 72

Hywel Livingstone
Y Capten Bach (The Little Captain) (2014)
Steel
60 x 50 x 50 cm

Interview:

JONATHAN GILDERSLEEVES

Studio assistant 2005–8

South London, UK

Email correspondence (September to December 2015)

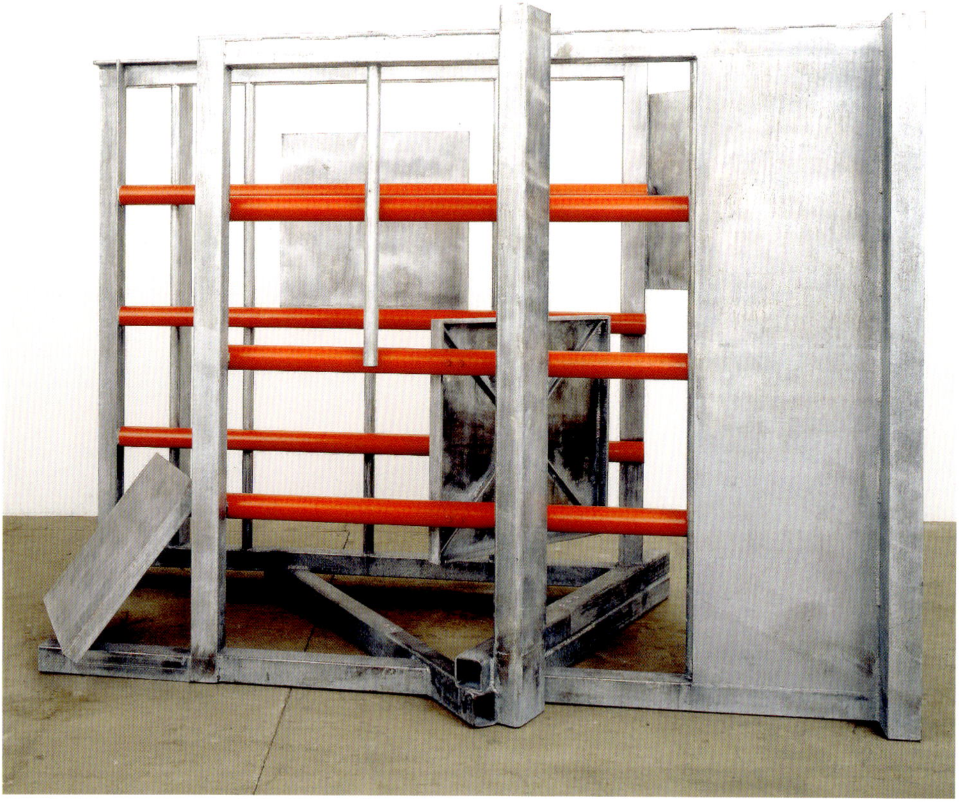

fig. 73

Anthony Caro
South Passage (2005)
Steel, galvanised and painted red
231 x 346 x 173 cm

How did the job with Anthony Caro come about?
I had a tip-off from a technician at Wimbledon School of Art, where I was studying, that previous students from the school had gone on to work for Tony some years ago. I contacted Barford Sculptures, was asked to pop in for a cup of tea (and biscuits) and started my probationary period the following week.

Why did you want to work for him?
I had finished studying, and this was a way not just to earn a living, but also to continue learning: an apprenticeship of sorts. It was a very privileged position to be in – a first-hand glimpse into the practice of an artist whose work I, as a student, had admired.

Which sculptures did you work on? And what was involved in the making?
The galvanised sculptures – specifically *The Yellow Room, Magnolia Passage, Jupiter* and then the planning for *The Chapel of Light* in Bourbourg. The process of making would generally involve the selection of a specific piece of steel, whether a machine part such as a guillotine or press, or an off-cut or piece of scrap. Tony would instruct us to offer up one piece of material to another, turning it by hand or with a crane, until it was in the correct position. The two pieces would then be tacked together with a weld and the process would be repeated, until a form began to appear in the studio.

Once this basic form was complete, the sculpture would be engineered so that it could be deconstructed and put back together. Alterations would be made as Tony saw fit almost daily – the piece would grow and evolve until it reached a point at which he was happy. A piece would then be sent for galvanising and return to be cleaned up and often painted.

Who else worked there?
John Wallbank, Will Fausset, Tom Willis, Neil Ayling, Jenny Dunseath, Kate McLeod... We are almost all still in touch.

Did you have an art school education? If so, where and to what level?
I studied at The University of Derby for my degree and then Wimbledon School of Art for an MA in Drawing.

Do you believe that a pedagogic relationship existed between Caro and his assistants?
If you work closely with someone over a period of time, there cannot fail to be some kind of exchange of knowledge and learning. As assistants we observed Tony's working process closely. Stories and snippets of advice would be commonplace in the tearoom during breaks, but it was in the studio that I began to gain an understanding of how one might construct large-scale work, how one might use steel, how one could work intuitively and sensitively with such heavy and cumbersome materials.

How has – or has – working for Tony influenced you?
Without a doubt, Tony has influenced my practice. He was in his early/mid 80s during my stint at Barford and he was in the studio more or less every day I worked for him. So at that level, his work ethic was pretty inspirational. Additionally, Tony's working process and methods of making have influenced how I work in my studio.

I have a particular fascination with his methods of making and their relationship with drawing. For me, the placement of each piece of metal was like making a mark. By joining, extending, altering and editing these marks, he was able to create a sculpture within the space of the studio. This link with drawing has enriched my practice as well as my teaching methodologies.

How was your role of assistant received by your contemporaries?
With considerable excitement, surprise and intrigue. It's not an opportunity that too many people get – a view into the world of such a well-respected artist.

Have you worked as an artist's assistant to anyone else?
Previously I worked with Ivan Smith, a Henry Moore Fellow, but no-one since Tony.

Do you still make work?
I do still make work, but don't have assistants.

Have you taught in art schools? Has being an assistant informed your teaching methods in any way?
I teach short courses at Central Saint Martins and West Dean College.

Being an assistant meant being part of a tight-knit group who discussed Tony's work, one another's work, and the work of contemporary artists. We also talked about and investigated practical processes on the job, and visited each other's studios and exhibitions. Functioning in this way reinforced in me the importance of dialogue and working as a part of a team in order to build a vibrant, creative workplace. Achieving this kind of working environment is pivotal to my teaching practice. It enables people to experiment, talk, express, make mistakes and learn.

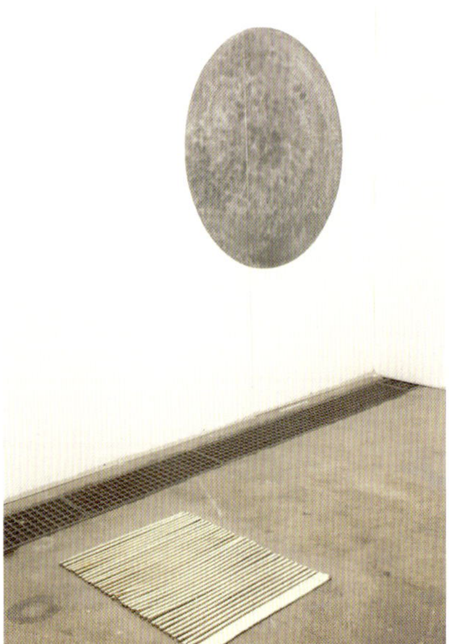

fig. 74

Jonathan Gildersleeves
Studio fragment (2013)
Wood, paint and graphite
168 x 215 x 98 cm

Interview:

WILLIAM FAUSSET

Studio assistant 2005–8

Hertfordshire, UK

Email correspondence (September to December 2015)

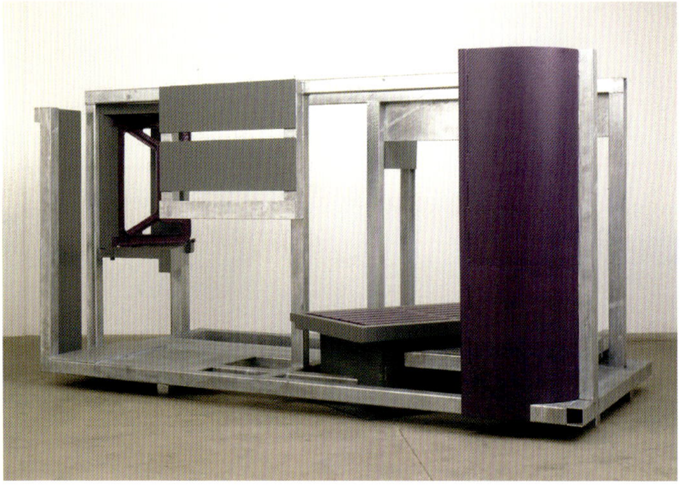

fig. 75

Anthony Caro
Magnolia Passage (2005-6)
Steel, and cast iron, galvanised and painted
222 x 401 x 236 cm

When did you work for Caro?
September 2005 to September 2008 full-time, and then I carried on part-time until the end of December 2008 to finish off the *Child's Tower* sculpture I was working on.

How did the job come about?
I had just graduated from the Slade and was looking to work for a sculptor for a few years to gain more hands-on experience. Jeff Lowe advertised a sculptor's assistant position in *The Artist's Newsletter*, which I applied for. I didn't get the job, but Jeff put me in touch with Pat Cunningham, because he knew at the time Tony and Pat were looking to take on new assistants. I went for an interview and got the job.

The fact that Tony had known my father, Shelley Fausset (1920–94), who was a sculptor, tutor, and contemporary of his, probably didn't hurt my chances of getting the job! Like Tony in 1951–53, my father had also been an early assistant to Henry Moore (1946–48), which was an interesting connection for us to discuss. However, I believe I had a strong portfolio at the time of my interview and wouldn't have got the job without showing I could do the work!

Why did you want to work for him?
I thought it would be a great learning experience at that stage of my life, which it definitely turned out to be. As long as I had been studying and practicing sculpture I had always been interested in Tony's work because

he was predominately an assembler of things, which is how I generally prefer to work in my own practice. I therefore felt very comfortable with and excited by the idea of learning his working methods and processes of construction.

Which sculptures did you work on? And what was involved in the making? The first series I worked on was the galvanised passages. I was particularly involved in the making of *Magnolia Passage, The Yellow Room* and *Jupiter*. It involved a lot of oxyacetylene cutting; fitting, grinding, welding and the making of bolted joints so they could all come to pieces for logistical reasons.

Then I worked for a long period on a new version of the wooden *Child's Tower* – a half-size, eight foot tall model that would be used as a template for Jo Oliver to make full size in oak. This initially involved scaling up and interpreting from a tiny model and photographs of the original *Child's Tower*. As the structure grew, Tony would make significant changes and fresh new revisions to the sculpture's form. I became skilled at translating Tony's instructions into the work – for example, he might indicate with a simple animated gesture of his hands how he wanted a number of planes to relate and angle. He would leave me to work on it for a few days, then come back and look at it with Pat and either say, 'Yes', or, 'Try it a bit more this way'!

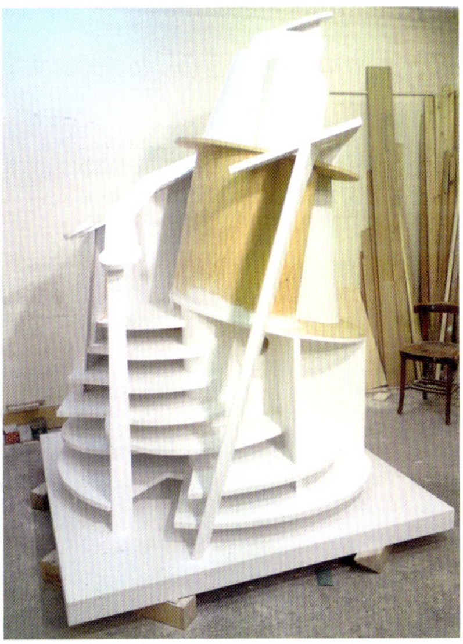

fig. 76

Scale model of *Child's Tower Room* in process (2007-8)

Technically, it required a lot of precise template-making to get all the different, mostly angled, components to join well. At the same time, the structure had to be easily dismantled and reassembled, at any point in the process, to incorporate the ongoing changes that Tony would make as the composition developed. It became a kit of adjustable components, which was also helpful when it was to be used as a template for the larger oak version and for its transportation.

Once this half-size model had come back to the studio, after it had been used as a template for the oak version, Tony asked for it to be finished into a sculpture in its own right so he could paint, colour and finish it. My final job at the studio was gluing, joining and preparing the structure for this process.

I also worked on the Bourbourg church commission [Eglise de Saint-Jean-Baptiste]. I was responsible for measuring and reconstructing the niches of the church, full size, back in the Camden studio, so Tony could work on the sculptures to be fitted into them. This involved a huge amount of measuring, surveying, template making and the reconstruction of the medieval stonework into timber and other mixed media, which the whole team helped me complete. Once the niches were finished, I helped with many of the sculptures for the commission, especially when wood working and joining was required.

In all the above, I had great support and tutoring, both technically and logistically, from Patrick Cunningham, the studio director.

Who else worked there?
Patrick Cunningham, John Wallbank, Jon Gildersleeves, Neil Ayling, Kate McLeod, Tom Willis, Piers Candy, Jenny Dunseath, Terence Kershaw, Trevor Harris; Hywel Livingstone and Edward Goolden at times too. I am still in touch with everyone, I'm glad to say.

Did you have an art school education? If so, where and to what level?
Yes: I completed my art foundation at the University of Hertfordshire, in which I specialised in sculpture. I received a BA (Hons) in Sculpture from Leeds University, and an MFA in Sculpture from the Slade School of Fine Art.

Do you believe that a pedagogic relationship existed between Caro and his assistants?
Yes, definitely. When working with Tony on his sculptures I felt that he taught more by example and body language than by discussion. However, when you brought your own work in to show him he was very generous with his time, willing to discuss at length what you were doing, and was a great teacher who gave you a lot of positive encouragement.

Most of the time spent working at the studio was like doing another degree, especially in the tea breaks, which became like informal art seminars in which Tony would encourage us to discuss ideas about art, and specifically sculpture, with him and among ourselves. He was very good at starting a debate or raising an interesting question for us to all talk about and learn from.

During long car journeys, driving Tony somewhere, were great opportunities to ask him all sorts of questions about art and to pick his brains and absorb invaluable knowledge about the process of making work.

How has – or has – working for Tony influenced you?
Working for Tony has influenced me strongly in many ways; the habits of his that I list below I have found seeping into in my own practice over the years and continue to this day… His example of redrafting the same piece of work over and over again, until after multiple changes and many months – sometimes years – of re-looking at it and living with it, it comes to a gradual state of completion.

His practice of working on a series of ten to fifteen or more sculptures at once. For example, working on one or two in the morning and then moving onto another one in the afternoon, to keep it fresh. Circulating between them over a long period of time, returning to them over and over again to bring them to a conclusion.

Discussing the work with the people that you have around you, and how valuable these people are in the process of editing – helping you see the way to move forward or when to leave it alone. In Tony's case, Sheila, Pat, Karen Wilkin and Michael Fried spring to mind.

To not believe in any artwork ideas unless you have tried it out in real material stuff, in actual space and time. The importance of really looking and seeing it clearly to know how it works in reality.

To have an idea and then have the openness to start with just some pieces of material stuff (often very carefully selected material stuff) that could have been lying around the studio, sometimes for years. To see the possible values in this raw stuff; that it can be incorporated into a sculpture at any point. Also the importance of having a lot of this material stuff around you to draw on when needed.

How was your role of assistant received by your contemporaries?
Fine, because often they were in similar roles working for other artists, or just getting any work they could to make ends meet and still make their own artwork. Some, I believe, would have liked to have had the opportunity to work for someone like Tony, to gain the experience, had they been able to find that kind of job.

Have you worked as an artist's assistant to anyone else?
Before I worked for Tony I worked at the Henry Moore Institute where, as part of the gallery technical team, I assisted Keith Wilson and other artists involved with the 'Object Sculpture' show in 2003. I have assisted Melanie Counsell, who was a tutor of mine at the Slade, with the construction of a solo show in 2005, and Meekyoung Shin with the installation of an exhibition at the British Museum again in 2005. Post working for Tony, I have briefly assisted Steven Pippin, helping him cut up some cameras for a project he was doing.

Do you still make work? Do you employ assistants in the making of your own work?
I still make work when I can, although full-time employment and family life have restricted this activity somewhat, but I keep things ticking over and hope one day to have more time.

I do not use assistants. I work in a very hands-on, immediate way, at a size and scale that doesn't require any help. However, if my situation changed and I was going to take on work that was more logistically demanding, I would absolutely consider the use of an assistant or two, if I could afford it!

Have you taught in art schools? Has being an assistant informed your teaching methods in any way?
I taught at Leeds University in the sculpture department for a day a week, for about a year in 2006/7, while I was working for Tony. Thinking back, the working practices of Tony's studio did inform my teaching methods; I would encourage the students to try it out, to test it, in real materials, space and time. To not get too caught up in their sketchbooks and over-thinking, which can lead to not doing or trying something.

I now run the model-making workshops at the Architectural Association. The way I teach students at the school to model-make is also heavily influenced by the time I spent as an assistant to Tony. Again, I encourage the students to learn by trial and error, to test things out, to learn from doing it in reality and not to try to plan it all out in their heads in advance. This allows the space for new things to happen, happy accidents, from which new directions and possibilities can emerge. Working for Tony gave me a huge amount of belief and confidence in this process of working.

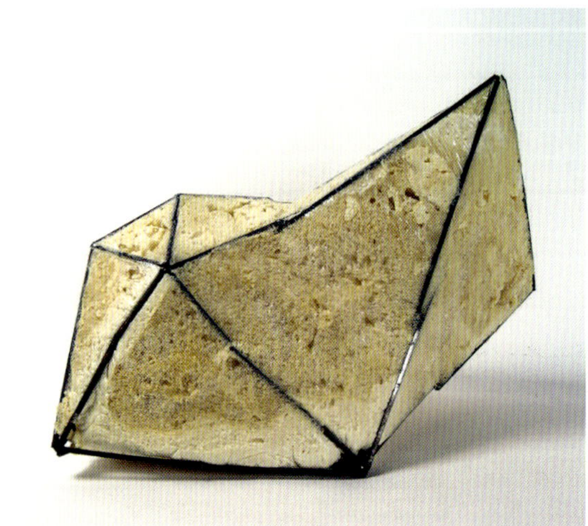

fig. 77

William Fausset
Foam & Rod Construction 2 (2010)
Expanded foam and mild steel rod
70 x 45 x 30 cm

Interview:

ANTHONY CARO, PATRICK CUNNINGHAM, JOHN WALLBANK, NEIL AYLING & OLIVIA BAX – PART TWO

Studio assistants 1968 to present day, 2005-13, 2005 to present day; 2010 to present day.

Camden studio, London, UK

Group interview (November 2010)

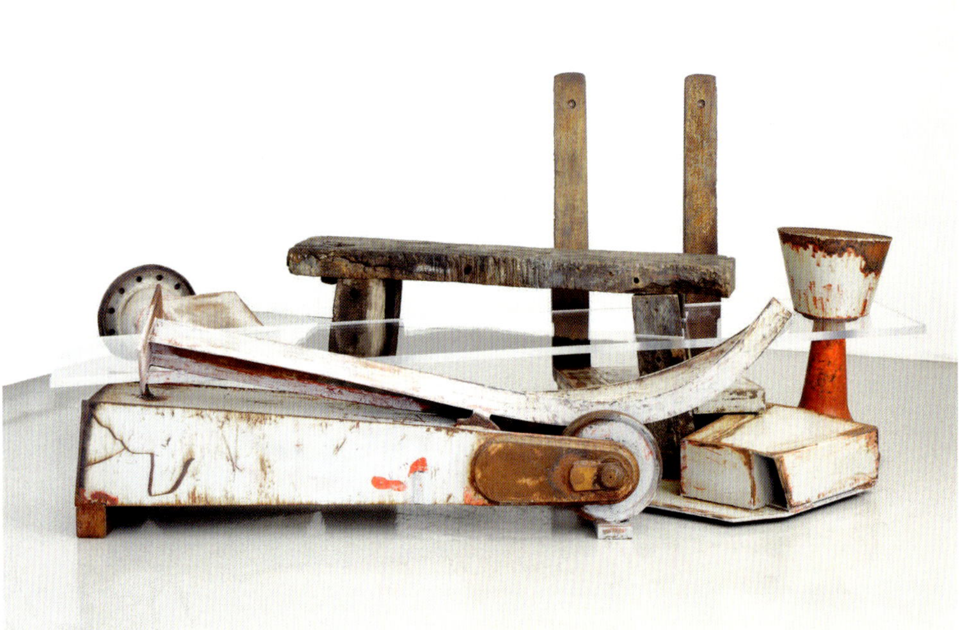

fig. 78

Anthony Caro
Bench (2011-13)
Steel, wood and clear Perspex
147 x 316 x 178 cm

JENNY DUNSEATH *Group cohesion and teamwork appears to be very important in the studio. Many assistants have talked about studio visits and how they were encouraged to bring in photos of their own work, and trips to see exhibitions to discuss sculpture together...*

ANTHONY CARO We should do it more often!

JD *Thinking of the group, let's open it up to you all. There are a several veins of thought about the artist's assistant. One, almost derogatory, position states that the artist's assistant (or apprentice) implies a withholding or deferral of the fullness of one's own practice. The other, more celebratory, position offers a version of an old-fashioned apprenticeship, falling between the period of completing art school and the precipice of an art career. It would be interesting to know what you think about these positions.*

AC These guys are all at different stages, but go ahead.

NEIL AYLING I started here when I was still studying for my BA at Winchester School of Art, so I didn't know what to expect really because I was still young. I knew I wanted to be a sculptor, I knew that for sure.

AC How long ago was it?

NA About five-and-a-half years. It was all new, and I didn't really know what to expect at that time, but I loved it. I think coming here made it real. That you're not just dreaming, 'I want to be a sculptor'; you can see how it's done in real life. I think you only really get a perspective on that after leaving art school, having six months of not being here and trying other work. Then when I went to do my MA at the Royal College it felt like a natural progression.

JD *You worked for Darren Almond as well, didn't you?*

NA Yes, over the summer I started here. That was pretty full on that summer, very surreal.

AC I actually – in your case particularly, and I think in Piers's [Candy] case too – am very conscious of how much you have grown over the years. I don't know how much of that is due to me. I think quite a bit is due to having a job. You've become so much more solid; you seem to know who you are and where you are. At the beginning, you were wobbly. You would hang around and you didn't quite know what to do, what you were meant to be doing or who you were meant to be, and somehow now you know it! There's a clarity that does make it felt.

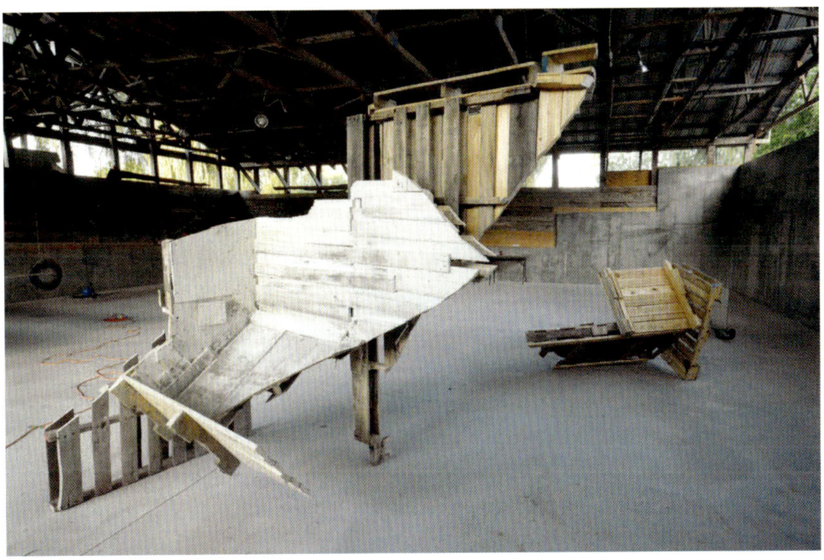

fig. 79

Neil Ayling
Untitled Triangle Workshop (2015)
Pallet wood and photographic emulsion
250 x 210 x 260 cm

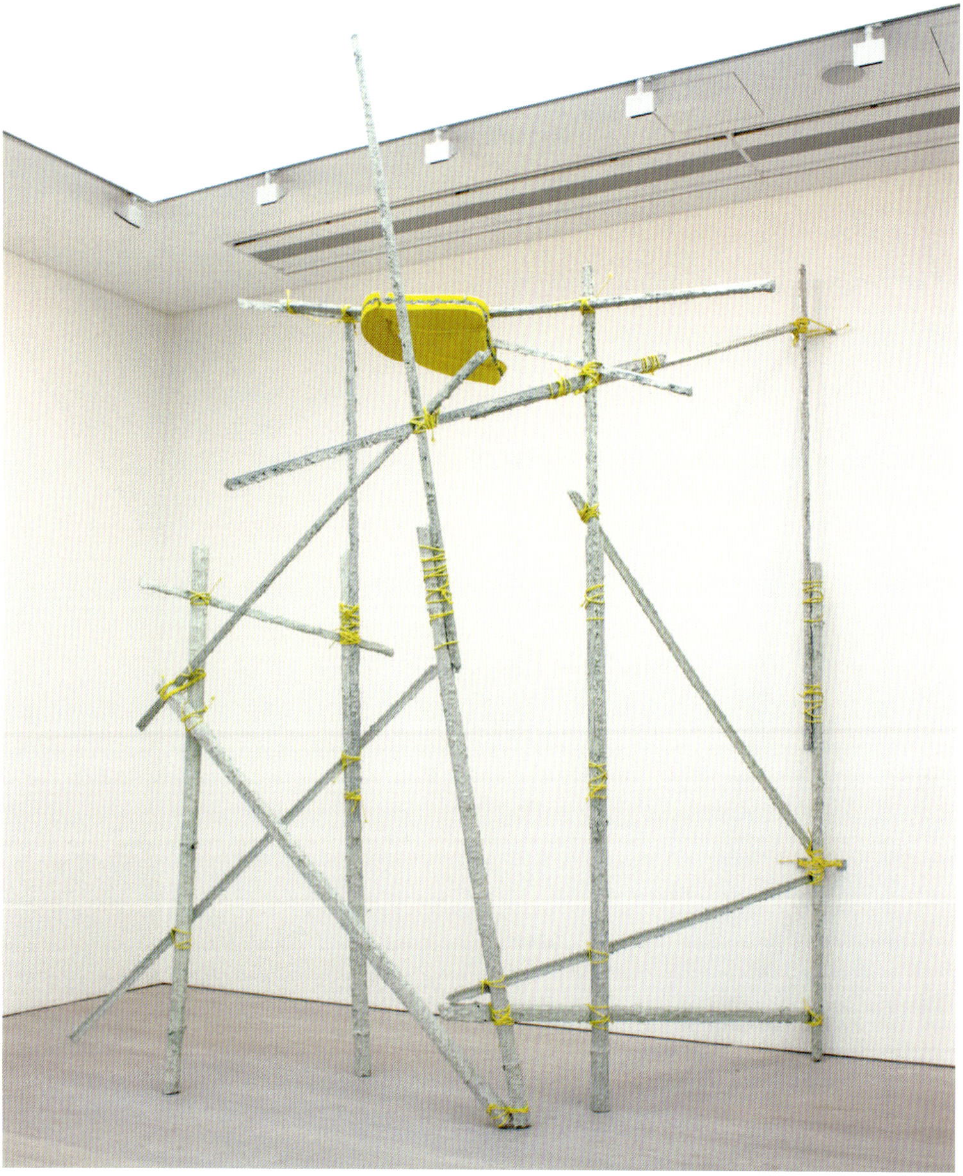

fig. 80

Olivia Bax
Sink or Swim (2015)
Paper, glue, paint, plaster, steel mesh,
bungee cord, foam and galvanised ring plates
420 x 266 x 245 cm

AC What about you, Olivia?

OLIVIA BAX I graduated from my BA in June 2010, so I'm new. At the start of my third year I was really conscious of almost graduating, and we started to have a lot of 'after art school' discussions about what we were going to do, how we were going to make a living. They were completely impractical, and I remember it suddenly dawning on me: 'When I leave college, how am I ever going to make work?' And that was what I really wanted to do, so the prospect of leaving art school freaked me out!

AC Where did you actually make metalwork?

OB At Byam Shaw. Tim Peacock, the technician there, taught me a lot. By the time I was graduating I still didn't know what I was going to do. So when this job came up, it was wonderful because I had admired Tony's work for a long time. And this gives me a chance to keep working on my own work.

AC Can you work on your own now?

OB Yeah, I sometimes come in here at the weekends and I've got my own studio now, too. And I also get Tony and Pat's input. It's really good having other people like all these guys around as well, to talk about art.

AC Is it also because Pat knows so much about how to make an idea real and he can find a quick way of doing things?

OB And all of the professional advice. Pat's good at knowing what opportunities we should pursue or, more importantly, what to avoid!

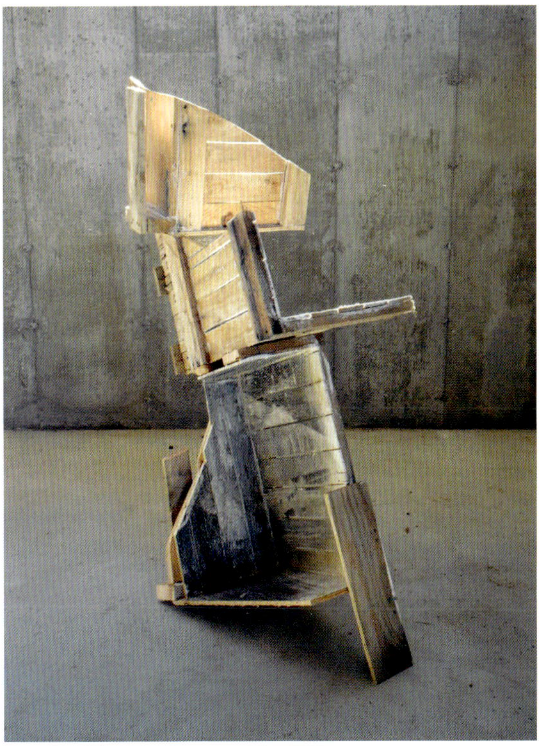

fig. 81

Neil Ayling
Untitled Triangle Workshop (2015)
Pallet wood and photographic emulsion
150 x 75 x 80 cm

AC What about you?

ANON. I finished at Central Saint Martins probably three or four years ago. I was definitely influenced by Tony's work, using certain aesthetics but moving along a slightly different path. When I left there I went straight into The Sculpture Factory – an art production firm. That was my first experience of working with artists. It was very different to working here, but still an insight. I was there for two years before having a few shows myself from that, because I was able to make my own work while I was there. Then I went to work at a bronze foundry, which was a different conversation with artists – because the turnover was so quick, you might be seeing three artists a day; it became very pointed, very specific, different choices from the forms of the bronze, or fixing and the practicalities.

AC What age are you?

AN. Twenty-six.

AC And you, Neil?

NA Twenty-seven.

PATRICK CUNNINGHAM Don't ask me!

JD Don't ask me either!

PC Now you'll have to reveal your age... How old are you Tony?

AC Twenty-six!
[*Lots of laughter*]

JD *The experience of working as a fabricator is very interesting in comparison to the role of a studio assistant. What do you feel the differences are?*

AN. Working here is a lot more valuable. A lot of decisions are taken out of the artist's hands when they are only coming into the studio once every two months or so. Some artists can work like that, and the work was designed before it was made, and I think that's the difference. Everything here happens on the spot; it's changed and moved and I think that's probably what makes the work so successful.

AC All sculptors are different; we've all got our different ways of doing things. There's not a right way of doing things, not just one way.

JD *How does working here affect your own practices?*

AC Yes. What about you, John?

JOHN WALLBANK For me, working here isn't like a job; it gives you the energy to carry on. I'll come here and then go to my studio afterwards because I enjoy making stuff. The daytime is like a warm-up for my own studio. I get to make stuff all day then I go back to my own studio to steal all Tony's ideas!
[Lots of laughter]

No, I think it comes down to this really hands-on approach; the thing is left open and that makes the fabrication more interesting for us. By saying it isn't working to design... Here you are not just a technician – you work it all out as you go along. That's what makes it interesting.

You don't know if it will be finished in a month or six months. The story is being made as you go along.

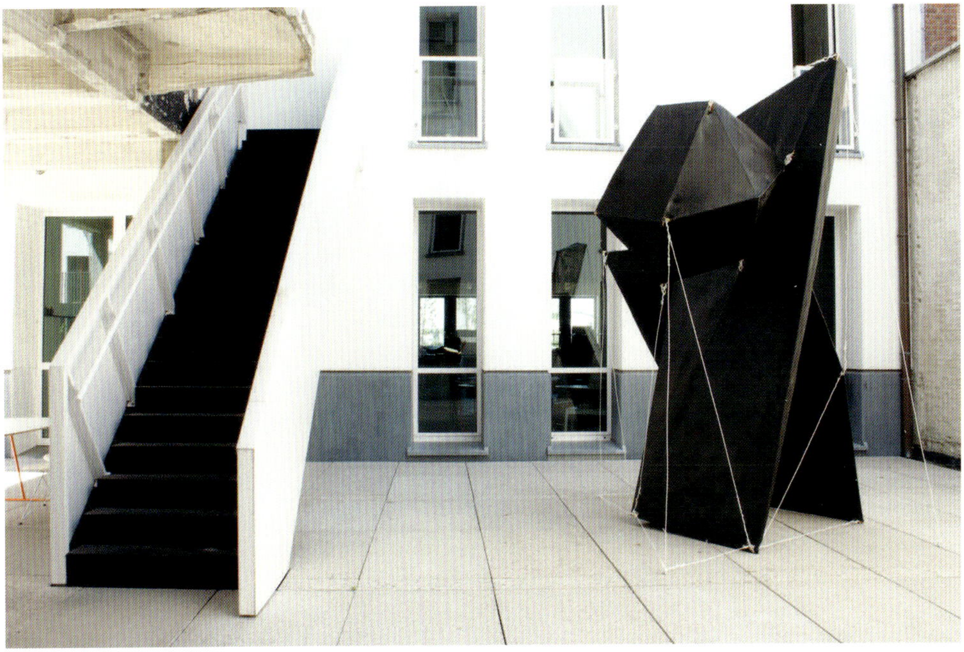

fig. 82

John Wallbank
Painting (Black & White) (2015)
Bituminous paint, cotton fabric, PVA glue, plywood, staples and PVC coated wire
350 x 250 x 250 cm

AC What about you, Jenny? What about the break between art school and where you are now? Do you feel that this was a bridge?

JD I certainly developed more practical skills here than I did at art school, because you're working outside the parameters of your own practice, and that was invaluable. As everyone has highlighted, it's an immersion in sculpture and you're doing something that you're completely involved with; you go home and feel satisfied and able to continue to make work.

AC Can you imagine, Jenny, leaving art school and going straight into teaching?

JD Personally, I felt it was important to have another view outside of working within an art school, and have a transition into teaching.

AC You say that, but you see at Saint Martin's, people like Philip King and all that lot, they finished their studentship and were hired for two days a week teaching. Frank Martin had a very hard time and said we were eating our own tail, but they did in those days and that's why I was asking Jenny. This isn't the way people are doing it now.

JD Personally, teaching provides me with a constant dialogue about current debate, sculpture and new concerns within art practices. I find it completely invigorating and, of course, that exists within this studio environment as well.

JW What do you see as the differences between art school discussions and these studio discussions?

JD There are several. Conversations in the 'institutional studio' within an academic context will, at times, have to address academic criteria. For example, we may talk in depth about material qualities, characteristics or the sensation of making, then the discussion may lead to the relationship between theory and practice, context around thinking and making perhaps...

AC Yes but you are talking about physical things and they're all very old-fashioned sculptures. You're not dealing with somebody singing.

JD You might be, and one could argue that sound is sculptural. Sound fills a space. Sound is shaped by the physical properties of the source of the sound (like the shape of musical instrument) and is also affected by the environment it's in, or received in.

AC I think sculpture is physical, well, not purely physical, but sculpture has to be very physical. I have a real problem with that sound idea even more than I have with visual things, computer stuff. I think it could be an art form but I don't think of it as sculpture.

JD *What about a physical gesture or action, as in Richard Serra's early films like* Hand Catching Lead *(1968)?*

AC I think that feeling the weight of things is a sculptural activity. I think I said before, somebody came to my studio – a painter, Bernard Cohen – to give me a hand and he said, 'It's heavy', and that's a funny feeling, something that a painter wouldn't feel that we feel. So I'm not sure that I agree with you; I think it's too big a jump towards sound for me. But still, the way you were talking, it was old-fashioned because it was to do with making, and nowadays it is not necessarily to do with making, is it?

PC But you're all talking about making by the artist's hand, and an awful lot of sculpture isn't made by the artist.

AC Not at all, not all. In fact, very much as Jenny was saying...

PC It's made in big factories, like The Sculpture Factory. They make it all, but it's not like that here. Everything here you have to pay attention to. You couldn't have it made outside, without you being down there. When we made *Promenade* we'd go to Benson's [Benson-Sedgwick Engineering] every day.

AC Yes, we did. But with that *Tower* that went to Japan, I was too close to it. Unlike being an architect... If one had designed it like an architect and said, 'Now I'm away from it, go and make it', it would have been better. I was poking my nose in all the time and saying, 'That's not right'!

OB I think there might be a bit of a 'making' revival in art education and more emphasis on the importance of it, because students were often frustrated by the lack of practical skills that were taught.

AC At Byam Shaw?

OB Yes, but both my flatmates were studying at different art schools and they were having the same frustrations. Students can't learn how to do things from a half-hour induction that's just: 'This tool does this, this tool does that'. Even in the short time I've been here I've had to use new tools, and that has been a huge learning curve.

JW Ultimately, if someone else does it for you...

OB Yes, exactly. If you're simply watching, you have no practical skills. That's another advantage to being here: you learn things that may end up being useful in your own work.

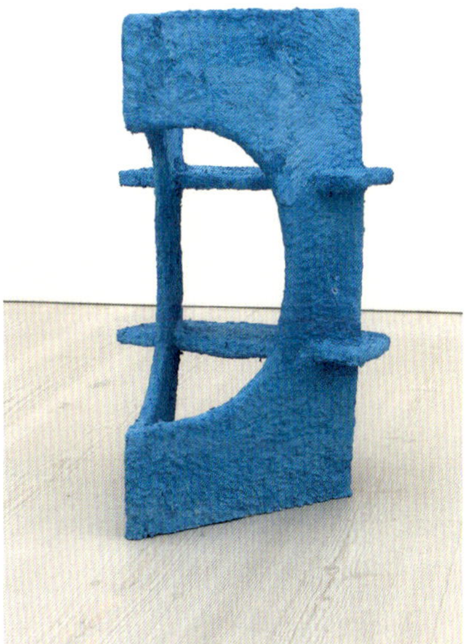

fig. 83

Olivia Bax
Slot & Groove (2015)
Paper, glue, paint, plaster and polystyrene
120 x 60 x 85 cm

PC You think you've missed out by not having more skill-based training? How to cast, how to model, how to make armatures... All that stuff?

OB Yes, maybe. I'm jealous of people starting art school now, because they have introduced these new exchanges, so if you want to do bronze work they'll send you to Romania to teach you how to do it. I think that's brilliant, to have the opportunity to learn as many different skills as possible. Whether they end up being useful or not, it's really beneficial.

JD *That's interesting Olivia: a push for a return to skills in making. Tony, what was the emphasis like at Saint Martin's? Was there a rigorous training in basic skills?*

AC Nobody knew anything! I was there for a few years before we got into welding at all. And when we got into it, nobody knew how to weld! Jim Sherriff, who had been the casting chap, was trying to help people to weld and to cast and he didn't know how to do it all!

JW I find it quite interesting when you get to a point where people don't know what they're doing, but are prepared to find out, because that's when invention happens. You might not end up making a technically brilliant work, but that's not what making art is about, is it?

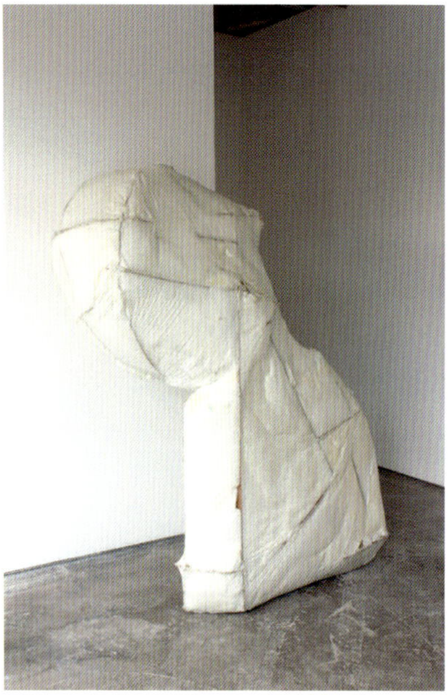

fig. 84

John Wallbank
Untitled (2013)
Polyurethane foam, polystyrene and plywood
182 x 160 x 100 cm

AC John, do you think if you had gone straight from university could you have known how to set up your own studio?

JW After I left Edinburgh I went to the Edinburgh Sculpture Workshop. I used to work there before I got my own studio, so it was quite an easy transition.

AC Is this whole thing anything like the Triangle Workshop?

JW Triangle was more like art school in a way, except that everyone knew what they were doing! It's a collection of like-minded people trying to make stuff.

AC Jenny, what else do you want to ask us?

JD *Well, Tony, you've talked a little about the difference between working here and working for Moore. We've talked about the professional experience that this provides and we've touched upon the similarities and complexities of an art education, either in the studio or in an institution. Perhaps we can talk about how the role of artist's assistant is viewed or perceived... How is it received by your peers, and professionally?*

AC I think it's very bad to be here too long. I remember asking one of Henry's assistants, 'How long have you been here?' – seventeen years! He wasn't going to be able to make his own work; he couldn't, he was imbued! He could only make Henry's work, not his own. One thing we haven't talked about is the practicality of the world and making money, and galleries, and so on. I think this is something we never talked about here and the reason is I'm no good at it! But it's a whole side of being an artist, which as teachers we have neglected entirely. They didn't neglect it at Goldsmiths. Career is part of the job; confidence too.

OB In answer to your question about people's reactions – this is a difficult time to get a job and there are only a small handful of students who have graduated and got an art-related job. People wonder what you're going to do after a fine art degree, so it's great to say I've got this job working for Tony.

AC Mind you, we don't pay them very much here, and we're going to keep it that way! I have had times when people have wanted to come really just to make money and then it's kind of soul-destroying. You don't want that, you want them to come because they love art, they want to learn something and do the whole thing as well as they can.

These days people want assistants far more than they used to.

JW I think they want fabricators.

Postscript by Olivia Bax, Neil Ayling and John Wallbank (August 2015):
Looking back on this interview, which was conducted in November 2010, we thought it would be worth adding how the dynamic developed over the months and years that followed. Tea breaks often turned into heated discussions about art and sculpture, and more time was spent visiting exhibitions and other artists' studios. It was apparent that Tony was aware that working in the studio facilitated our own practices. Indeed he made it clear that it was important to him that we treated our own work as the priority. We will always be very grateful for the support and generosity from Tony in the last few years of his life.

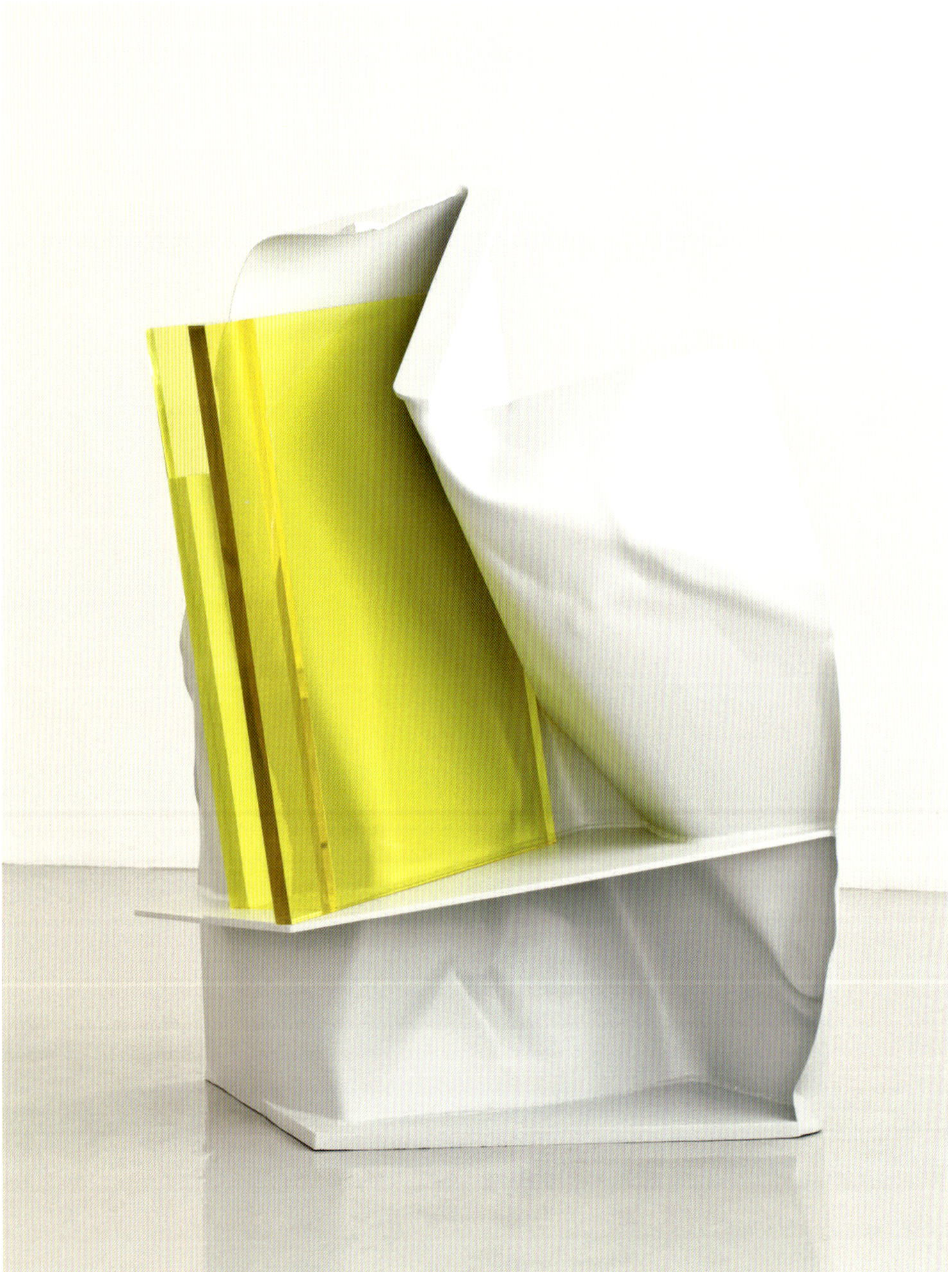

fig. 85

Anthony Caro
Alpine (2012)
Steel and Perspex
151 x 125 x 66 cm

Interview:

PATRICK CUNNINGHAM

Studio assistant 1968 to present day

Camden studio, London, UK

Interview (September 2015)

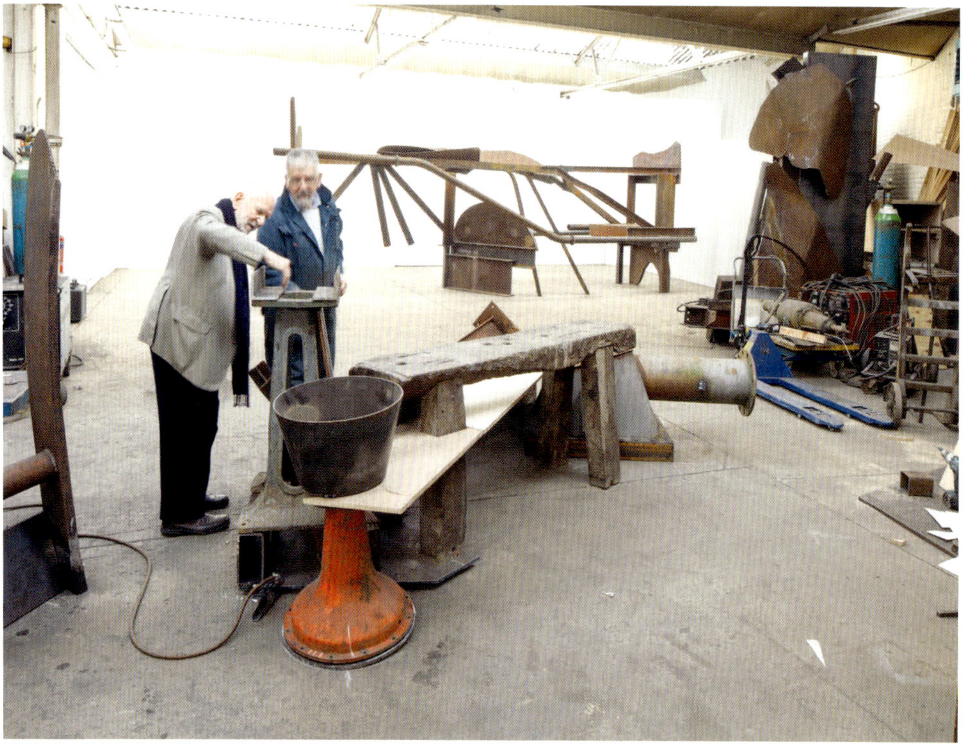

fig. 86

Anthony Caro in Camden studio
with Patrick Cunningham (2013)

JENNY DUNSEATH *I am interested in your experience as a studio assistant to Anthony Caro and your role as studio manager. Can you tell me when you started, and how the job came about?*

PATRICK CUNNINGHAM It was about 1968/69 and I was at Aeromet, a fabrication company. We worked a lot doing things like the motor show and the boat show and that was all in Olympia in those days. Tony came in one day with a *Table* piece tacked together and he wanted someone in the factory to make it. It sat on my bench and that was the first time I had seen anything of Tony's. Everybody looked at it and asked, 'What is it?!' Tony said, 'It's a sculpture!' 'A sculpture of what?' they asked. I said, 'Well, the man wants it made, so let's get the job done.' So I made that sculpture. He came back a couple of weeks later and wanted it rubbed down and sprayed with red oxide. He didn't want any of the welds to show.

It was hanging on the wall when he came in; he took it down and placed it on the bench – it sat off the table edge. He said, 'You've done a wonderful job.' He was very polite, and that's how it started.

JD *How did you get into welding?*
PC Oh, I grew up with it. My father had a farm, so we had to learn how to repair all our own machines, including tractors and ploughs. I was very young. Welding was my thing. I knew how to cut and grind and how to make things work. I loved doing that, and made my own things like gates and stuff.

JD *You had practical knowledge...*
PC I did, and my father was a very practical person. He was a builder and a farmer and he was very good at teaching people how to do things properly and well. There were never any shortcuts, you know. It was no good just cutting it and sticking it – it had to be beautifully done. I learnt a lot from him, a tremendous amount.

JD *How soon did you start at Aeromet?*
PC That's when I came to England. I had a sister in Chelmsford, it was a real bad winter and I was working on a building site as a hod carrier. I went to London, to the job centre, and said, 'I'm looking for a job in welding; it's too cold outside, I want to work inside.' They sent me to Aeromet in West Hampstead at 11.30 in the morning. The man there asked when I could start, and I said, 'When do you want me to start?' 'What are you doing this afternoon?' he asked, and I said, 'If you've got a boiler suit, I'll stay'.

JD *From there, how did you go on to work full-time for Tony?*
PC I had been working for Aeromet for about six months. I wasn't really happy there, and one Friday morning I told them I would leave that evening.

Who should come in an hour later, but Tony with another sculpture! He came straight to me and said, 'I want you to work on this for me, and I'm in a bit of a hurry.' And I said, 'Sorry Tony, I'm not going to be here next week – you better give it to one of the other boys.' He asked why not, and I said that I hadn't been paid for the last three weeks. He said 'How much does Tom owe you?' 'About £75,' I replied. Then he pulls out a chequebook, puts it on the bench and says 'I'll pay you'. I said, 'Haven't you got real money?' – I was sick of cheques!

Tony asked where I was going to work next, because he wanted to bring the work to me. So I explained that I had no other job to go to. Tony asked if I would work for him and I said, 'Yeah, I think so'.

JD *And that was it? You started full-time in his studio?*
PC Yes, that week.

JD *What were your first days like, working in the studio?*
PC I never did anything! I would sop around in the office, or in the tearoom that was in the corner of the studio. I swept the studio five times a day. There was nothing to do. I used to go to the pictures in Camden in the afternoon!

But Tony was teaching three days a week then. He would come in, sit on this stool and look at his work. I didn't know what he was doing – I would help him move things around. And then the next day he'd move it back again!

He was very nice to work for and he was very happy with what I was doing, but I needed to earn so much to be able to live. So I said to Tony, 'It's really a waste of my time being here – we're not doing anything. I can only clean the studio so many times!' But then he wanted to play around with metal in a different way and do things quicker and I made that possible for him.

I made all the adjustable stands so that he could hold things up in mid air and see things float. He thought that was amazing.

JD *To have that option?*

PC Yes, to see things stand, floating in mid air.

JD *You seemed very accommodating...*

PC It was fun! But Tony was always good at inviting you in. He would ask your opinion: 'What do you think?' I would say, 'Well, I wouldn't have done it like that I would have done this... Try it the other way up or something.' And the dialogue between us grew that way.

JD *How long was it from those early days of not being busy to the shift in production and prolific making?*

PC Within six months.

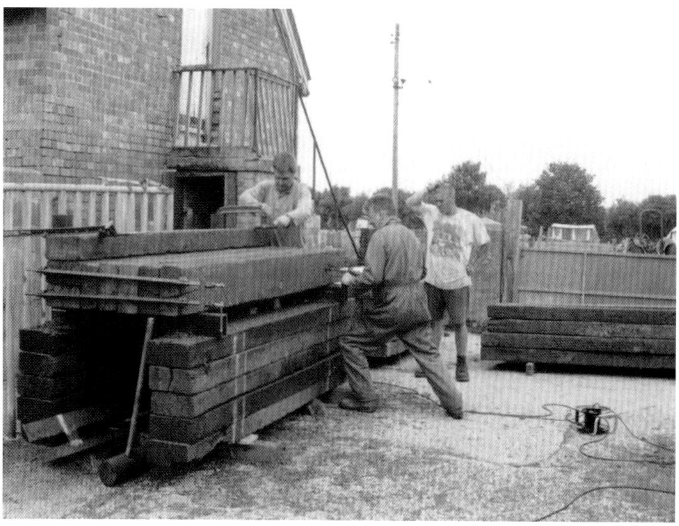

fig. 87

Patrick Cunningham and others working on *Ziggurats* (1997)

JD *There was a noticeable shift in being able to produce and test work?*
PC Yes – and being able to work on many things at one time. And I think that Tony learned that you could tack stuff together, leave it, bring it back out and have it all welded, cleaned up. Have a look at it and change it.

I think the one thing he always praised me for was that I didn't get upset when he would change something I was making. Poor Charlie would make things beautifully – every weld was ground, finished, filled, primed – then Tony would say, 'That thing isn't quite upright', and would put a level to it and it would be perfect. But Tony would want it different... And that would break Charlie's heart. It didn't bother me in the slightest; I didn't care, it's just another job – just do it. If you're not happy, change it; cut it off.

I also think Tony learnt more about steel. He didn't really know how to work quickly with steel before I came. We had oxyacetylene. He'd never done a lot of cutting before but I could cut well – any circle or shape. I remember him saying that he wanted the line to be soft. I said, 'Well, you just draw the line on the piece of steel and I'll cut it.' So easy!

JD *At that time, which other assistants were there?*
PC At that time there weren't any. Charlie Hendy and Guy Martin had gone; there was only me. Then Lofty came because we needed a lot of welding done. Tony had about two or three sculptures that he needed welded or ground and I couldn't keep up with the production so we got Lofty. I also knew Sue Brown, who worked at Saint Martin's. We'd ask Sue if they had any students who were good at welding and she'd send us people – that's how we got lots of people... From John Gibbons and so on.

JD *You would invite them in for an interview; what were you looking for?*
PC Well, we'd get them in for a cup of tea and Tony would do his bit. He had to like them and that was important. And I would ask, 'Can you weld, grind, and cut?' Not a lot of them knew how to do it incredibly well, but I'd spend a bit of time with them and they would pick it up very quickly.

But it was important that they fitted in with the place.

JD *There was a high turnover of assistants – you must have worked with hundreds.*
PC Yes, over many years. But Tony's thing was that he didn't want people to stay for too long because it would ruin their art lives. So some had to go away, and they felt they couldn't come back and talk to Tony for years – until they had their own identity. It was harder for the younger artists. It was always great fun having a lot of different people around. I liked having people around.

JD *And how was that role for you? You often had to teach and show people skills and how to work here.*
PC I loved it. I was always happy to teach what I know, and show people how to do stuff – it never worried me. Nobody ever took over my job here. *[Laughs]*

JD *How do you describe your job here?*

PC Well, Sheila always called me the studio manager. Tony gave me the title of studio director but, you know, the truth is my job wasn't that really... I guess I was head technician at the Anthony Caro studio.

JD *You were the constant throughout all of Tony's practice.*

PC Yes, that's what Tony always said to people. You know, he'd be talking to other artists about their studios and he'd say, 'Ah, but you don't have a Pat!' It was a constant thing between Tony and me. It was great.

JD *How do you describe that relationship?*

PC I have great respect for Tony and I grew to love him very much. Not in a fatherly way, but he was always very good with his advice and Sheila was the same. We used to rub knuckles from time to time – not physically, but, you know, I'd tell him what I thought of him and I'd go away and be pissed off for a couple of days and then come back. We fell out quite a few times. Tony was quite a force in the studio because it was his domain, and he wouldn't have any problem giving me a dressing-down. And whether that was right or wrong, it was his space, his studio and his life. But there were always very good times; working together and doing shows together.

JD *Were there any times when you were tempted to leave?*

PC I did leave. I left Tony for over a year, but I was very unhappy and came back. I phoned Tony and said, 'I'm back in London'. He had Charlie Brown, I think it was, there at the time.

I went to see Sheila in Hampstead, and she said, 'Tony's in America; he'll be back next week.' So I went back the next week and he was very reluctant; he was upset that I'd left him. He said, 'You won't stay', and I said, 'You'll have to take your chance on me and see how long I stay. I'm here, I'm ready to work – if you want me. If not, I'll find something else.'

He didn't answer me right away. He thought about it overnight and rang me the next day and said, 'Yes, come on back'.

JD *How long ago was that?*

PC The mid 1970s – forty-something years ago!

It was quite strange, when he had the fire in Hampstead and wrote to me in Ireland, I came over for a few days to give him a helping hand. It was a wreck and I was there for three or four days. But he wrote to my mother a lot and always had a great affection for me. It was different then: I was very young and stupid.

JD *You have worked on thousands of pieces of work. When speaking to other assistants, many talk of an affinity to a particular work. Is there is any piece, or body, of work that you feel close too, or would even describe as a collaboration?*

PC I never liked that word, collaboration, because the truth is: it isn't. We'd talk about everything – 'Hold that there, try that there, stick that up...' I think I was facilitating Tony's ideas; 'facilitator' is a much better way of describing it.

I think Tony could work with anybody; he was that sort of person. I think when I got involved I could orchestrate Tony's way of working and make things happen quickly.

Every day, my role was to make sure that when Tony came to the studio there was something for him to work on, to see, or to get an idea. Tony wasn't interested in hearing about ideas, he would always ask you to show him. He just wanted to see it. I think what he liked about having me around was that I could make things happen quickly for him.

JD *You picked up on collaboration. Was it more about facilitation, orchestrating and managing?*

PC I'm not saying that Tony didn't collaborate. He did with people like Hans Spinner and David Pelham or Ken Noland. Tony would make sculptures and Ken would paint them – that I'd call collaboration.

But, you know, what I did: anyone could have done it. But I'm glad it was me! In the early days Sheila would ring down to the studio because we never had a clock so we would keep on working. Sheila would say, 'That young man [me] has a wife and a daughter, can't you let him go home?'! But I was so involved in Tony's thinking and the way he worked, I didn't mind.

JD *You mentioned that, in the early days, you felt you didn't understand or know what he was doing. How do you feel now? Do you feel you understand the decisions? Or were there constant surprises?*

PC I did understand Tony's decisions in the last twenty years working with him. I could tell what he was thinking. I could look at a sculpture and see what he was trying to achieve. He'd always have a bit of chalk in his pocket and he'd be like, 'Let's try...' And it might not be anything like what he wanted to do, it might be totally different and that was a great surprise to both of us!

JD *If you were both on the same wavelength, did it increase the pace at which you were able to work?*

PC Yes, but he could see it... You know, he'd walk back over across the yard, the steel would be out there, and he'd put an 'X' on one and say, 'Take that piece in'. I think he did a lot of that in the evenings – looking at books and getting ideas and thinking about which way to go.

Working on things like *The Last Judgement* and *The Trojan War*, I was intrigued by the stories; Tony had read all the books and he'd love to tell me about them. I found it incredibly interesting.

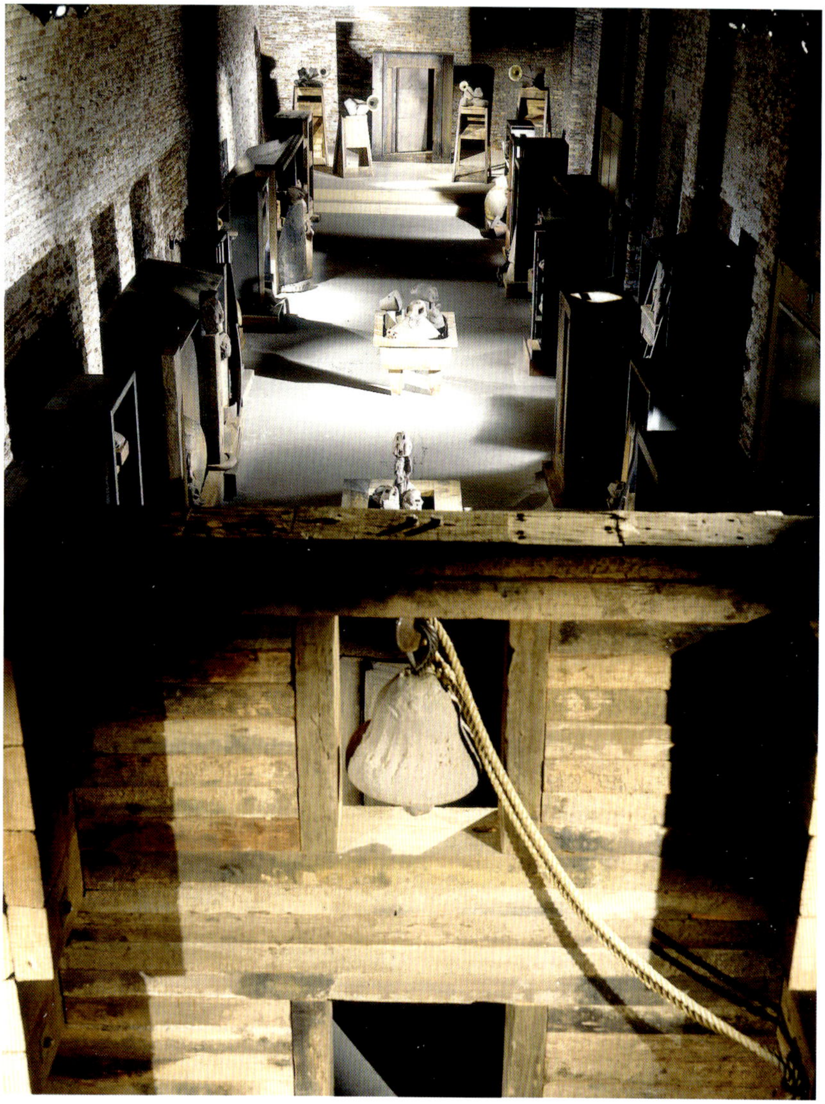

fig. 88

Anthony Caro
The Last Judgement (1996-99)
Stoneware, wood, steel, brass,
bronze, concrete and plaster

JD *Have you worked for any other artists?*

PC No, not really; not in the way I worked for Tony. I worked on a few bits for John Gibbons and Peter Hide, for artists in the Triangle Workshops, but not in a creative way.

JD *You spoke earlier about how some assistants had to leave for a time before being able to make their own work. Because you are free of that, what's your view on those complexities?*

PC I think that an awful lot of people who came enjoyed the experience of working here, and it was always very easy-going, but you worked your arse off. I don't know how many of the people who came went on to be artists in their own right... A lot of people gave up.

There are so many, back through the years, who just went off and did other things.

JD *Is being a studio assistant like an apprenticeship? Does it set you up for a career in the art world?*

PC That's a tough question. I think being a studio assistant does set you up. Most people who have worked here have learned a lot of practical skills, and they've learned a lot about how to work – how to move stuff, easily and safely. You know, I've always been very proud of my safety record. I broke two toes, and Piers had a sleeper dropped on his leg... Oh, and Tony dropped a steel bar on Sheila's foot and broke a bone in it! But that's out of how many people who have been through this place? Nobody ever lost a hand or a finger. I've always been very health and safety conscious by making sure the studio was run properly, that everyone had the right equipment.

JD *During your time here, you've worked with a lot of students and recent graduates from art school and have spent time with them, teaching them skills... What would be on your art school curriculum?*

PC I think that the practical skills of making, and knowing how to make things, are very important. It's difficult, because as a young artist you can't afford to pay people to help you. Tony was incredibly lucky in that he'd made enough money to keep all this going; he made enough sales. Not many artists do.

Mind you, Tony always said, 'Don't make it too well, you'll take the art out of it!'

[Laughs]

Michael Fried came to the studio one day and Tony complained about my welding. He said, 'Pat welds too well – they're too nice, can't you rough them up a bit?'!

JD *If we had all those practical skills, would we still have assistants?*

PC I think Tony knew the practical skills, but it never interested him. I think Tony was the last of the artists now who worked in that way: with his eyes, just what he saw. He'd take that, put that there, it's right, it's wrong... I think sculpture has gone a very different way now. I don't think people make sculpture like that anymore. But he was so prolific in his lifetime; he's worked in every medium, in every way! Painted steel, Perspex, wood, steel, silver, gold, paper... Everything. So it's very hard for someone else to come in and do the same. As soon as you pick up a piece of a machine – it's an Anthony Caro! It's hard.

Practical skills in life are good. I used to take the engines out of cars when I was fourteen, take the whole engine into the house, into the kitchen. I'd be grinding the valves, and my mother would be like, 'Get that bloody thing out of here!' But that's all I was interested in – just working, having fun.

JD *You both had the desire to make, to find out more, how it worked and what was next...*

PC But he was amazingly open to suggestions and interested in people. He was like a sponge. He'd listen to you and take everything in. Somehow it would all come out in a sculpture.

JD *And the rate at which he would process ideas?*

PC I remember when John Wallbank started the head sculptures with Tony, and I wasn't in the studio. Within two days they had two or three of these on the go. Just sitting there with bits of wood, put together.

He loved to make art, that's all he wanted to do.

Some dealers would say that he was too prolific, there was too much stuff – that it devalued his prices. But if you're having fun there's never too much!

JD *Are there any bodies of work that really stand out for you from your time as an assistant?*

PC The thing I find the most moving is the Bourbourg chapel [Eglise de Saint-Jean-Baptiste].

JD *Why is that?*

PC I don't know. I think because it's in a church and I'm Catholic. I didn't feel it at the time of making it – it was just another project. I went back with Neil, and it was incredible to see it again. To think that we were all part of making this great thing... It's there and it's going to be there forever. I know that sculptures will be there forever too, but it's not the same.

JD *Bourbourg was different, in a way, because it was a commission, although Tony had a lot freedom. Did the commissioning process change things?*

PC It was quite difficult, but it was great working with Pierre Bernard and Francis Bassemon (the Mayor), who told Tony to do whatever he wanted. We didn't have to show anyone anything until it was all in place. When we were installing it we put up the screens and kept the doors locked. When Sheila came over to help with the last bit of painting, that's when it was finished. It was only after that the whole town was invited to see it and to meet Tony. Everyone was so moved.

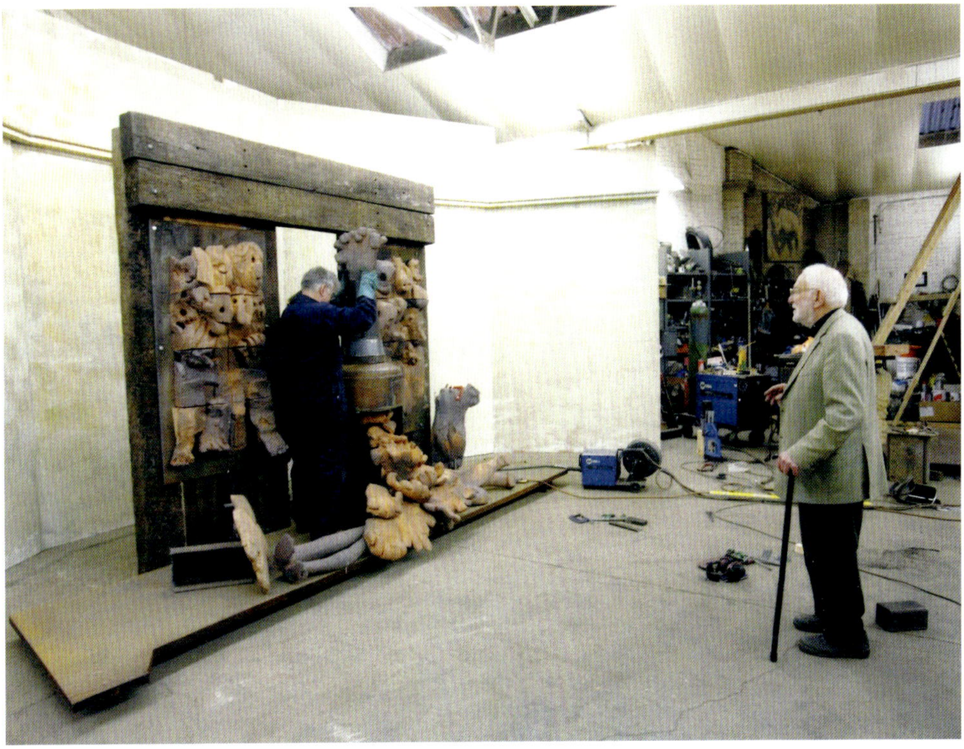

fig. 89

Anthony Caro and Patrick Cunningham in Camden studio preparing for Bourbourg (2008)

I am always amazed, seeing shows finished and in place. The Yorkshire Sculpture Park and Hepworth shows [2015] were incredible.

JD *What was it particularly about those show do you think?*

PC It was the variety of works – Longside, sculptures in the grounds and then over to Hepworth. Just wonderful.

JD *You mentioned earlier how you and Tony had the same eye...*

PC Sheila too... I would say something in the studio, and she would come in and say exactly the same thing. She'd say something and Tony would say, 'Pat said that earlier', or I would go in and Tony would say, 'Sheila said that'. It was reassuring to know that you were on the same wavelength.

Someone once said to me, you should put your name on those sculptures because they have come from between the two of you; but there was no doubt about it – it was Tony. He had the power to say 'Yes that's right', or 'No that's wrong'. I may have participated and helped, but he said when it was finished.

JD *How do others perceive the role of an assistant?*

PC Well, all my friends in Ireland think that I'm looney, because they don't understand art and you can't spend time trying to convert them. I'll show them books and things, but all they think is, 'Oh you've just been to Spain, New York, Madrid... That's great!' But I'm working my butt off every day. They don't understand it and it's a funny thing, trying to explain abstract art.

JD *How have you been able to stay for so long?*

PC I have always felt a great pride in the work, and also Tony was very kind. I think Tony understood me better than I understood myself. He would always say, 'Well done, thank you'. They weren't just words: he meant them, and that's what kept me going. It's the same for Sheila; I've stretched her paintings for years.

Also I think it's amazing when I see a sculpture finished; what a great achievement. I've been very lucky in that I've worked for someone who has been a great artist and whom I've admired forever. I've done very well. I'd say we've been very good for each other.

He's had a long career in sculpture. I very much grew into this job. I came as a young kid but was always very keen to learn about things – running a business... Looking after Tony and Sheila; taking care of them like family.

JD *When it came to decisions about which shows to do, commissions and projects, how did that work? What was the business side like?*

PC It came through me. It's about good business-sense and a good sense of people. I think you can take stock of people very quickly, and realise if a project is right for Tony's work.

JD *How about the archive and database? Were you involved with that?*

PC Tony always drew every sculpture he ever made. He did a sketch, documented it, had it photographed. He was always good at that. He recorded everything; he kept every letter, every note. But now it has become even more valuable.

JD *And what now?*

PC Now I'm not in the studio so much, I'm running around organising shows. I'm happy to stay for as long as I'm needed.

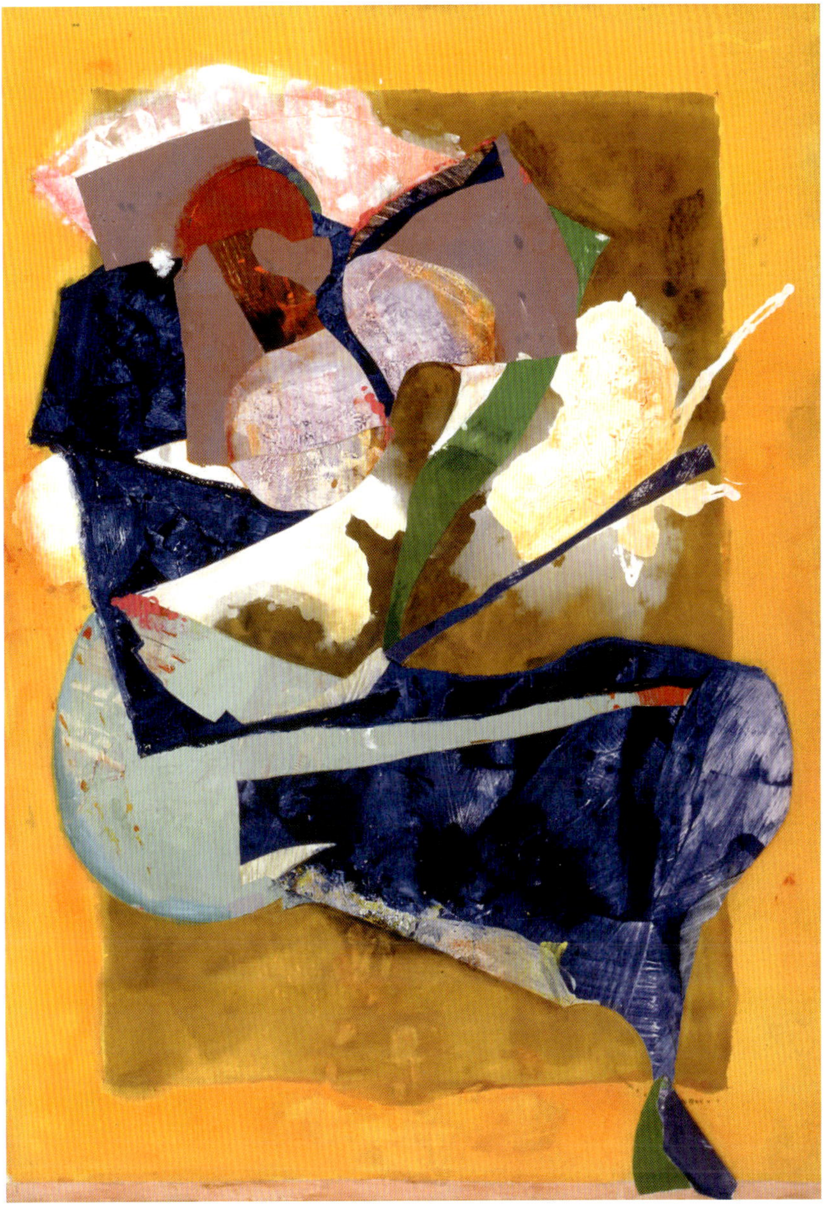

fig. 90

Sheila Girling
Sitting in the square (1991)
Acrylic and collage on canvas
241.3 x 170.2 cm

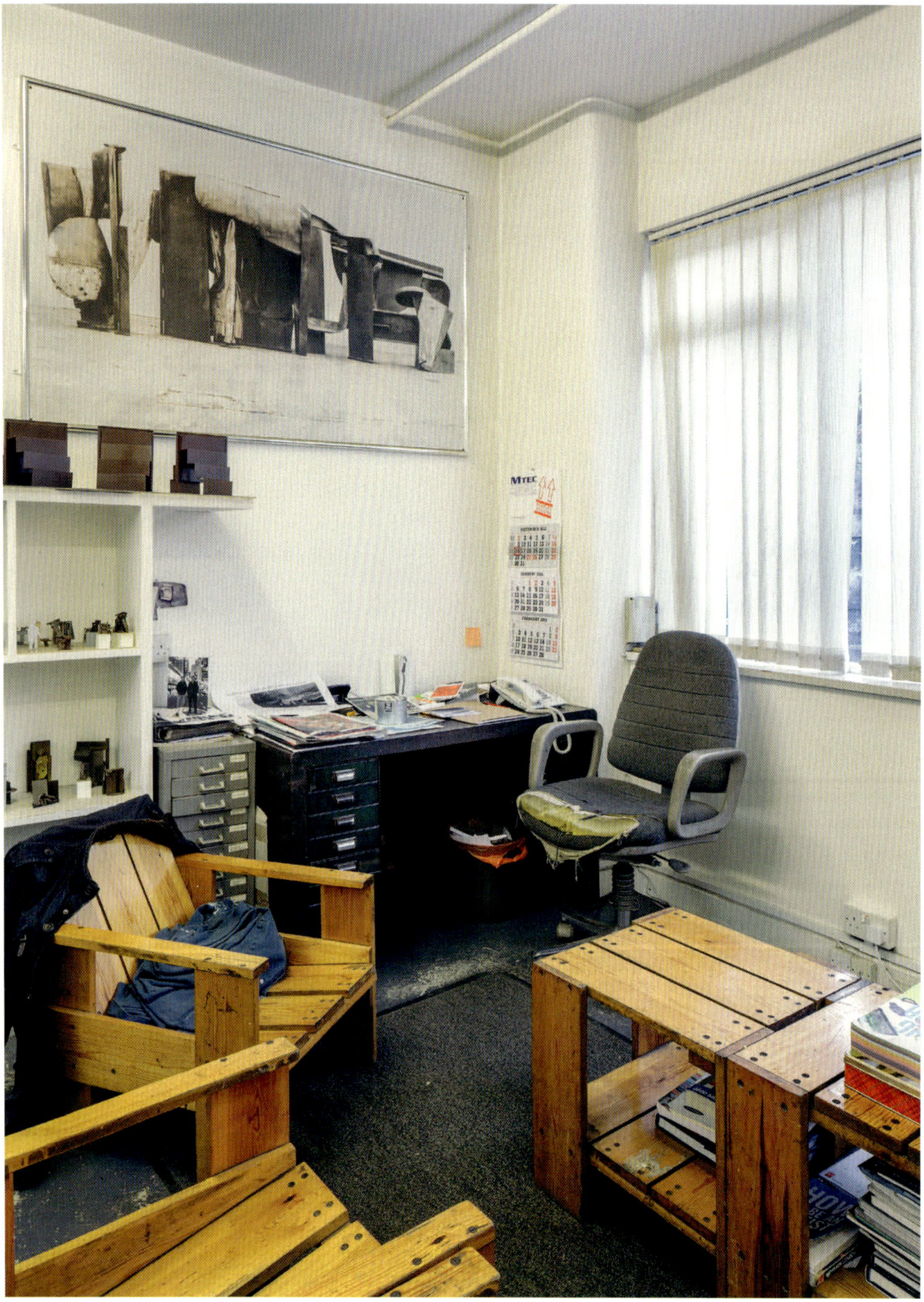

fig. 91

Tearoom at Camden studio (2013)

Contributors & Acknowledgements

Neil Ayling graduated with an MA in Sculpture from the Royal College of Art in 2010. Solo exhibitions include a Frieze Week off-site project at the Berloni Gallery, London (2015), 'Composite Order' at the Berloni Gallery (2014) and 'Flection' at EB & Flow – now the Berloni Gallery – (2011). Recent group exhibitions include 'Mind Out', APT Gallery, London (2016); the RBS Bursary Award Show (2014); 'Summer Mixer' at the Joshua Liner Gallery, New York (2013); 'Objectify' at the High House Gallery, Oxford (2013); and 'The Thing is the Thing' at the ASC Gallery, London (2011). Ayling unveiled a permanent public sculpture in King's Cross entitled *Vert* (2013). He received the Royal British Sculptor Bursary Prize (2014) and the Broomhill Sculpture Prize (2014) and participated in the Triangle Artists' Workshop, New York (2015).

Olivia Bax graduated from Byam Shaw School of Art in 2010 and completed an MFA in Sculpture from the Slade School of Fine Art in 2016. Recent group exhibitions include 'UK/raine' at the Saatchi Gallery, London (2015/16); 'Ellipse' at the A3 Gallery, Moscow (2014); 'Signs of the City' at the Drawing Room (in association with UBM), London (2013). Solo exhibitions include 'Unfurled' at The Foundry Gallery, London (2012); and 'Structural Shift' at ArtMoorHouse, London (2011). Bax was awarded a full fellowship residency at Vermont Studio Center, USA, in 2013 following her participation in the Triangle Artists' Workshop in Brooklyn, New York, in 2012. In 2015 she was the recipient of a British Council residency to the University of Dhaka, Bangladesh.

Willard Boepple grew up in Berkeley, California. He studied at the Skowhegan School of Painting and Sculpture, New York (1963), the University of California, Berkeley (1963–4), Rhode Island School of Design (1967) and The City College of the City University of New York (1968). After teaching at Bennington College and the School of the Museum of Fine Arts in Boston, he returned to New York, where he has lived for over thirty years. He has exhibited widely here and abroad, at galleries including Acquavella Galleries, New York; the André Emmerich Gallery, New York; Tricia Collins Contemporary Art, New York; and Broadbent Gallery, London. His work belongs to such noted institutions as the Metropolitan Museum of Art, New York; the Museum of Fine Arts, Boston; the Storm King Art Center, New York; and The Fitzwilliam Museum, Cambridge, UK. Boepple served as chairman of the Triangle Artists' Workshop for twenty years, an artist residency program that he helped replicate in Africa and the Caribbean.

Sir Anthony Caro (1924–2013) studied sculpture at the Royal Academy Schools and worked as assistant to Sir Charles Wheeler and Henry Moore. He came to public attention with a show at the Whitechapel Gallery in 1963. Caro taught at Saint Martin's School of Art in London (1953–81). Major exhibitions include retrospectives at the Museum of Modern Art, New York (1975);Trajan's Market, Rome (1992); the Museum of Contemporary Art, Tokyo (1995); Tate Britain, London (2005); and three museums in Pas-de-Calais,

France (2008), to accompany the opening of his *Chapel of Light* at Eglise de Saint-Jean-Baptiste, Bourbourg. He has been awarded many prizes, including the Praemium Imperiale for Sculpture in Tokyo in 1992 and the Lifetime Achievement Award for Sculpture in 1997. He holds many honorary degrees from universities in the UK, USA and Europe. He was knighted in 1987 and received the Order of Merit in May 2000. Retrospective exhibitions include Museo Correr, Venice, (2013); and Yorkshire Sculpture Park, Leeds Art Gallery and The Hepworth Wakefield (2015).

Shaun Cassidy studied sculpture at Norwich School of Art and finished his graduate studies in sculpture at the University of Alberta, Canada. Cassidy's sculptures have been exhibited extensively throughout the USA including at Socrates Sculpture Park, New York; Franconia Sculpture Park, Minnesota; the Forum for Contemporary Art (now the Contemporary Art Museum), St Louis; the Columbia Museum of Art, South Carolina; and at the deCordova Sculpture Park and Museum, Boston. Cassidy has been awarded residencies at over ten venues including the McDowell Colony, Peterborough, New Hampshire; Djerassi Resident Artists Program, Woodside, California; the McColl Center for Visual Art (now the McColl Center for Art and Innovation), Charlotte, North Carolina; and Sculpture Space, New York. His work has been reviewed and featured in *Art in America, New Art Examiner, The Wall Street Journal* and *The New York Times*. Cassidy serves on the Board of the McColl Center for Art and Innovation and is a lead artist for the Innovation Institute. He is a professor of sculpture in the Department of Fine Art at Winthrop University, Rock Hill, South Carolina.

Sam Cornish is a writer on abstract art and a curator. Recent projects include a book and exhibition on the artists who worked at the Stockwell Depot; a monograph and exhibition on the New-Zealand-born, London-based sculptor John Panting; and the editorship of a two-volume survey of the paintings of Gary Wragg. He organised the symposium 'Collaborating with Caro' and is currently working on the John Hoyland *catalogue raisonné* and a monograph on the sculptor Tim Scott. From 2012 to 2014 he was editor of www.abstractcritical.com.

Professor K. Patricia Cross is a scholar of educational research and emerita professor of higher education at the University of California, Berkeley. She studied BS Mathematics, MA Psychology and PhD Social Psychology at the University of Illinois. Throughout her career she has explored adult education and higher learning, discussing methodology and pedagogy in terms of remediation and advancement in the university system. Publications include: with Elizabeth F. Barkley and Claire Howell Major, *Collaborative Learning Techniques: A Handbook for College Faculty*, (San Francisco: Jossey-Bass, 2005); with Mimi Harris Steadman, *Classroom Research: Implementing the Scholarship of Teaching*, (San Francisco: Jossey-Bass, 1996).

Beth Cullen-Kerridge studied at Liverpool John Moores University and the Royal College of Art. She honed her craft working in foundries and has produced works for Eduardo Paolozzi, Elisabeth Frink and Alberto Giacometti. For eight years she worked closely with Mike Bolus as a studio assistant for Sir Anthony Caro, on large-scale projects for the likes of Sir Norman Foster, Richard Rodgers, and the Tate, as well as working on shows at the Venice Biennale and the Marlborough Gallery, New York, and the Eglise de Saint-Jean-Baptiste, Bourbourg, France. She continues to make and exhibit work internationally.

Patrick Cunningham was raised on a farm in Ireland, and early in life learned practical skills from his father. On moving to England, he worked for a short time as a hod carrier before becoming a welder at Aeromet in London. He began working for Caro in 1968, leaving only once (for approximately a year), to return and continue working at Barford Studios to the present day.

Ian Dawson is a London-based artist and head of sculpture at Winchester School of Art, University of Southampton. He studied at the Royal College of Art and first came to prominence in the 1990s with a series of large-scale melted plastic sculptures that celebrated creativity through the destructive act. He is the author of *Making Contemporary Sculpture* (Marlborough: The Crowood Press, 2012). His practice remains intensely experimental, involving different processes and diverse materials. Dawson has exhibited internationally, and his work is held in both public and private collections worldwide including the Saatchi Collection, London; the ABN Amro Collection, Amsterdam; the SEI Collection, USA and UK; the Ti Group, London; and Skadden, Arps, Meagher & Flom, New York.

Jenny Dunseath is a London-based artist and senior lecturer in fine art sculpture at Bath School of Art and Design, Bath Spa University. After graduating from the Royal Academy of Arts she worked as an assistant in the Caro studio, and it is this first-hand insight that triggered this project's interest in master/pupil relations, practical pedagogy and legacy. She continues to make and exhibit work internationally. Exhibitions include The Royal Academy of Arts, Bloomberg New Contemporaries, Cornerhouse, Korean Cultural Centre, Gana gallery Seoul, Flat Time House, OUTPOST and Spike Island. Awards include the Royal Society of British Sculptors bursary award and Red Mansion Art Prize, Beijing.

William Fausset studied sculpture at the University of Leeds and the Slade School of Fine Art, University College London. He has worked as technical assistant at the Henry Moore Institute and the University of Hertfordshire. He has run sculpture workshops at Norwich University of the Arts, has been a visiting lecturer of sculpture at the University of Leeds, and is head of workshops at the Architectural Association School of Architecture, London. He continues to make and exhibit work.

André Fauteux is a Canadian-born artist who studied at Upper Canada College and Central Technician School, Toronto. He has exhibited internationally, including 'The Condition of Sculpture' at the Hayward Gallery, London (1975), and is held in collections by the Art Gallery of Ontario, Canada's National Gallery, and the Art Gallery of Hamilton in Ontario, among many others. Fauteux also has a permanent installation of a sculpture in Barcelona, Spain, and has won numerous Canada Council Awards as well as the Canada Council Art Bank.

John Gibbons studied at Limerick School of Art, Crawford Municipal School of Art and Saint Martin's School of Art. He was a studio assistant to Anthony Caro and Oscar Nemon. He is a member of Aosdána and fellow of the Royal British Society of Sculptors, and emeritus professor at Winchester School of Art, University of Southampton. Gibbons's work is in numerous public and private collections around the world, including: Tate, London; Arts Council England; Edmonton Art Gallery, Alberta; the Calouste Gulbenkian Museum, Lisbon; the Museum of Contemporary Art, Barcelona; the Czech Museum of Fine Arts, Prague; Crawford Art Gallery, Cork; Jesus College, University of Cambridge; Syracuse University, New York; and the University of Limerick.

Jonathan Gildersleeves is a practicing artist based in South East London. A masters graduate in drawing from Wimbledon School of Art, he teaches at Central Saint Martins and West Dean College, specialising in drawing and sculpture. He co-founded the artist collective The Drawing Factory, continues to exhibit throughout the UK and has been artist-in-residence at Wimbledon College of Art and Construction Gallery, London.

Jon Isherwood is professor of sculpture at Bennington College, Vermont. He studied at Leeds College of Art, Canterbury College of Art, and Syracuse University, New York. His work has been widely exhibited in public museums and private galleries around the USA, Canada, Europe and China. He is the recipient of a Jerome Foundation Fellowship, Pollock-Krasner Foundation grant, and an honorary doctorate from the University of New York at Plattsburgh. His sculpture has recently been exhibited at the National Archaeological Museum, Florence; the National Museum, Beijing; The deCordova Sculpture Park and Museum, Boston; and Belgrave Square, London. He has had more than 20 solo exhibitions, including Reeves Contemporary, New York; John Davis Gallery, New York; The C. Grimaldis Gallery, Baltimore; and Pyramid Hill Sculpture Park and Museum, Hamilton, Ohio. He has been featured in many group exhibitions, including the Peggy Guggenheim Museum, Venice; the McNay Art Museum, San Antonio, Texas; Derby Museum and Art Gallery; and Kunsthalle Mannheim, Germany. He has lectured at numerous colleges and universities in the USA and Europe, and is the founder of the Digital Stone Project.

Hywel Livingstone is a practicing artist based in Cheltenham. He studied sculpture at Winchester School of Art in 2003 and gained an MA in Art History at the University of Bristol. He was awarded the Royal Society of British Sculptors Bursary Award in 2003. Livingstone has had residencies in Holland Park School, London, and Franconia Sculpture Park, Minnesota. Recent exhibitions include a solo show at Line Gallery, Stroud (2016); Oriel Davies Open, Newtown, Wales (2014); and The London Group Open at Menier Gallery, London (2009).

Tim Marlow joined the Royal Academy of Arts in 2014 as artistic director. His remit includes the RA's exhibition programme and collection, as well as learning, architecture and publishing. Prior to this, Marlow was director of exhibitions at White Cube (2003–14). Over the past decade he has played a major role in White Cube's evolution into one of the pre-eminent contemporary art galleries in the world, with new spaces in São Paulo, Hong Kong and London. He has also worked with many of the most important and influential artists of our time, including Jake and Dinos Chapman, Chuck Close, Tracey Emin RA, Gilbert and George, Antony Gormley RA, Damien Hirst, Gary Hume RA, Anselm Kiefer Hon RA, Julie Mehretu and Doris Salcedo. Marlow is an award-winning radio and television broadcaster who has presented over one hundred documentaries on British television. He was the founder editor of *Tate Magazine* and is the author of numerous books and catalogues. He has lectured, chaired and participated in panel discussions on art and culture in more than forty countries.

Guy Martin was brought up on a converted motor torpedo boat moored at Hayling Island. He studied at Portsmouth School of Art and Saint Martin's School of Art. He was a studio assistant to Caro from 1966, and in 1984 he established a contemporary furniture design practice. From 1988–94 he was principal design tutor at Parnham College in Dorset, during which period he developed a strong interest in environmental concerns, which underpinned his design philosophy. He applied this to making interior domestic furniture and garden buildings. In recent years he has returned to making sculpture and drawings.

Gavin Morris studied sculpture at Winchester School of Art and completed an MA at the Royal College of Art. After working in Caro's studio, he worked at Mike Smith Studio and went on to teach sets, props and scenic construction at the Central School of Speech and Drama. He now teaches art, design and photography at a secondary school in Devon and continues to make and exhibit work.

Tim Peacock studied sculpture at Winchester School of Art. After working for Caro, he proceeded to run the sculpture workshops at Byam Shaw School of Art, and later taught adult and children's short courses. He went on to help set up KCL Fine Arts in London, managing the studio for the Greek artist Kalliopi Lemos.

Dr Michael Petry studied at Rice University, Houston (BA), London Guildhall University (MA), and has a Doctor in Arts from Middlesex University. Petry is an artist, author and director of the Museum of Contemporary Art (MOCA) London, and guest curator for Futurecity. He co-founded the Museum of Installation, was guest curator at the Kunstakademiet, Oslo, research fellow at the University of Wolverhampton and curator of the Royal Academy Schools Gallery. Petry co-authored *Installation Art* with Nicholas de Oliveira, Nicola Oxley and Michael Archer (London: Thames & Hudson, 1994), and *Installation Art in the New Millennium* with Nicholas de Oliveira and Nicola Oxley (London: Thames & Hudson, 2003), and authored *Abstract Eroticism* (New York: Academy Editions, 1996) and *A Thing of Beauty is…* (New York: Academy Editions, 1997). *The Touch of the Oracle* (with Adrian George and Katherine Plake Hough, London: MOCA London, 2012) is a recent survey of his work. Petry's book, *The Art of Not Making: The New Artist Artisan Relationship* (London: Thames & Hudson) was published in hardback in 2011 and paperback in 2012. His current book (and travelling exhibition) *Nature Morte: Contemporary Artists Reinvigorate the Still-Life Tradition* (London: Thames & Hudson, 2013) was published in four hardback editions. Petry's libretto for *A Prussian Requiem* had its world premiere in March 2016 at the Royal Festival Hall, where it was performed by the Philharmonic Orchestra and Choir, commemorating the dead of the First World War.

John Wallbank is a London-based artist. He received an MA from Edinburgh School of Art in 2000 and an MFA from the Slade School of Fine Art, London. He won the Mark Tanner Sculpture Prize in 2010 and was awarded a six-month residency at the Triangle Artists' Association, New York, in 2013. Recent solo exhibitions include 'Diptych' at Arcade Fine Arts, London (2015); Hub, Antwerp (2015); Arcade Fine Arts, London (2014); Islington Mill Studio, Salford (2012); 'Masticate' at Arcade Fine Arts, London (2011); and 'Hazard All' at Studio 1.1, London (2010). His work is in the Saatchi and Zabludowicz collections. He is currently represented by Arcade Fine Arts, London.

Karen Wilkin is a New-York-based curator and critic. Educated at Barnard College and Columbia University, she is the author of monographs on Anthony Caro, Willard Boepple, Stuart Davis, Helen Frankenthaler, Hans Hofmann, Giorgio Morandi, Kenneth Noland, David Smith and Isaac Witkin, and has organised exhibitions of their work internationally. She is contributing editor for art for *The Hudson Review*, a regular contributor to *The New Criterion* and *The Wall Street Journal*, and teaches in the New York Studio School's MFA program. Recent projects include the touring exhibition 'American Vanguards: John Graham, Stuart Davis, Arshile Gorky, Willem de Kooning and their Circle, 1927–42' for the Addison Gallery of American Art, Andover, Massachusetts (named best exhibition of 2012 by *The Boston Globe*) and 'Hans Hofmann: Magnum Opus' for the Museum Pfalzgalerie Kaiserslautern, Germany. Ms Wilkin is preparing a retrospective of Hofmann's works on paper for the Museum of Contemporary Art, Jacksonville, Florida, and the Portland Art Museum, Maine.

Dr Mark Wilsher is an artist and regular writer for *Art Monthly*. He is a lecturer at Norwich University of the Arts on undergraduate and postgraduate courses. He has had solo exhibitions at OUTPOST, Norwich; the Henry Moore Institute, Leeds; CHELSEA Space, London; and has participated in exhibitions at the Institute of Contemporary Arts, London; Picture This, Spike Island, Bristol; the Arnolfini, Bristol; Wysing Arts Centre, Cambridge; Leeds City Art Gallery; and EAST International, Norwich. From 2003–5 he was curator at the Tablet Gallery in Notting Hill, and curated projects for Camberwell College of Art from 2005–7. Recent projects include a solo exhibition looking at the negotiation of visual culture and the mass reproduction of fine art at The Minories Galleries, Colchester (2015); a sculpture project with the Department of Philosophy at the University of East Anglia, Norwich; and researching representations of contemporary art in the mainstream media.

James Wolfe is based in Northport, Maine. He has had solo exhibitions at galleries in Germany and Canada, and in the USA at the André Emmerich Gallery, New York; Meredith Long & Company, New York; the Baumgartner Gallery, Washington DC; Marion Meyer Contemporary Art, Laguna Beach, California; the Rubiner Gallery, Bloomfield, Michigan; Turtle Gallery, Deer Isle, Maine; and the New York Studio School of Drawing, Painting and Sculpture. His sculpture has also been shown in solo exhibitions at the James A. Michener Art Museum, Doylestown, Pennsylvania, and the Civic Center Plaza, Palo Alto, California. His work is included in many public and corporate collections including the Whitney Museum of American Art, New York; Hirshhorn Museum and Sculpture Garden, Washington DC; the Museum of Fine Arts, Houston; the Museum of Fine Arts, Boston; the Storm King Art Center, New York; and the Creative Arts Guild, Dalton, Georgia. He has received awards from the National Endowment for the Arts and the Saint-Gaudens Foundation.

Studio assistants and collaborators listed in the Barford database

Paul Chaleff, Charlie Hendry, Roger Mack and students from Syracuse University, Isaac Witkin, David Annesley, Michael Bolus, Shorty Griffin, Patrick Cunningham, Glynn Rudich, Guy Martin, Jim Wolfe, Willard Boepple, Mario Rigamonti, André Fauteux, Jane W, William Noland, Douglas Bentham, Steve Reeves, Tom Strianese, Barton Myers, John Gibbons, Jon Isherwood, Pat Hoystracht, David Gooding, Peter Verstigo, Gary Gradis, Jordi Dedeu, John Crossley, Barbara Lander, Carlo Mantegazza, Jane Clarke, Richard Lander, Philip Medley, Christopher Williams, Guy Hardern, Garry Doherty, Shaun Cassidy, Simon Black, Clay Ellis, Roy Mills, Berg Kikonian, Isla Burns, John Hock, Tony Scialo, Jaana Fowler, John Riddy, Shap McDonnell, Sheila Vollmer, Elizabeth Wright, Julia Whiston, Dan Rappaport, Duncan Kerr, Neil Evans, Paul Smith, Giorgio Sadotti, Stephen Thompson, Kirstie Reid, Gideon Peterson, Ian Dawson, Alastair Leslie, Susannah Oliver, Tom Roberts, Derrick Robinson, Simon Black, Derek Haworth, Hans Spinner, Gavin Morris, Dan Frye, Richard Trump, Kees van der Graaf, David Pelham, Beth Cullen-Kerridge, Tim Peacock, Richard Trupp, Jim Coverley, Tony Stone, Kenneth Tyler, Michael Mueller, John Hutchison, Elena Foster, Hans-Magnus Enzenberger, Ralph Oliver, Christopher Wise, Jolyon Oliver, David Pelham, Norman Foster, Gavin Morris, Ed Goolden, Hywel Livingstone, Neil Ayling, William Fausset, Jonathan Gildersleeves, Jenny Dunseath, Terence Kershaw, Piers Saxby-Candy, Trevor Harris, Oliver Cheyne, John Wallbank, Tom Willis, Rafa Rablancci, Olivia Bax.

Acknowledgements

The research on studio assistants grew out of the experience of working for Anthony Caro and an interest in studio culture. Over time, conversations grew into discussions, and collaborations between researchers, educators and practitioners formed.

Our gratitude is due to everyone involved in the various stages of this project, which began in 2010 and continued, with interviews, studio visits, conferences and seminars at aligning institutions, through to 2016.

Sincere thanks are due to all the contributors to this publication for their time, insight and considered reflection so graciously shared. Particular thanks to Barford Studios Ltd: Paul Caro, Patrick Cunningham, Sile Stuttard and Olivia Bax for their generosity and patience. Thanks to Tim Marlow, Karen Wilkin, Dr Michael Petry, Sam Cornish and Professor K. Patricia Cross for their valuable insight and perspectives; to all featured artists and artists' estates for giving permissions; to Annely Juda Fine art and the private donors for their support.

We are grateful to our respective departments and institutions for their backing and funding. To participants and colleagues at Bath School of Art and Design, Bath Spa University; Norwich University of the Arts; Winchester School of Art, University of Southampton; and Bennington College, Vermont. To Professor Anita Taylor, Dr Graham McLaren, Naomi Box and Professor Jon Isherwood.

Thanks to Wunderkammer Press at Bath Spa University. To Extra Strong for the book design and production. To proof reader Angela Rivers and picture researcher Lorraine Beck for their support in bringing this publication to fruition.

To our respective families, we are in your debt.

Picture Credits

fig. 1
Courtesy of Barford Sculptures Limited
Photo: John Hammond
fig. 2
Courtesy of Barford Sculptures Limited
and Gagosian Gallery
Photo: Mike Bruce
fig. 3
Courtesy of Barford Sculptures Limited
and Gagosian Gallery
Photo: Mike Bruce
fig. 4
Courtesy of Barford Sculptures Limited
Photo: John Hammond
fig. 5
Courtesy of Barford Sculptures Limited
Photo: John Hammond
Private collection
fig. 6
Courtesy of the artist
Photo: Guy Martin
fig. 7
Courtesy of the artist
Photo: Guy Martin
fig. 8
Courtesy of Barford Sculptures Limited
Photo: John Riddy
fig. 9
Courtesy of Barford Sculptures Limited
Photo: William Noland
fig. 10
Courtesy of the artist
Photo: Tom Jones
fig. 11
Courtesy of Barford Sculptures Limited
Photo: John Goldblatt
fig. 12
Courtesy of the artist
Photo: Jessica Pages
Collection: Metropolitan Museum of Art, New York
fig. 13
Courtesy of the artist
Photo: Etienne Frossard
Private collection, France
fig. 14
Courtesy of Barford Sculptures Limited
Photo: Mick Hales
fig. 15
Courtesy of André Fauteux
Photo: André Emmerich
fig. 16
Courtesy of the artist
Photo: André Fauteux
fig. 17
Courtesy of Barford Sculptures Limited
Photo: John Riddy
fig. 18
Courtesy of the estate of Oscar Nemon
Photo: Falcon Stuart
fig. 19
Courtesy of the artist
Photo: John Gibbons
Collection: Arts Council England, 1978
fig. 20
Courtesy of the artist
Photo: John Gibbons
Flowers East, London, 1994
fig. 21
Courtesy of the artist
Photo: John Gibbons
fig. 22
Widener Collection/courtesy National Gallery of Art, Washington
fig. 23
Alamy Stock Photo/dpa Picture-Alliance
fig. 24
© Damien Hirst and Science Limited.
All rights reserved, DACS 2016
Image courtesy of Gagosian Gallery
Photo: Mike Parsons
fig. 25
© Anish Kapoor. All rights reserved, DACS 2016
Image courtesy of the City of Chicago and
Gladstone Gallery
Photo: Patrick Pyszka
fig. 26
Courtesy of the artist and CarrerasMugica
fig. 27
Image courtesy of Joana Vasconcelos
Collection of the artist; courtesy Galerie Nathalie Obadia, Paris/Brussels and Haunch of Venison, London
Photo: Luís Vasconcelos/courtesy Unidade Infinita Projectos/ courtesy of the Palace of Versailles
fig. 28
Courtesy of the artist
Photo: Michael Petry
fig. 29
Courtesy of Barford Sculptures Limited
Photo: John Goldblatt
Collection: Yale University Art Gallery, New Haven
fig. 30
Courtesy of Barford Sculptures Limited
Photo: Desmond O'Neill
fig. 31
Courtesy of the artist
Photo: Jon Isherwood
fig. 32
Courtesy of the artist
Photo: Michael Fredericks
fig. 33
Courtesy of the artist
Photo: Michael Fredericks
fig. 34
Courtesy of Barford Sculptures Limited
Photo: John Riddy
Collection: Tate, London
fig. 35
Courtesy of the artist
Photo: Shaun Cassidy

fig. 36
Courtesy of Barford Sculptures Limited
Photo: John Riddy
Collection: Museum of Contemporary Art, Tokyo
fig. 37
Courtesy of Barford Sculptures Limited
fig. 38
Courtesy of Barford Sculptures Limited
Photo: John Hammond
fig. 39
Courtesy of the artist
Photo: Ian Dawson
fig. 40
Courtesy of the artist
Photo: Ian Dawson
fig. 41
Copyright: estate of Michael Bolus
Collection: Tate, London
fig. 42
Courtesy of Barford Sculptures Limited
Photo: John Riddy
Private collection, UK
fig. 43
Copyright: estate of Michael Bolus
Collection: Tate, London
fig. 44
Courtesy of Barford Sculptures Limited
Photo: John Goldblatt
fig. 45
Courtesy of the artist
Photo: courtesy of the Whitworth, The University of Manchester
fig. 46
Courtesy of Barford Sculptures Limited
Photo: Patrick Cunningham
fig. 47
Courtesy of the artist
Photo: Exhibition at Kasmin Limited, London, 1970
Collection: Lewis Cabot, Boston, Massachusetts
fig. 48
Courtesy of Barford Sculptures Limited
Photo: Carlos Granger
fig. 49
Courtesy of Barford Sculptures Limited
Photo: John Riddy
fig. 50
Courtesy of the artist
Photo: David Evison
fig. 51
Courtesy of the artist
Photo: courtesy of *The Architects' Journal*
fig. 52
Courtesy of Barford Sculptures Limited
Photo: Carlos Granger
fig. 53
Courtesy of Barford Sculptures Limited
Photo: John Goldblatt
fig. 54
Courtesy of the artist
Photo: Ray Sacks
fig. 55
Courtesy of Barford Sculptures Limited
Photo: Geoffrey Clements
fig. 56
Courtesy of the artist
Photo: courtesy of Waddington Custot Galleries
fig. 57
Courtesy of Barford Sculptures Limited
Photo: Carlos Granger
fig. 58
Courtesy of Barford Sculptures Limited
Photo: Carlos Granger
fig. 59
Courtesy of the artist
Photo: Carlos Granger
fig. 60
Courtesy of Barford Sculptures Limited
Photo: David Buckland
Collection: Kunsthalle Würth, Künzelsau
fig. 61
Courtesy of Barford Sculptures Limited
Photo: John Hammond
fig. 62
Courtesy of Barford Sculptures Limited
Photo: John Riddy
fig. 63
Courtesy of Barford Sculptures Limited
Photo: John Riddy
Collection: Kunsthalle Würth, Künzelsau
fig. 64
Courtesy of the artist
Photo: Gavin Morris
fig. 65
Courtesy of the artist
Photo: Gavin Morris
fig. 66
Courtesy of Barford Sculptures Limited
Photo: David Buckland
Collection: Kunsthalle Würth, Künzelsau
fig. 67
Courtesy of Barford Sculptures Limited
Photo: John Riddy
fig. 68
Copyright: estate of Michael Bolus
Collection: Tate, London
fig. 69
Courtesy of Tim Peacock
fig. 70
Courtesy of Barford Sculptures Limited
Photo: John Riddy
fig. 71
Courtesy of Barford Sculptures Limited
Photo: John Riddy
fig. 72
Courtesy of the artist
Photo: Hywel Livingstone
fig. 73
Courtesy of Barford Sculptures Limited
Photo: John Riddy
Private collection, Korea

fig. 74
Courtesy of the artist
Photo: Jonathan Gildersleeves
fig. 75
Courtesy of Barford Sculptures Limited
Photo: John Riddy
fig. 76
Courtesy of the artist
Photo: William Fausset
fig. 77
Courtesy of the artist
Photo: William Fausset
fig. 78
Courtesy of Barford Sculptures Limited
Photo: John Hammond
fig. 79
Courtesy of the artist
Photo: Neil Ayling
fig. 80
Courtesy of the artist
Photo: Olivia Bax
fig. 81
Courtesy of the artist
Photo: Neil Ayling
fig. 82
Courtesy of the artist
Photo: John Wallbank
fig. 83
Courtesy of the artist
Photo: Olivia Bax
fig. 84
Courtesy of the artist
Photo: John Wallbank
fig. 85
Courtesy of Barford Sculptures Limited
Photo: John Hammond
fig. 86
Courtesy of Barford Sculptures Limited
Photo: John Hammond
fig. 87
Courtesy of Tim Peacock
fig. 88
Courtesy of Barford Sculptures Limited
Photo: David Buckland
Collection: Kunsthalle Würth, Künzelsau
fig. 89
Courtesy of Barford Sculptures Limited
Photo: Claire Greenway
fig. 90
Courtesy of Barford Sculptures Limited
Photo: John Riddy
fig. 91
Courtesy of Barford Sculptures Limited
Photo: John Hammond

Index

A

B

C

D

E

F

G

H

I